BRITISH
RAILWAY Disasters

Ian Allan
Publishing

First published 1996 Third impression 2004
Based on *The World of Trains*
© Eaglemoss Publications Ltd 1996

ISBN 0-7110-2470-7

Published by Ian Allan Publishing

an imprint of Ian Allan Ltd, Terminal
House, Shepperton, Surrey TW17 8AS.

Acknowledgements

Photographs: Front cover (top) Syndication
International; Front cover (bottom) Press Association;
Back cover (top) Press Association (bottom left)
Popperfoto (bottom right) Illustrated London News; 1
PA; 3 Glasgow Herald and Evening Times Picture
Library; 4 Topham; 5,6 The Scotsman Publications; 7-
9 SI; 10 Rex Features; 11,12,13 PA; 14-15(t) SI; 15(b)
PA; 16-18 ILN; 19 PA; 20 SI; 21 PA; 22 SI; 24-26 PA; 27-
30 Hull Daily Mail Publications; 31-33 British
Library/Times Newspapers Ltd; 34 Topham; 35-38
Associated Press/Topham; 39 PA; 40,41 SI; 42 PA; 43-
46 H-D; 47-50 SI; 51 PA; 52-54 Glasgow Evening
Herald; 55 PA; 56 SI; 57 PA; 58 H-D; 59 H-D; 60 PA; 61
Popperfoto; 62 H-D; 63 PA; 64 H-D; 65 SI; 66 PA; 67 SI;
68-70 PA; 71-74 H-D; 75,76 SI; 77 H-D; 78 SI; 79 H-D;
80 PA; 81,82 SI; 83 PA; 84 Yorkshire Evening Post; 85
PA; 86 Yorkshire Evening Post; 87 PA; 88,89 SI; 90 PA;
91 K&J Kelley; 92 Topham; 93 PA; 94 K&J Kelly; 95
Popperfoto; 96 Topham; 97 National Railway
Museum; 98 Popperfoto; 99,100,101 Topham; 102
Topham; 103 H-D; 104,105 PA; 106 Millbrook House;
107 Topham; 108 Popperfoto; 109 Topham; 110 H-D;
111 Topham; 112 PA; 113 Topham; 114 Popperfoto;
115-117 H-D; 118 SI; 119-121 ILN; 122 Popperfoto;
123(t) SI; 123(b) Popperfoto; 124 SI; 125,126 H-D; 127
SI; 128-130 Popperfoto; 131-134 Topham; 135 ILN;
136-138 PA; 139 Topham; 140-142 H-D; 143 H-D; 144
ILN; 145 British Library Reproductions; 146 ILN; 147
ILN; 148 British Library Reproductions; 149 H-D; 150
British Library Reproductions; 151 SI; 152 ILN; 153,
154(t) H-D; 154(b) SI; 155 SI; 156-158 ILN; 159 H-D;
160-161 David St John Thomas (Gretna: Britainís
Greatest Railway Disaster); 162 Topham; 163,164
Anthony J Lambert Collection; 165 A.G.Ellis
Collection; 166 Anthony J Lambert Collection; 167
ILN; 168 Geoffrey Kichenside Collection; 169 ILN; 170
H-D; 171-173 H-D; 174 Millbrook House; 175 ILN; 176
H-D; 177 Mary Evans Picture Library; 178 H-D; 179,180
ILN; 181 H-D; 182 ILN; 183-186 H-D; 187-189 ILN; 190
Jim Fleming; 191 British Library; 192 ILN.

Key: H-D = Hulton-Deutsch Collection; ILN =
Illustrated London News; PA = Press Association; SI
= Syndication International.

The diagrams on the following pages are based on
Crown copyright and are reproduced with the
permission of the Controller of the HMSO: 32-33, 36-
37, 44-45, 48-49, 68-69, 72-73, 84-85; 96-97; 112-113;
123-124; 148-149; 184-185.

All illustrations by Paul Kellet/Eaglemoss.

Contents

Newton 1991

**Dusk was falling on a July evening in Newton when a
three-car electric train started against a signal at danger
and hit another train head-on, killing four people. This was a
newly signalled junction with single points and the latest
micro-processor controls – so what went wrong?**

Newton is a junction station on the West Coast main line, about 7 miles (11km) south-east of Glasgow Central. Apart from the double track main line running from Glasgow Central to Carlisle, which has no platform faces at Newton, a second pair of tracks on the south-west side of the main line forms the through route from Glasgow Central via Kirkhill to Hamilton, which then circles back to join the main line at Motherwell. These two tracks have separate platform faces, one for up trains towards Motherwell (by either main line or via Hamilton) and one for down trains towards Glasgow (by either route).

From the early 1970s, pairs of parallel single crossovers gave access at both ends of Newton station to the West Coast main line, so trains running on the main lines could cross to the platform tracks, known as the Cathcart or Kirkhill lines, and back to the main lines. This allowed trains running from the suburban lines north of the city to Motherwell to connect with trains running in the southern suburbs on the Kirkhill route, and formed

part of the electrified suburban network north and south of the River Clyde.

During the late 1980s, to cut costs, plans were drawn up to simplify layouts and remove redundant track, taking into account altered service patterns and travelling habits. During the 1960s and early 1970s layout alterations had been undertaken in conjunction with the electrification and resignalling of the Glasgow south side suburban services. These culminated in the electrification of the West Coast main line from the south to Glasgow Central in 1974.

Also in 1974, the signalling at Newton was taken over by the new centralized power signalbox at Motherwell, which controlled lines by what had become conventional relay interlocking. Routes were set on the Motherwell panel by the signalman pressing buttons at the entrance and exit of each signalled route along a mimic track diagram. The signalman's instructions were then conveyed from the panel by what were called non-vital electric circuits to the interlocking electro-mechanical

▼ The combined force of the collision at an impact of 60mph (100km/h) wrecked the leading coaches of both trains. The Class 314 front coach is above and to the left with the roof hanging over the wrecked body.

could a signalman change his mind unless there was no train present; if there was, and it had not passed the signal, a time delay prevented the signalman from changing the route. This time delay was normally two minutes.

The interlocking relays also prevented the signalman from setting two conflicting routes at the same time, so one train could not be signalled across the path of another.

More non-vital electrical circuits carried information back from the points, signals and track circuits to the signalbox panel. This showed the signalman where the trains were by displaying red lights on his track diagram, which way the points were set and whether signals were at danger or proceed. White lights along the tracks showed routes set. This system is in use on most British Rail (BR) main lines and suburban networks today.

New technology
At Motherwell, when plans were made to alter the layout at Newton with simpler track layouts, it was also decided to adopt new technology to control the signalling, this being solid state interlocking (SSI), with micro-processors. It was a new world of computers, as far as the vital interlocking functions were concerned, with specially programmed software designed to take signalmen's route setting and train location inputs and route-setting outputs to point motors and signals.

Computers had been used in BR signalling for train describers and information technology for nearly two decades by this time, but use of computers for safety interlocking functions was only just being accepted for general use by the late 1980s. It followed several years of trials, with solid state running alongside relay interlocking at a few locations, to assess reliability and cost. At Motherwell, the signalman's panel controls were adapted to work with the SSI.

From 1986 onwards the new layout proposals were being drawn up. Both of the new BR business sectors involved, InterCity and Provincial Services ScotRail, had their own ideas, which had to be merged into the final scheme. InterCity wanted to lift the speed limit through Newton from

▲ The front coach of the Class 303 unit lies on its side with the front coach of the Class 314 on top of it.

relays that controlled points and signals. These were the vital circuits that, through the relays, determined whether it was safe for points to be changed and signals to clear.

As part of the system, the track circuit relays detected whether trains were on a particular section of line. They also ensured that, once set and the route cleared for a train with the signal at yellow or green, the points could not be changed. Nor

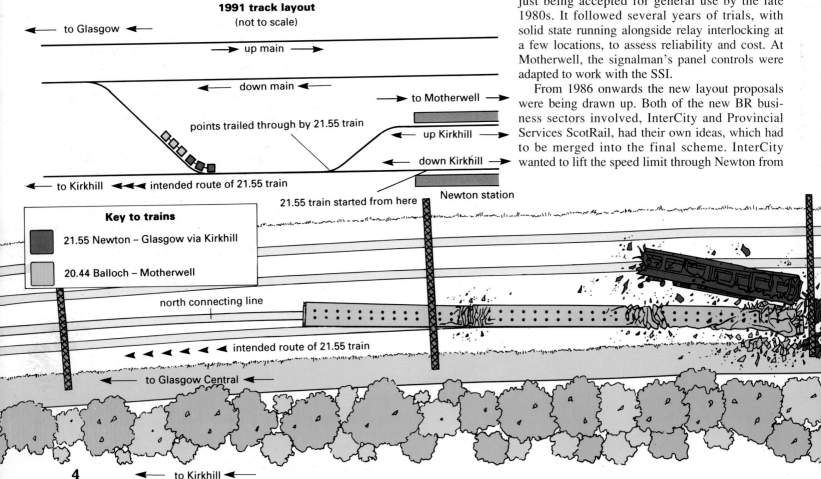

1991 track layout
(not to scale)

to Glasgow ←

→ up main →

← down main ←

→ to Motherwell →

points trailed through by 21.55 train

← up Kirkhill →

← down Kirkhill →

← to Kirkhill ←◄◄ intended route of 21.55 train

21.55 train started from here

Newton station

Key to trains

21.55 Newton – Glasgow via Kirkhill

20.44 Balloch – Motherwell

north connecting line

◄◄◄ intended route of 21.55 train

to Glasgow Central ←

4 ← to Kirkhill ←

70mph (113km/h) to 90mph (145km/h), which could not be achieved on the old layout. This meant simplifying crossovers, and it was planned to have a simple facing crossover from the up main to down at the north-western end, then single trailing points in the down main (but facing to a train crossing from the up main), leading to a single north connecting line to single points on the Kirkhill lines.

Here was a remarkable layout: the double line Kirkhill route became single as it approached the station from Glasgow, the connecting line joined it, and it became double again into the platforms. But at the Motherwell end, the two platform tracks remained double towards Hamilton, a single trailing crossover linked down and up lines and single points led to the south connecting single line back to the main line with, again, single points and crossover. There was also a reversing siding off the up Hamilton line for trains terminating at Newton. Only one train could now use the junction at the Glasgow end of Newton at one time, instead of the two as before.

The final Newton alterations and solid state interlocking were brought into service in June 1991. Drivers were given a diagram and instructions on the new layout, but not given training on site. The first they saw of the new system was when they drove over it in service.

Lead up to disaster

On the evening of 21 July 1991, a fine summer Sunday, suburban trains on the main line were running a little late. But an electric train from Glasgow Central via Kirkhill, terminating at Newton, arrived at the down platform on time, just before 21.50. The train was a three-car electric multiple unit (EMU), No 303 037, operating under driver-only conditions (although the train also had a ticket examiner on board). After the passengers had left, the train went forward into the reversing siding. The driver changed ends and within two minutes was signalled back into the down platform, ahead of a late running Motherwell – Balloch train, which normally went first.

The EMU then stood with its doors open for three or four minutes. The ticket examiner in the back coach looked out to see if passengers were joining, but he did not look at the platform starting signal – he was not required to do so. In fact, his duties involved no part in the operation of the train, control of the doors, or signalling to the driver. The driver closed the sliding doors and the train moved away fairly rapidly in the falling light.

▼ After the removal of the major wreckage, one of the motor bogies from the Class 314 unit is examined before being removed from the track. It is standing on the points linking the north connecting line to the Kirkhill line, with the West Coast main line tracks in the background. Newton station is just out of sight in the far background.

Single lead to disaster

In the late evening of a July Sunday, a driver-only EMU left Newton station towards Kirkhill, apparently passing the platform starting signal at danger.

Only a month earlier a new track layout and computer signalling had been commissioned. The routes towards Glasgow over a single line were shared with trains in the opposite direction through the single lead junctions, so on this occasion a collision was inevitable, as a train in the other direction, running under clear signals, was already occupying the single line; four people died.

Both trains had AWS, but the driver of the one that passed the signal at danger would have acknowledged the warning before the train had stopped in the platform.

The inquiry criticized many safety aspects of the layout design and found that the workmanship in some wiring, together with equipment faults, was responsible for the many failures that occurred before and after the accident. The solid state interlocking was checked thoroughly and found to be in good working order.

→ up main line →

← down main line ←

→ to Motherwell →

→ to Newton and Hamilton →

▲ The leading coach of the train from Balloch, a Class 314 unit, was ripped apart in the head-on collision. Here it is seen after it had been disentangled from the other train and left alongside the West Coast main line, ready for cutting up.

Causes for concern
While the Newton planning was still underway, two accidents occurred elsewhere: the Clapham disaster in December 1988, which showed up poor wiring and testing procedures (and brought in new guidelines), and the Bellgrove collision in March 1989, which took place on a single lead junction. Questions were asked whether single lead junctions were safe if a train passed a signal at danger. There was a searching assessment by BR and the Railway Inspectorate, which concluded that they were little different from reversible lines at terminus stations but relied on drivers obeying signals.

The Inspectorate gave the go-ahead to resume Newton alterations in July 1990. A month later, there was another single lead head-on collision, at Hyde Junction near Manchester, caused by a signal being passed at danger.

'Explosive' impact
Almost immediately there was a sharp brake application and what the ticket examiner described as an explosion. The train stopped. The 21.55 from Newton had hit another train head on, the 20.44 Balloch – Motherwell (running two minutes late), formed of a later pattern three-car EMU, No 314 203, on the single track north connecting line.

The combined speed of the trains was about 60mph (100km/h) and both leading coaches were demolished. The drivers and two passengers were killed, and 22 further passengers were injured. The 20.44 train was double manned with a guard, and both trains were equipped with the automatic warning system (AWS) and cab-to-signalbox radio. But with new signalling just a month old, what had gone wrong? There was no guard on the 21.55 train, so it was not a case of 'ding-ding and away' as had caused the accident at Bellgrove Junction. The driver had control of the doors, he had to look at the signals and then drive the train.

A complex inquiry
Mr D C T Eves, Deputy Director General of the Health & Safety Executive (HSE), chaired the inquiry, rather than one of the railway inspecting officers of the HSE. His job was not easy. The driver of the 21.55 train was fully aware of the new layout, and had discussed with other staff the potential for danger at single lead junctions. Had he passed the down platform starting signal at danger? Had the signalman changed his mind by deciding to let the Kirkhill line train go before the up Balloch train arrived? Or had there been a wrong side failure, allowing the signal to show green when it should have been red?

Evidence from the Motherwell signalman and the guard of the Balloch train showed that there had been insufficient time for the signalman to have set the route for the 21.55 train and then can-

cel it without telling the driver of the 21.55. But there was clear evidence of many faults and failures – some 34 between the commissioning of the system in late June and late September – both before and after this accident. Some were faulty electronic modules or loose connections, but there were three cases of points moving on their own with no train present. These were traced to faulty wiring, with short circuits caused by wires touching a metal plate. Guidelines on installation and testing evolved after the Clapham disaster had not been followed properly; that was enough. With so many faults occurring even after this accident, the Newton layout was partly taken out of use. Only three routes were available, points were locked out of use and speed limits were applied until the faults were overcome.

But Mr Eves concluded that despite the faults there was no interlocking failure. The 21.55 train must have passed the platform starting signal at danger, trailed through the points set towards the up platform line and been diverted on to the north connecting line, where it met the incoming Balloch train head on. It was unfortunate that the data logger working from the processors failed earlier on the day of the accident, otherwise there would have been a record of the routes set. There had been no time to warn drivers by radio.

The inquiry raised many questions about safety at single lead junctions, standards of workmanship and testing of the new signalling at Newton and Motherwell and safety management generally.

Recommendations
This accident raised questions about the use of single lead junctions, the accident potential of signals passed at danger, signalling reliability, staff training and human factors. There were no fewer than 21 recommendations.

Almost immediately, BR undertook a risk assessment of single lead junctions and identified 10 locations, including Bellgrove, Hyde and Newton, where immediate additional protection was needed. At Newton the double line junctions were restored.

Better management of installation and testing procedures should be instigated to give confidence and reliability in new systems, and safety and risks in new layouts should be assessed with co-ordination between all departments. There should be better links between installation and maintenance staff, and with operators. This would include driver training on new features, and improved training on the use of train-to-signalbox radio. There should be technical developments to the radio links for rapid transmission of an emergency stop message, as well as more reliable data recorders.

As in other recent accidents the report urged the provision of automatic train protection (ATP), which would have stopped the 21.55 train from passing the platform starting signal at danger.

Purley 1989

On a spring afternoon, residents of Glenn Avenue in Purley were working in their gardens below a high railway bank when a resounding crash rent the air above them. Two trains had collided and, to their astonishment, five coaches hurtled down the slope, killing five passengers.

Purley is on the London – Brighton main line, just over 13 miles from Victoria in the suburbs south of Croydon. The ground here is undulating, rising from the Thames basin towards the North Downs. There are some quite steep hills and valleys, not high in themselves but enough to cause the railway builders problems in the last century.

To cross over the Downs entails an almost continuous climb soon after leaving Victoria. From East Croydon there is an unbroken seven mile rise of 1 in 264 through Purley to the summit of the line at the parallel Merstham and Quarry tunnels. But, because of the undulations, massive embankments up to 60ft high had to be built between South East Croydon and Coulsdon to maintain an even gradient.

The history of the line was complicated because two railways – the South Eastern line to Dover and the Brighton line – originally had to share tracks to Redhill. By 1900 four tracks were provided in the area. Purley was also the junction for the Caterham and Tadworth (later Tattenham Corner)

branches, so the station had six platforms in all.

During the early 1980s, the track layout was altered in connection with resignalling. New crossovers were installed at Purley and further south to rationalize layouts and operating practices (which had largely dated from the Brighton electrification on the third rail system in 1932-33). This provided more flexibility and higher speed crossovers.

Just north of Purley are crossovers from the up slow line to the up fast and from the down fast to down slow, both sets also giving access to the up and down loop lines for the Caterham and Tattenham Corner branches. All the signalling in the area is modern and controlled from Three Bridges Signalling Centre, 16 miles to the south, through relay interlockings.

The signals themselves are colour lights, mostly four-aspect types with white light junction indicators for those controlling moves through the junctions ahead. All the running signals are equipped with the automatic warning system

▼All five of the coaches which careered down the embankment can be seen in this aerial shot. A sixth was hanging over the edge behind, the seventh was derailed, while only the eighth and last remained on the tracks. The rear two coaches of the Horsham train were also derailed.

through the crossovers from the up slow to the up fast lines.

Meanwhile, another train was approaching Purley on the up fast line. This was the 12.17 from Littlehampton to Victoria, an eight-coach formation comprising two four-coach main line Class 421/2 EMUs, originally known as 4CIGs in the SR code. It was running non-stop from Gatwick airport to East Croydon and had been routed on the Quarry line, avoiding Redhill, and continuing on the up fast line from Coulsdon towards Croydon.

The signals had been green all the way from Gatwick to Coulsdon. But at Stoats Nest Junction, just north of Coulsdon, where high speed crossovers allow trains to be switched between fast and slow lines, the up fast line signal approaching the crossovers, No 182, was displaying a double yellow aspect without a junction indicator. This meant that the Littlehampton train was continuing on the up fast line, but that its driver should prepare to slow down as the next signal was likely to be showing a caution aspect.

With the signals at Purley clear for the train

▲One of the coaches was set down between two houses on Glenn Avenue before being hoisted on to a trailer and removed by road. It was surrounded in the meantime by rescue service personnel who were later criticized for not allowing BR engineers access to the wreckage in a misguided attempt to preserve evidence.

Key to trains

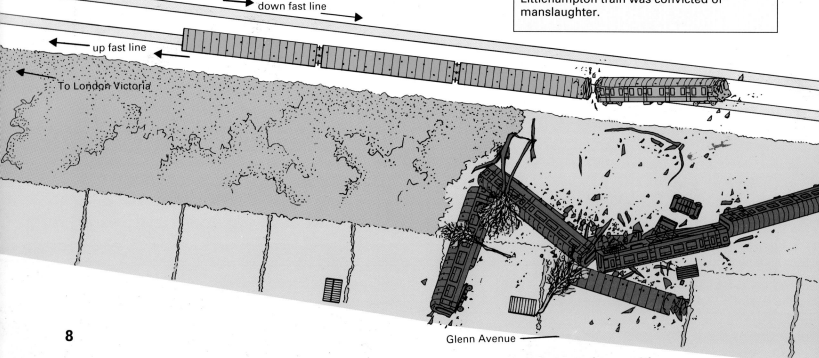

12.17 Littlehampton – London (Victoria)

12.50 Horsham – London (Victoria)

(AWS) while the track magnets for operating the cab equipment are placed about 200yd before the signal to which they apply.

The semi-fast to Victoria

On the afternoon of Saturday 4 March 1989, the 12.50 semi-fast train from Horsham to Victoria drew into platform 3 at Purley, running on the slow line. It was formed by a four-coach EMU of Class 423, originally known under the Southern Region (SR) code as a 4VEP.

As the train ran into the platform at 13.39, the signal at the departure end was red, but it then changed to a single yellow aspect with the junction indicator displayed. This meant that the train was to be switched from the up slow line to the up fast line when it departed. With the station work complete, the guard gave the starting bell signal to the driver who accelerated the train out of the platform. He allowed for the 25mph speed restriction

A lapse of concentration

As the 12.50 Horsham – London train was switching from the up slow to the up fast line, it was rammed by the 12.17 Littlehampton – London train travelling at about 50mph. The inquiry conclusively proved that the Littlehampton driver had ignored signals at caution and unconsciously cancelled automatic warning system (AWS) indicators in his cab. Having passed signal No 182 at double yellow and No 178 at single yellow, he finally saw No 168 at red on the approach to Purley station. He slammed on the brakes, but by then it was too late to avoid the collision. The leading five coaches flew down the bank and into the back gardens of Glenn Avenue below, the sixth hung on the edge and the seventh was derailed, leaving only the last coach on the tracks. A total of 88 people were injured and five passengers died. The driver of the Littlehampton train was convicted of manslaughter.

down fast line

up fast line

To London Victoria

Glenn Avenue

from Horsham to cross from the up slow to the up fast line, the up fast line signal approaching Purley, No 178, was indeed showing a single yellow and the next up fast line platform starting signal ahead of No 178, No 168, was at red, meaning that the Littlehampton train would have to stop.

The Horsham train swung over the crossover but, with about three coaches on the up fast line, there was a violent impact at the back. Its driver shut off power and applied the brakes but the train had almost stopped anyway. The Littlehampton train had failed to stop at signal No 168 and had hit the back coach of the Horsham train at a speed of around 50mph. Estimates suggest that the speed difference of the two trains was between 30 and 40mph on impact.

The results for the Littlehampton train were catastrophic as the impact derailed it to the left, straight down the high embankment and through the trees into the gardens of Glenn Avenue. Five coaches went completely over the edge while the sixth stopped partly down the bank. Witnesses suggested that the train actually flew through the air.

Residents had a lucky escape as debris, bogies and complete coaches landed around them. The passengers were not so lucky. Five were killed and no fewer than 88, including three railway staff, needed hospital treatment. The Littlehampton train driver also escaped, although he was injured.

What went wrong?

The press reports on the following day had no doubts as to why it happened. Coming just three months after the Clapham Junction disaster (when a stray electric wire in a relay room had caused a signal to show clear instead of red, resulting in the death of 35 people), they decided that the Purley accident must have resulted from the same thing. In fact, it didn't.

There being no technical fault, it was much more basic than that – simply a case of driver error. The driver of the Littlehampton train had seen green signals approaching Coulsdon but was then totally oblivious of the aspects shown by signals 182 and 178. He must also have unconscious-

▼Residents of Glenn Avenue were horrified by the sight of the eight-coach Class 421/2 EMU leaving the rails and, according to witnesses, flying through the air, before landing in their back gardens. Miraculously, no residents were injured.

point of impact

From Horsham and Littlehampton →

▲The residents of Glenn Avenue in Purley had never seen anything like it. One of the coaches from the 12.17 Littlehampton – Victoria train had to be hoisted aloft between the terraced houses after the accident occurred.

ly cancelled the AWS warnings. As his train approached Purley at about 70mph, he saw the platform starting signal at red and made an emergency brake application. He realized, however, that the train wasn't going to stop in time and it ran into the back of the Horsham train.

Although it appeared that a driver's mistake had caused the collision, BR technical departments carried out a thorough check of all the signalling equipment. This included counting all the wires and making sure all the relays were operating correctly so as to be certain that they didn't have another Clapham Junction on their hands. The equipment was shown to be in full working order.

The inquiry
There was no doubt now that the accident had been caused by the driver of the Littlehampton train not observing the caution signals and not slowing down in time. Nevertheless, the inquiry, chaired by the Deputy Chief Inspecting Officer of Railways, Mr Alan Cooksey, heard that a number of signalling faults had occurred in the area since installation in 1984. Most, however, were right side failures (signals showing danger when they should have shown a proceed indication). There had also been several cases of signal No 168 being passed at danger. Two wrong side failures had occurred because of design faults, but they had been spotted before they caused accidents.

Mr Cooksey was critical of this early unreliability of the new signalling equipment, but his report showed that it was working normally at the

time of the accident. He said that witnesses had seen the signals working normally at the time and, since no fault was found by tests after the accident, he considered that the signals were showing the correct aspects when the Littlehampton train approached Purley. Its driver had never claimed that signal No 168 was showing any indication other than red. Mr Cooksey concluded that he had failed to heed the meaning of the double yellow and single yellow aspects of signals 182 and 178, and the alarms of the AWS which he must have reset without thinking.

The report examined the unusually large number of cases in which signal No 168 had been passed at danger. Although the sighting time – 7 seconds – was within the limits for seeing a signal on a 90mph line, he felt that the view to drivers was poor since it was obstructed by the station buildings as a train approached. In contrast, the view of the two previous signals was excellent and No 178 (approaching Purley) could be seen for 1100yd (1006m). He thought the indication shown by No 168 should be enhanced by a banner repeater signal approaching the station.

His two main recommendations were aimed at further enhancing safety. The first was that black box incident recorders be fitted, as in aircraft. Investigators could then have evidence of what had happened just before an accident, including the speed of the train, whether power or brakes were applied and whether there had been an AWS warning.

His primary recommendation was for the development of an automatic train protection (ATP) system. This would override the driver if he exceeded speed limits or if he failed to slow down enough to stop at a danger signal, and would also prevent the train from overrunning such a signal. Mr Cooksey felt that ATP shouldn't be delayed so that BR could develop its own unique version, and that an existing system, of which there were several around the world, could be used.

Clapham Junction 1988

The Clapham disaster was an accident waiting to happen. Human error during rewiring works prevented a signal from showing red, resulting in a crowded commuter train running into the rear of another, which was stationary, and then veering to the right and striking a second oncoming train.

The morning of Monday, 12 December 1988 dawned chilly and bright. As darkness gave way to daylight over the south-west London suburbs, the rush hour on the main lines into Waterloo began to build up. Several trains were on the up main line from starting points in the south-west – not just from the outer suburbs, but on the longer distance services coming in through Surbiton and Wimbledon. Before they reached Clapham Junction, trains would slow down from the 90mph allowed further out to around 60mph and, given green signals, drivers would begin to brake for the 40mph restriction through Clapham Junction itself.

The driver of the 06.14 Poole to Waterloo train was running under green signals from Wimbledon. After passing signal WF138 – the second signal out from Clapham Junction, which was showing green – the driver let the train coast round the left-hand curve ready for the 40mph restriction ahead. There was a steep bank and retaining wall to his left which limited his view of the line ahead – suddenly he saw a train standing on the line in front of him.

It was unthinkable – the last signal had been green. He put the brake handle into the full emergency position, but from 50mph there was barely time to slow down, let alone stop. His train smashed into the back of the standing train at about 35mph.

The train ahead was the 07.18 Basingstoke to Waterloo, a 12-coach train of three outer suburban type electric multiple units. The rear two coaches were trailers and lighter than the heavy motor coach at the front of the 12-coach Poole electric train. Although the Poole train hit the Basingstoke train squarely in the back, it continued along the right of the stationary train, throwing the rear coach of the first train up on to the retaining wall and bank.

But worse was to come, for as the Poole train

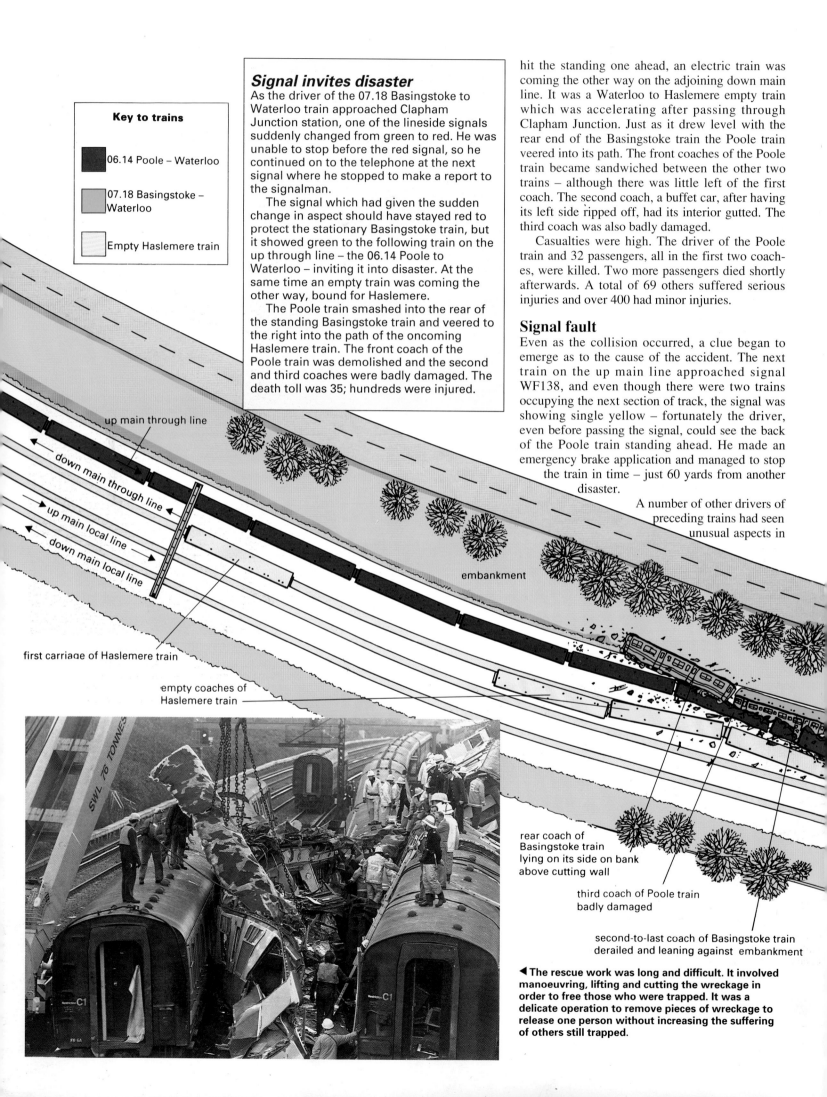

Signal invites disaster

As the driver of the 07.18 Basingstoke to Waterloo train approached Clapham Junction station, one of the lineside signals suddenly changed from green to red. He was unable to stop before the red signal, so he continued on to the telephone at the next signal where he stopped to make a report to the signalman.

The signal which had given the sudden change in aspect should have stayed red to protect the stationary Basingstoke train, but it showed green to the following train on the up through line – the 06.14 Poole to Waterloo – inviting it into disaster. At the same time an empty train was coming the other way, bound for Haslemere.

The Poole train smashed into the rear of the standing Basingstoke train and veered to the right into the path of the oncoming Haslemere train. The front coach of the Poole train was demolished and the second and third coaches were badly damaged. The death toll was 35; hundreds were injured.

hit the standing one ahead, an electric train was coming the other way on the adjoining down main line. It was a Waterloo to Haslemere empty train which was accelerating after passing through Clapham Junction. Just as it drew level with the rear end of the Basingstoke train the Poole train veered into its path. The front coaches of the Poole train became sandwiched between the other two trains – although there was little left of the first coach. The second coach, a buffet car, after having its left side ripped off, had its interior gutted. The third coach was also badly damaged.

Casualties were high. The driver of the Poole train and 32 passengers, all in the first two coaches, were killed. Two more passengers died shortly afterwards. A total of 69 others suffered serious injuries and over 400 had minor injuries.

Signal fault

Even as the collision occurred, a clue began to emerge as to the cause of the accident. The next train on the up main line approached signal WF138, and even though there were two trains occupying the next section of track, the signal was showing single yellow – fortunately the driver, even before passing the signal, could see the back of the Poole train standing ahead. He made an emergency brake application and managed to stop the train in time – just 60 yards from another disaster.

A number of other drivers of preceding trains had seen unusual aspects in

Key to trains

■ 06.14 Poole – Waterloo

▨ 07.18 Basingstoke – Waterloo

□ Empty Haslemere train

up main through line

down main through line

up main local line

down main local line

first carriage of Haslemere train

empty coaches of Haslemere train

embankment

rear coach of Basingstoke train lying on its side on bank above cutting wall

third coach of Poole train badly damaged

second-to-last coach of Basingstoke train derailed and leaning against embankment

◀ The rescue work was long and difficult. It involved manoeuvring, lifting and cutting the wreckage in order to free those who were trapped. It was a delicate operation to remove pieces of wreckage to release one person without increasing the suffering of others still trapped.

the two or three signals approaching Clapham Junction that morning. One saw signal WF138 go from yellow to green, but thought that a train ahead had been side-tracked at Clapham Junction. Another passed one signal at green and the next at single yellow and assumed that the signalman at Clapham Junction had put a signal back to danger ahead of him.

But the driver of the 07.18 from Basingstoke had seen a more serious change of aspect. Signal WF138 was green when he first saw it, travelling at over 60mph, but it changed to red when his train was no more than 30 yards from it. He could not stop the train before passing the signal. As all cases of signals passed at danger must be reported, he stopped his train at the next signal (WF47, just outside Clapham Junction station) to call the signalman from the signalpost telephone. The signalman told him that there was nothing wrong with the signal – but just as the driver turned to get back on to his train, the Poole train ran into the back of it, pushing it forward by 10 feet.

The driver of the standing Basingstoke train picked up the handset again and told the signalman that his train had been rammed in the rear and that the emergency services should be called. The signalman immediately put all the controlled signals in the area to danger to stop all trains.

What went wrong?

Modern British colour light signalling has an excellent safety record. Each signal protects the stretch of track beyond it (known as a block section) by detecting the presence of a train in the section – or on a further distance called an overlap – by means of electrical circuits in the tracks. As the wheels of a train enter the section, the track circuit is shorted out and the

▲As darkness began to draw in, council electricians provided floodlighting to the scene. The London Borough of Wandsworth was commended by the chairman of the investigation for the speed and scale of the assistance it gave to the emergency services.

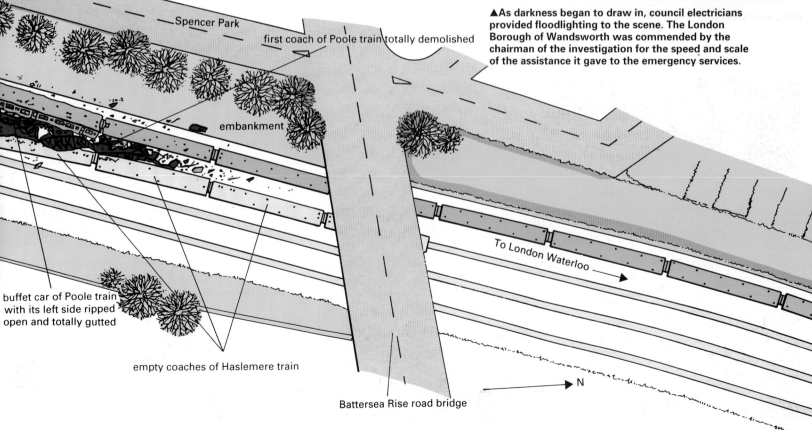

Spencer Park

first coach of Poole train totally demolished

embankment

buffet car of Poole train with its left side ripped open and totally gutted

empty coaches of Haslemere train

Battersea Rise road bridge

To London Waterloo

N

electric supply to the track circuit relay is cut. This action changes the electric circuits to the signal, and switches off the control current to the signal. It makes the signal change automatically to a red aspect and is designed to be a totally fail-safe system. But on the morning of 12 December 1988 signal WF138 did fail – so what went wrong?

The controls on signal WF138 included two track circuits: DL running from just beyond signal WF138 to just beyond signal WF47, and DM through a set of points just beyond signal WF47. Both track circuits had to be clear for signal WF138 to show a proceed aspect. If there was a train on either or both track circuits DL and DM, the control current would be cut off and signal WF138 would show red.

While investigating the accident, signal engineers examined the wiring in the Clapham Junction relay room. There they discovered the cause of the accident – a stray wire. It was attached to a fuse at one end, but its uninsulated loose end was touching a terminal on the relay designed to repeat track circuit DM through the points. This meant that although a train standing on track circuit DL at signal WF47 was correctly operating the track circuit – and therefore showing the correct indication to the signalman – the stray wire touching repeater relay DM provided a path

▲Rescue efforts were hampered by a steep wooded bank sloping down from the adjoining road, followed by a 10 foot high concrete retaining wall down to the track. Steel railings had to be cut away and many trees and shrubs chopped down to allow rescuers to reach the site.

The wiring error

In wiring up new signal WF138, connections had to be made between the track repeater relay for track circuit DM – via another track repeater relay for track circuit DL – to a fuse.

The wire for the old signal which was being replaced should have been disconnected, cut back and insulated – but it was not. Instead the wire was left attached to the fuse, and although the other end was pushed away from the terminal, it sprang back to make contact once again when it was disturbed.

The stray wire permitted a disastrous false feed of current from track repeater relay DM to the fuse and then on to signal WF138, bypassing relay DL. This meant that when the Basingstoke train was standing on track circuit DL it could not be detected by the signal that was designed to protect it. The control current did not switch off, so the signal did not show a red aspect to the following Poole train.

for the control current to bypass relay DL and go straight to signal WF138.

Any train standing on track circuit DL was invisible to signal WF138. Only when a train occupied the following track circuit – DM – through the points just beyond signal WF47 did signal WF138 show red. This accounted for the unusual aspects seen by the drivers of earlier trains. When the driver of the 07.18 from Basingstoke saw signal WF138 at green it was because the train ahead was still on track circuit DL – and not far in front of him. As that train moved on and occupied track circuit DM, signal WF138 detected it and changed to red – just as the Basingstoke train approached it. When the driver stopped at signal WF47 to report the red signal he had passed, his train had become invisible to the signal behind him. Therefore WF138 had changed back to green, inviting the Poole train into disaster.

Signal WF138 had only just been installed. It replaced an old signal as part of work which was being carried out to update old electric signalboxes, colour light signals and track circuits in the Waterloo area. Alterations to the wiring in the Clapham Junction signalbox were needed to bring

rogue wire making contact with terminal

path for false current bypassing relay DL

fuse

wire carrying false electric current to WF138

track repeater relay DM energized

proper path for electric current

other electrical equipment

Key
- ● Red signal
- ● Amber signal
- ○ Green signal

electric current should have stopped here

track repeater relay DL de-energized

Signals as they should have looked to the Poole train

| Clapham Junction | DM | | DK | BN | |
| WF47 ○ | DL | WF138 ● | WF142 ○ | WF148 | |

07.18 Basingstoke – Waterloo train

06.14 Poole – Waterloo train

Sequence of signals at the time of the disaster

| Clapham Junction | DM | | DK | BN | |
| WF47 ○ | DL | WF138 ○ | WF142 ○ | WF148 ○ | |

07.18 Basingstoke – Waterloo train

06.14 Poole – Waterloo train

track circuit repeater relay DL and another piece of equipment into the existing control circuit from relay DM to signal WF138. On Sunday 27 November the technician took off the old wire from the DM relay and pushed it aside as he attached the new wires to the extra relays. But he did not cut off the old wire or insulate it.

Two weeks later, on Sunday 11 December, more work was done in the relay room on the relay next to that for track circuit DM. In the process the old wire was disturbed and it sprang back into the position which it had occupied for so many years – to the terminal from which it had been disconnected. It was just resting on top of the terminal, but the contact was enough to cause that fatal false feed to the signal.

Accident investigation

The Secretary of State ordered a judicial investigation, chaired by Anthony Hidden QC. Many aspects were unearthed by the inquiry – not least the amount of overtime worked by signal engineering staff. There was a slippage of working practices to dangerous standards, lack of adequate testing, proper supervision and training, and inadequate communication between management and men on the ground.

▼Spencer Park was used as a base for the emergency services. Assistance was also given by council workers, the Salvation Army, Emanuel School and the British Association for Immediate Care (BASICS), a charity which provides medical help at scenes of major disasters.

Recommendations

Mr Anthony Hidden QC made 93 recommendations. The main ones directly relating to the accident included requirements that wiring practices be improved and standards adopted nationally; drawing office standards had to be improved; proper testing had to be adopted, including wire counts by independent qualified testers; a national testing instruction had to take place, with testing engineers being independent of installation staff. Also recommended were effective instructions, proper initial and refresher training for technical staff, better management and organization and proper safety monitoring.

Mr Hidden welcomed BR's move to adopt an automatic train protection system (ATP) to prevent speed limits being exceeded and signals passed at danger – although the accident might not have been prevented even if ATP equipment had been linked to the controls of signal WF138.

Communications between signalboxes and electrical control rooms were to be improved so that the track surrounding an accident site could be electrically isolated immediately. Communications generally, including those to emergency services, were to be reviewed also. Modifications to rolling stock design were to be examined.

Generally, the recommendations amounted to the need for BR to improve its overall safety systems.

Hawes Junction 1910

It was a dark and stormy Christmas Eve when two engines, coupled together, were forgotten by a busy signalman, causing a serious collision with the overnight Scotch Express and a major fire on the wild Pennine moors. Though the signalman accepted the blame, locomotive crews had also ignored basic rules.

▼*The Sphere* magazine produced a graphic illustration of the disaster for its New Year edition. After the driver of the Scotch Express had emerged from Moorcock Tunnel in the centre of the diagram, he had less than 6 seconds to react after seeing the slowly moving light engines straight ahead. Similarly, the light engine drivers had no time to accelerate away.

Disasters at Christmas always seem to be more poignant because they usually involve families visiting relations for the festive season. In the past there was perhaps more risk of accident when staff were stretched with far more extra trains than today added to the normal service to cope with heavy traffic. The Midland Railway in the early years of this century was no exception.

For Christmas 1910 it had arranged several extra services on its Anglo-Scottish main line between London and Scotland. But it had the added handicap on the section between Leeds and Carlisle of having to climb across the Pennines with the 10 mile stretch from Blea Moor Tunnel to Ais Gill, around 1100ft above sea level.

Hawes Junction (today known as Garsdale), a bleak moorland station about 3 miles south of Ais Gill Summit, was operationally the centre of the area with three platforms, a branch to Hawes, a signalbox on the down platform, and a turntable reached from a siding on the down side. The reason for the turntable was the height, for the Settle & Carlisle section included long climbs at 1 in 100 from near sea level at Carlisle, and from the lower areas of Yorkshire around Leeds. The Midland Railway had small engines only, nothing larger than 4-4-0s of varying design and power, most not able to take more than 180 tons (six or seven coaches) unaided over the Settle & Carlisle line. The heavier services needed a second engine to help lift them up the steep gradients. Ais Gill, the summit of the line, was the point where the trains stopped to uncouple the assisting engine from both Carlisle and Leeds directions. The assisting engines then ran light to Hawes Junction where

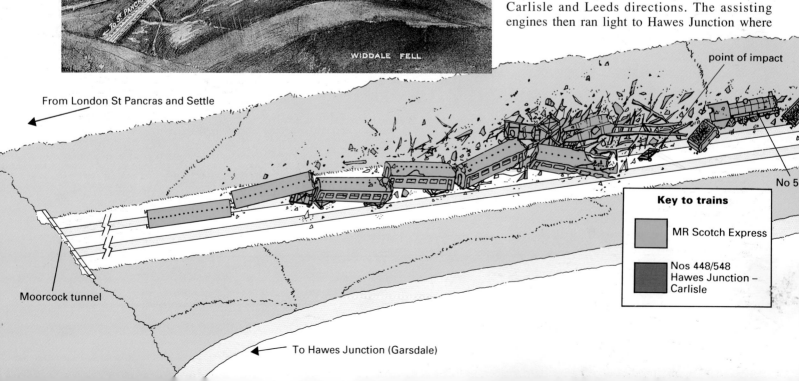

From London St Pancras and Settle

Moorcock tunnel

To Hawes Junction (Garsdale)

point of impact

No 54&

Key to trains

MR Scotch Express

Nos 448/548 Hawes Junction – Carlisle

◄Railway staff work to replace track on the down line which had been torn up by the second of the Scotch Express locomotives. Almost 400 yards of track were destroyed. The charred remains of the coaches lie beside the line after being cleared from the tracks. All the coaches except for the rear two brake vans were consumed in the inferno.

they turned and worked back without a train.

The night of 23 December 1910 was wild and stormy with fierce winds blowing across the exposed moorland, driving the rain hard against anyone out there. It must have been uncomfortable on the engine footplate, with little protection other than a canvas storm sheet stretched from the cab roof to the tender.

Soon after 4am on Christmas Eve morning, there were no fewer than nine engines at Hawes Junction. A pair of Class 2 4-4-0s, Nos 448 and 548, had just arrived from Ais Gill off trains from Carlisle. They had been turned fairly quickly, but the signalman could not send them back straight away because of other trains on the down line. He set them back over the crossover to the branch platform to await a path.

Before 5am a down goods and an up goods had passed and several light engines had been shunted. But the signalman still couldn't send Nos 448 and

548 back to Carlisle as he was expecting an extra down express. When it finally swept past at 5.20, he had his chance. He changed the points from the branch platform across the up to the down line and signalled the two engines on to the advanced starting signal. This was at danger behind the extra express, so they waited for it to clear Ais Gill.

But then, with all the other engine movements, the two light engines slipped his mind. And with the night pitch black and rain sheeting across, he couldn't see the rear tail lamp. Nor did he have any mechanical or electrical equipment to remind him of the two engines. Such equipment was rare then.

The two engines were held at the signal for over ten minutes, far longer than was needed for

To Carlisle and Scotland

To Ais Gill Summit

No 548

No 48

down main line

up main line

No 448

A lapse of memory

The accident was caused because the signalman at Hawes Junction forgot that he had sent two light engines, coupled together, to wait at his down advanced starter signal. He then cleared that signal for the overnight sleeping car express from St Pancras to Glasgow. The two engines, thinking the signal clearance was meant for them, moved off. Tackling the summit slowly, they were not travelling at more than 30mph when the express, thundering up behind at about 60mph, caught them up 1½ miles beyond Hawes Junction, and collided with them. The Hawes Junction signalman was blamed for the 12 deaths.

Train lighting

Very basic oil lamps were used for primitive lighting from the early days of the railways in the 1830s. From the 1860s, a few companies used coal gas, carried in containers under the coaches, but this proved erratic. A decade later the German, Julius Pintsch, invented a system using compressed oil-gas in cylinders fitted beneath each coach, at a pressure of around 80lb/sq in. But by the 1880s the first experiments with electric lighting had been undertaken on new Brighton line Pullman cars, and by the end of the century electricity was a serious rival to gas.

The problem was that heavy batteries and axle driven dynamos added to train weight so that electrically lit coaches were heavier than gaslit ones. This influenced the Midland Railway with its small engine policy. It continued to build gaslit coaches up to World War I and even a few after that. The LMS built a few gaslit coaches in the 1930s, but these were kitchen cars with gas for cooking.

The last gaslit coaches were phased out during the 1950s, except for a few on the short Devon line to Hemyock. They were needed until the early 1960s because speeds on the line were so low that electric dynamos couldn't keep the batteries charged.

▼With the bleak fells in the background, a tangled mess of bogies and underframes litters the embankment beside the down line. The cylinder in the top left of the photograph is one of the pressurized tanks used to hold fuel for the Pintsch gas lighting system. It was a pipe leading from one of these tanks which ruptured, causing the gas to ignite and burst into a ball of flame.

the express to have cleared Ais Gill. Yet the crews failed to remind the signalman by sounding the engine whistles or carrying out one of the most famous rules in the book, Rule 55, by one of the firemen going to the signalbox to remind the signalman.

At 5.39am, the signalman accepted the midnight London sleeping car express from Dent, the next signalbox to the south, and immediately offered it on to Ais Gill, which accepted. He then cleared all his down line signals for the express.

The drivers of the two light engines naturally took the clear advanced starting signal as theirs and started off. But they were in no great hurry.

The sleeping car express was working hard, even on the short falling gradient through Hawes Junction, ready for the final climb to Ais Gill a short distance ahead. It was double-headed and travelling at around 60mph, but would stop at Ais Gill to detach the assisting engine.

Poor visibility

It never reached Ais Gill, catching up the two light engines around 1½ miles beyond Hawes Junction. Emerging from Moorcock Tunnel, the leading driver had almost no time to react after seeing the tail lamp on the rear light engine, and the express hit them at an impact speed of around 30mph. They were pushed forward for about 200 yards before the tender of the leading engine and all of the second engine left the track. The leading engine of the express was derailed, while staying more or less in line, but the second engine overturned and the wooden-bodied coaches were wrecked as they piled up against it, the first two being telescoped. Seven out of the eight coaches were derailed and badly damaged.

But worse was to follow because all but the two sleeping cars were gaslit and one of the gas pipes fractured, allowing the whole of the gas supply in one coach to escape and ignite in a ball of flame, setting all the wreckage on fire. Nine passengers died immediately, with the death toll rising to 12.

Back at Hawes Junction, the first stages of the impending disaster had been seen by the crew of another light engine, waiting to go to Hellifield. They had watched the two light engines go down to the advanced starter and later had seen that signal go to clear. But it did not go to danger behind the two engines as they started off towards Carlisle. A moment or two later the sleeping car express roared through the station and they realized that it would soon catch up with the two light engines. The driver rushed to the signalbox and asked the signalman where the two engines were and told him what he had seen. The signalman looked stunned. He checked his train register book and telephoned Ais Gill to ask if the engines had arrived. But the glare in the sky told its own tale. Just then the morning turn signalman arrived. The night duty signalman just said to him, 'Go and tell the stationmaster I have wrecked the Scotch Express'.

The inquiry

Colonel Sir John Pringle carried out the inquiry. He didn't have far to look as the Hawes Junction signalman admitted his mistake. But he also put some of the liability on the two drivers of the light engines for not carrying out Rule 55.

Two features in his report marked milestones in railway safety: one concerning the causes of the loss of life and the other concerning the prevention of accidents of this kind in future. Action to phase out gaslit coaches and to introduce track circuits was undertaken following his recommendations.

But the root cause of the Hawes Junction disaster, the small engine policy of the Midland, did not change for the next 20 years.

Colwich Junction 1986

With modern signalling systems it should be impossible for two trains to meet head-on, but that is exactly what happened at Colwich in 1986. A train on its way to Manchester ran through a red light on the approach to a diamond crossing – straight into the path of an express coming the other way at 100mph.

Friday afternoons on British Rail are usually busy, and Friday 19 September 1986 was no exception. The 17.00 Euston to Manchester Piccadilly via Stoke train, hauled by electric locomotive No 86429, had 13 coaches carrying over 370 passengers, with seats to spare. In the opposite direction the 17.20 Liverpool Lime Street to Euston train, with locomotive No 86211 at the head, had one coach fewer but around 500 passengers, so most seats were filled.

Both trains had uneventful journeys until they approached Colwich Junction on the West Coast main line between Lichfield and Stafford, where the Manchester via Stoke line diverges from the West Coast route. There they met disaster in a spectacular high speed head-on collision, which was one of the most destructive of recent years in terms of rolling stock damage. Tragically, the driver of the Liverpool train was killed, but none of the passengers died in the accident – so what

saved the 870 passengers in the two trains from death? And with modern signalling, some of which had just been updated, what circumstances led to two express trains meeting head-on?

Main line junction

Colwich lies 127 miles from London on the West Coast main line. When approached from London there are four tracks: the down fast, down slow, up fast and up slow. The down fast line heads towards Stafford on the West Coast route, while the down slow line diverges on the flat through a diamond crossing over the up fast line towards Stoke. Trains on the up fast line can travel across the diamond at the full 100mph line speed, but trains on the down slow line are limited to 45mph because of curvature and track geometry.

There is a 50mph crossover from the down fast to the down slow line approaching Colwich, about $\frac{1}{2}$ mile from the diamond crossing. This feature

▼Following the head-on collision between two express passenger trains, the second, third, fourth and fifth coaches of the Liverpool to Euston train flew up, skewed sideways and came to rest on top of coach M5990 of the Euston to Manchester train. Because of the strength of the coaches, none of the passengers from either train was killed.

▲Damage to the coaches of both trains was extensive. Many of the Liverpool train's carriages, including those seen here, were beyond repair. The impact of the collision on the rear of the Manchester locomotive ripped it from its rear bogie (seen here on its side, right of picture).

offers the signalman unusual flexibility, as he can pass a train towards the branch heading for Stoke and Manchester in two stages: first from the down fast to the down slow, and then, if necessary, the train can be stopped on the down slow if its way over the diamond crossing is not clear. This layout avoids delays to following trains on the down fast line heading towards Stafford. Four-aspect colour light signals, all worked from Colwich signalbox, control the area.

Signals at Colwich Junction

The signalbox at Colwich was an old style type, with a lever frame adapted to work colour light signals when it was resignalled in the early 1960s. All lines were track circuited so that even though

the method of working the signals was old-fashioned, all the modern controls were used.

For the last 40 years most junctions on BR controlled by colour light signals have been protected by approach control. This is to ensure that the speed of a train taking a diverging route off a principal line is reduced correctly.

For a low speed divergence (generally less than 50mph) the junction signal is held at danger – even though the signalman may have set the route on to the diverging line. As the train occupies the track circuit approaching the signal, a timing device is started which is set to hold the signal at danger until the train speed is at the correct level for the junction ahead; then the timer is released and the signals clear to yellow, double yellow or

Key to trains

■ 17.00 Euston - Manchester

▨ 17.20 Liverpool - Euston

Coach strength

The crash scene at Colwich looked horrendous, but the strength of the Mark 2 and Mark 3 coaches meant that although they suffered extensive damage – many beyond repair – they saved the lives of the passengers. Out of a combined total of 870 passengers from both trains, only 75 sustained injuries, few of which were serious; the driver of the Liverpool train was the only fatality.

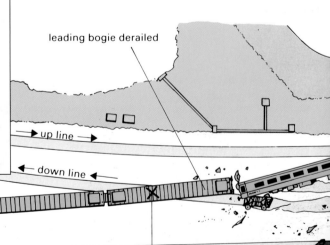

To Manchester via Stoke ←

N

← up fast line →

→ From Liverpool via Stafford →

← down fast line ←

leading bogie derailed

→ up line →

← down line ←

point of impact— switch diamond points

green (depending on the signals ahead), with a white light junction indicator.

At medium speed junctions, where trains can leave an otherwise high speed line at around 50mph or more, approach control from red would be too restrictive and difficult to apply in some cases – a driver could not see the signal change from red without slowing down too much – so BR adopted approach control from single yellow. The signal beyond the junction is held at red and the junction signal is first seen at single yellow with a junction indicator. In some cases, however, this could be dangerous – if a driver did not see the junction indicator until too late, he might take the divergence too fast.

In 1977 BR adopted a new positive signal indication as an advance warning to drivers that the route was set to a lower speed divergence off an otherwise high speed straight route. This uses flashing yellow indications at the two signals before the junction signal (there is no flashing double yellow aspect on lines with three-aspect signalling). At the signal next but one before the junction signal, the display is of flashing double yellows. This means that the line is set for a diverging route ahead and that the next signal will be a flashing single yellow.

A flashing single yellow aspect means that the driver must be prepared to find the next signal at single steady yellow, with a junction indicator for the highest speed diverging route. As the train approaches the junction signal, giving the driver time to see the junction indicator, it may clear to double yellow or green, depending on whether the line beyond the next signal is clear. If the junction signal stays at yellow the next signal must be assumed to be at red.

At Colwich Junction, about a month before the accident, the signal aspects advising drivers of trains to be switched from the down fast to the down slow line were changed from the approach control system to indications by flashing yellow aspects. Notices were issued to inform drivers of this important change, but there was still some confusion on its use in the mind of the driver of the 17.00 Euston to Stoke/Manchester train.

Into disaster

On that fateful Friday evening in 1986, the first signal approaching Colwich to be seen by the driver of the 17.00 train from Euston was CH105, just under 1¼ miles from the fast to slow junction signal. CH105 was displaying flashing double yellows. This was his first advice to confirm that he was being switched to the down slow line and that the junction signal was showing a proceed aspect.

The driver braked from the 100mph he had been doing to about 80mph, and then to 60mph when he saw the next signal, CH103, displaying a flashing single yellow as a reminder of the junction ahead. He continued to brake as he passed junction signal, CH28, showing a steady single yellow with a right-hand white light junction indicator for the fast to slow line crossover ahead.

The next signal on the down slow, CH23,

▼The rescue services arrived within minutes of the call from the signalman on duty in the signalbox, who had witnessed the horrific collision. A senior technician, who was also in the signalbox at the time of the crash, was a valuable witness in the investigation which followed.

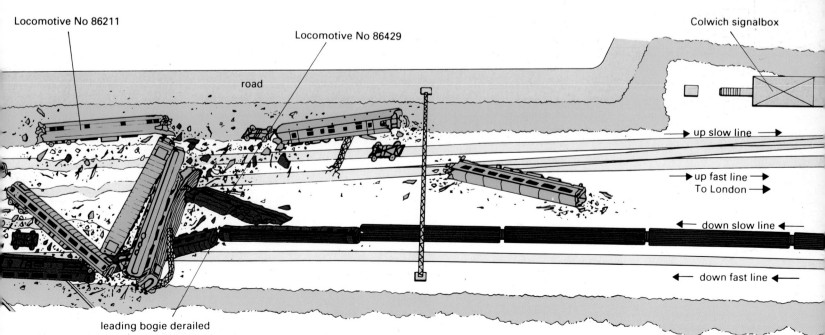

Locomotive No 86211

Locomotive No 86429

road

Colwich signalbox

→ up slow line →

→ up fast line →
To London →

← down slow line ←

← down fast line ←

leading bogie derailed

Driver's view of signals

As the Manchester train approached Colwich the signals were set for it to cross from the down fast to the down slow line. Signal CH105 was a flashing double yellow, which meant that the junction signal was showing a proceed aspect. The next signal, CH103, was a flashing single yellow as a reminder of the junction ahead.

The driver slowed to cross from the fast to slow line, and passed junction signal CH28 – a steady single yellow aspect. This should have warned him that the next signal would be at red. But the driver thought that signal CH23 was approach controlled and would change to a proceed aspect as he drew near. When it did not he made an emergency brake application, but was unable to stop before the crossing with the up main line. The Liverpool train, having just passed a signal at green and travelling at 100mph, could not avoid a collision and smashed into the front of the Manchester train.

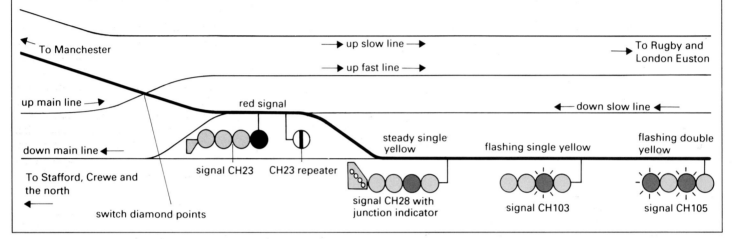

259yd before the diamond crossing, was at red. The Manchester train was still travelling at about 45mph when its driver saw first a banner repeater of the signal, and then the red of signal CH23 itself. At first he thought the signal was approach controlled and could change from red to yellow or green, but suddenly he realized that it was not going to change. He immediately made an emergency brake application, but the train was not able to stop before the locomotive reached the diamond crossing with the up fast line.

The 17.20 Liverpool to Euston train was already in sight, running at 100mph, having passed the last signal at green. Its driver did not stand a chance of avoiding the locomotive of the 17.00 from Euston which was blocking the crossing in front of him. The Liverpool engine hit the Manchester locomotive and was hurled into the air, landing on the far side of the up slow line. The obstructing engine, No 86429, was flung back alongside its own train for three coach lengths.

The front two coaches of the Liverpool train went even further, the second Liverpool coach landing alongside the fifth coach of the Manchester train. The next four coaches of the Liverpool train jack-knifed on top of the second coach of the Manchester train, while several more coaches from both trains were derailed and overturned. In all, seven coaches were damaged

▶ An aerial view of the accident scene shows how the impact of the collision scattered the coaches of both trains right across all the tracks. Road cranes were brought in to assist the rail cranes in removing the wreckage.

▲Three overhead electric structures were demolished, and approximately three miles of contact and catenary wire and associated fittings were destroyed in the accident. It was four days before the overhead line equipment could be re-energized.

read the notices as inexcusable, the inquiry report also criticized the reduction in the numbers of motive power inspectors (due to cut-backs) which Major Olver felt had led to less efficient supervision on vital safety matters. It is the role of these inspectors to check the correct handling of locomotives by drivers, including their knowledge of signalling procedures.

During the investigation, doubts were expressed about the braking efficiency of the Manchester train. Most of the coaches were of the Mark 3 pattern with wheel-slide protection equipment. This means that, to prevent damage to the wheel tread by the wheels locking and sliding in a heavy brake application, special equipment releases the brakes slightly.

It was suggested by witnesses that the wheel-slide protection system was operated as the Manchester train was being braked, which meant that the brakes might have been eased on individual coaches. The inquiry report said that there was no substantial evidence to confirm whether the brakes were or were not working with normal efficiency, but witnesses thought that the deceleration was slower than expected. If the Manchester train had stopped just 15yd sooner, the Liverpool train would have missed it and the accident would not have occurred.

beyond repair; some were later cut up on site, while four more needed heavy repairs.

Yet, despite their damage, the main body structures of the coaches withstood the accident so that the passenger saloons were not crushed or ripped open and most windows remained unbroken. It was undoubtedly the great body strength of BR's Mark 3 coaches – and to a lesser extent the Mark 2s – involved in this accident that prevented major fatalities. In all, 75 passengers were injured, the majority needing no more than hospital treatment for cuts and bruises; only two seriously injured passengers remained in hospital for more than a month.

There was just one fatality, the driver of the Liverpool train. He was an innocent victim and could have done nothing to save himself or his train. The driver and another driver, who was an unauthorized passenger in the cab of the Manchester train, escaped injury – they jumped off the locomotive as it came to a stop, with the Liverpool train fast approaching.

What went wrong?

The inquiry inspecting officer, Major Peter Olver, concluded that the driver of the 17.00 train from Euston to Stoke/Manchester had passed signal CH23 at danger and, although he had made a full brake application, had not been able to stop until his locomotive had reached the diamond crossing.

The reason for the driver's mistake was his ignorance of the new signalling system. Although he had received notices telling him of the new flashing yellow signals, he had not read them and thought that the flashing yellows meant that the train was clear to go right across the junction and not just into the first stage. He was also confused by what he thought was an approach controlled signal, which CH23 was not.

Although denouncing the driver's failure to

Lichfield 1946

**When a local passenger train arrived at the platform
on the up loop at Lichfield the signalman reset the points
and cleared the signals for a fish express to overtake it
on the up main. But the fish train swung over the points
and rammed the passenger train, killing 20 people.**

▼ Railway gangs shovel up the debris of the wooden bodied coaches from the up platform line at Lichfield on 2 January 1946, the day after the collision. Part of the third coach of the former Midland Railway set, dating from about 1912, lies on the platform. Above are the high level platforms and bridge.

New Year's Day in 1946 was a Tuesday and a normal working day in England, with an ordinary weekday train service. At Stafford, industrial plants included English Electric, shoe factories and a works where salt was extracted from brine. Although many of the workers at these plants lived locally, at the end of the day some would have caught the 6.08pm stopping train to Rugby.

Stafford was the junction between the original Grand Junction main line – opened in 1837, between the Liverpool & Manchester Railway of 1830 and Birmingham, where it linked to the London & Birmingham Railway of 1838 – and the Trent Valley Railway, opened in 1847. The Trent Valley Railway formed an alternative route from London to the north between Rugby and Stafford. It avoided Birmingham and eventually became the principal route for through trains from London that didn't need to call at Birmingham or Wolverhampton.

The 6.08pm train ran on the Trent Valley route, calling at most stations. Like many local stopping trains of the steam era it was very slow, taking a minute or two under two hours for the 51 miles. For the first few stops to Rugeley and Lichfield it was a commuter train for people working in Stafford. Beyond, it provided a station to station service for locals, a few of whom might have gone on to Rugby for the last connection to an express from Birmingham to Northampton and Euston.

The Trent Valley route was a curious mixture of double, triple and quadruple track sections. On the four-track sections the fast lines were mostly in the centre and the slow lines on the outside. Other than at Nuneaton, only the slow lines had platform faces at the intermediate stations. Stopping trains either had to run on the slow line throughout, where slow lines existed, or run on the fast line, switch to the slow line at the crossovers just before the station, then run out again on to the fast line when they left.

But at Lichfield there was double track to the north and south, plus additional platform loops, giving four tracks through the station. A bridge over the Trent Valley line here carried the railway from Wichnor Junction on the Derby – Birmingham line, through Sutton Coldfield to Birmingham.

to Derby

brake van   fish vans   Lichfield station   point of impact

fish train should have continued on up fast →   signalbox

Trent Valley platforms

high level platforms

to Birmingham

The connections between the fast lines and the platform loops at the north end of Lichfield Trent Valley station were controlled by No 1 signalbox, one of two signalboxes at the station. The signalling was mechanical, though the up fast outer distant signal was a colour light.

The evening of 1 January 1946 was frosty, but the Lichfield signalman hadn't had any trouble with points freezing. At about 6.40pm he was offered the 6.08pm stopping train by the Armitage signalman. He accepted it with the points set for the crossover from the up fast into the up platform loop, and cleared the home signal to allow it in. It wasn't signalled out again as it was to be overtaken by the 2.50pm fish express from Fleetwood to London Broad Street.

The stopping train had just four coaches, all old wooden bodied non-corridor types hauled by a former London & North Western Railway Prince of Wales Class 4-6-0, No 25802. Because of World War II the London Midland & Scottish Railway (LMS) had to keep stock in service much longer than was normal, and this train was no exception.

Countdown to disaster

As soon as the stopping train was clear of the loop points the Lichfield signalman put the signals back to danger and caution, sent the 'train out of section' bell signal to the signalbox in the rear, and cleared the block indicator. The fish train was immediately offered, accepted by Lichfield, and offered forward to continue its journey on the up fast while the stopping train was standing in the platform loop.

The signalman pulled the lever to unlock the bolt on the facing points of the up fast to loop crossover, pushed back the lever to reset the crossover points to normal – giving a straight run along the up fast – pushed back the lever to re-lock the facing points for the up fast, then pulled the home, starting and distant signal levers for the up fast, ready for the fish train.

The fish train was a lightweight formation of seven four-wheel fish vans and a brake van, hauled by one of the fairly new Stanier Class 5 4-6-0s, No 5495. It had been following the

stopping train for some time, a block section or so behind, and had been getting caution indications on the distant signals. But as it approached Lichfield the colour light distant was at green. At last it had a clear run, and its driver started accelerating to the maximum permitted speed for fish vans, which was generally 55-60mph.

The signalman saw the headlights of the fish train as it approached the station. To his horror it didn't continue on the up fast, but veered sharply to the left over the crossover towards the up platform line. The driver had no chance to apply the brakes before his engine rammed the back of the stopping train at full speed.

The three rear coaches of the stopping train were virtually demolished as the engine ploughed through them, and the fourth was severely damaged. The impact was so great that the passenger train engine was hurled forward beyond the overbridge by no less than 90yd. Twenty passengers were killed and many others injured. Remarkably, the driver and fireman of the fish train survived, despite being thrown about in the engine cab.

Just how had the fish train got over to the plat-

▲ Lichfield, looking south towards Rugby and London the day after the accident. The remains of the wooden bodied coaches of the local train from Stafford lie among piles of debris, all that was left of the rest of the bodywork. Of the two pairs of tracks prominent in this picture, the one on the right is the up fast line that the fish express should have taken.

Key to trains

6.08pm stopping passenger train

2.50pm fish express

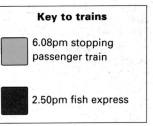

Prince of Wales 4-6-0 No 25802

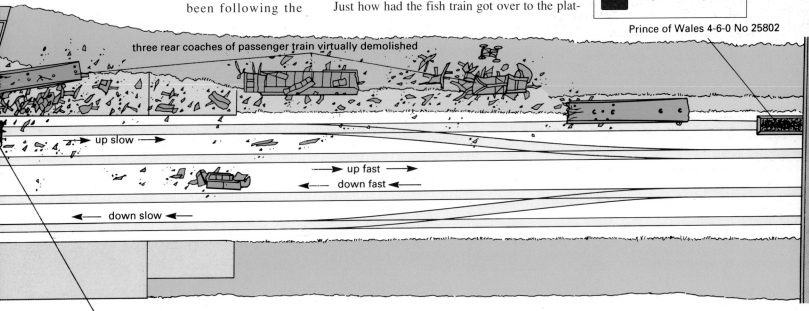

three rear coaches of passenger train virtually demolished

up slow →

up fast →

← down fast

← down slow ←

▲ On the night of the accident at Lichfield station, firemen search the wreckage of the devastated coaches of the local stopping passenger train.

Points to disaster
The signalman at Lichfield changed the locking and points levers and cleared the signals for a fish express to overtake a passenger train waiting at the loop platform, but the points remained locked and set for the crossover to the loop when frozen ballast got in the way of the locking mechanism. The express, running at speed with the distant signal at clear, swung over the crossover and rammed the standing train, killing 20.

The point rodding to the points was found to be buckled, and there were signs of strain in the fittings to the facing point lock. There was doubt whether the home signal arm was at clear, but even if at danger it was too late for the fish train to stop.

form loop with the signals standing clear for the up fast line? Clearly, the safety interlocking and detection features – a legal requirement ever since the Regulation of Railways Act of 1889 – hadn't worked. But why not? This was the question facing Lieutenant Colonel Woodhouse, the inspecting officer who inquired into the accident.

The two principal safety features that should have prevented the false clear indications being displayed on the signals were interlocking between the levers in the signalbox and the detection between the point blades and the wires leading to the home signals that read through the points of the crossover. But there was a third safety device, the facing point lock, designed not to prove which way the points were set, but to ensure that whichever way they *were* set they were fully home and locked with the switch blade on one side or the other firmly against the running rail.

The facing point lock comprised the lock itself, with a bolt inserted into a steel bar linking the two switch blades, and a long steel fouling bar just longer than the distance between the wheels at each end of the longest coach, lying on the inside edge of one of the running rails immediately approaching the facing points.

The fouling bar was carried on pivoted rocking bars so that, while it was normally below rail level, it rose up to rail level and down again when the facing point lock bolt was being operated. It was linked to the lock bolt by rodding and the whole assembly was worked by the facing point lock lever in the signalbox. If a train was standing on the fouling bar the wheel flanges prevented it from rising, so that the points couldn't be unlocked and changed.

The facing point lock lever was interlocked by mechanical tappets or wedges sliding in channels to the points and signal levers concerned in the signalbox lever frame. The points lever had to be

in the correct position, and the facing point lock lever in the 'points locked' position, for the signal levers to be free to be pulled.

As for the third safety feature, steel slide bars with slots cut in them were taken from the switch blades and the facing point lock into the detector mechanism, where other steel slides attached to the signal wires crossed them at 90°. Only if the slots in the bars from the points and the lock were lined up could the signal slide pass through, the other signal slide for the route not set being held so the signal arm wouldn't clear.

The crossover points at Lichfield were clearly wrongly set. But Lieutenant Colonel Woodhouse and the engineers found that operation of the facing point lock mechanism had been impeded by frozen ballast. After the passenger train arrived in the platform loop line the signalman put all the signals back to danger and caution. He then pulled the facing point lock lever to unlock the points.

But frozen ballast stopped the movement of the fouling bar, and that in turn prevented the lock bolt from being withdrawn. However, he got the facing point lock lever fully over, and that released the interlocking with the points lever. He pushed that lever back but, since the point blades couldn't move, the rodding in the signalbox buckled. With the points lever fully normal, he was able to push the locking lever back, which merely eased the strained rodding to the points. With the points and locking levers in their correct position he was able to clear the signals for the up fast.

But the detector should still have prevented the up fast home signal arm from showing clear, even though its lever was pulled. It was never established whether the arm was actually at danger. With a clear distant signal the fish train driver was expecting a clear line. Even if he had seen the home signal at danger he would have had no chance to stop. It was a remarkable and very rare failure of mechanical signalling equipment.

Recommendations
The inspecting officer didn't blame any of the staff. The signalman correctly operated the levers, though he didn't look at the back light of the up fast home signal when he pulled the lever, to see if the arm had responded. Whether the home signal was at clear as the fish train driver claimed was unclear. Afterwards the detector, which would have prevented the arm from moving to the clear position, was found to be working properly.

The inspecting officer recommended securer guidance to the rodding, not only at Lichfield but elsewhere, to prevent any chance of bowing or buckling. Also discussed was electrical detection on points, to prevent a false clear being given on the home signals, and detection of the home signal arm being clear before the distant signal could be cleared. But although there were developments in electrical detection they weren't used for arm to arm locking in British signalling.

Lockington 1986

**On a rural line in Humberside, a van drove over a
level-crossing in front of a four-coach DMU train doing
around 60mph (100km/h). The van was wrecked, and its passenger
killed. The train derailed, and the leading coach turned front
to back and overturned. Eight rail passengers died.**

At its southern end, the cross-country railway from Hull through Bridlington to Scarborough runs through the flat countryside of Humberside. The area around the route is largely agricultural, with one or two small towns and a few villages.

When the railway was built, in the 19th century, it was not thought worth the immense cost of building embankments to carry roads crossing the railway up to bridges over the line. Instead, many roads, particularly little-used lanes, were taken over on level-crossings. In less than five miles (8km), between Hutton Cranswick and Beverley, there were no fewer than five crossings. At one time, most would have needed a signalman or crossing-keeper to supervise them. At Lockington, the fourth level-crossing south from Hutton Cranswick, the crossing had a signalbox with manually controlled barriers until the end of 1985. But using a signalbox to look after the crossing was expensive in manpower and, since the signalbox

was not really needed for block signalling (the train service was not all that frequent), British Rail (BR) decided to automate the crossing operations as an economy measure.

From the beginning of 1986, Lockington crossing lost its signalbox and barriers and was converted to an automatic open crossing – as were the next three crossings to the north. The main feature of open crossings is that there is no physical barrier for road traffic – just a set of signs and warning lights to advise and instruct road users that they are approaching a railway crossing.

The AOCL system

Two types of open crossing were devised, supervised in different ways. In the first, the crossing is monitored locally, that is, by the driver of an approaching train. This kind of crossing is known as an automatic open crossing locally monitored (AOCL). At just over braking distance from the crossing is a rail signal, normally dark, but show-

▼Following the initial impact with the van on the level-crossing, the leading diesel car of the 09.30 Bridlington to Hull train not only fell on its side but was turned end to end in the subsequent derailment. The casualties occurred in this coach as they were hurled through the windows.

▲The tremendous forces involved as the derailed train came to rest can be gauged by the distortion to the tracks caused when the diesel cars spreadeagled across both up and down lines.

To the left of the picture is the rear car; the third is hidden from view. The second car has gone through the hedge to the right.

would trigger an alarm in Beverley signalbox, after which the signalman would halt approaching trains and caution them to approach the relevant crossing slowly, and to stop and check that the road was clear before going over it. Otherwise, trains were free to go over the crossing at the normal line speed of 70mph (113km/h). Although the crossings between Hutton Cranswick and Beverley had been modernized, including track circuit control of the warning sequence, the ordinary signalling consisted of normal block working between Hutton Cranswick and Beverley signalboxes.

Road traffic signals consist of a display of a steady yellow light, then two flashing red lights, all of which are dark until triggered by an approaching train. The yellow light shows for about three seconds, as on normal traffic lights, followed by the flashing red lights for at least 24 seconds before the train reaches the crossing. An audible warning, usually a bell or warbler ('yodalarm'), sounds continuously while the lights are illuminated as a warning to pedestrians.

A vehicle approaching the crossing would first encounter a fixed road sign, indicating that there is an automatic crossing ahead, and that vehicles must stop when the lights flash. Then there would be signs instructing drivers of large or slow road vehicles on what action to take in an emergency.

ing a flashing white light to an approaching train – provided that the crossing road signals have been correctly triggered by the train (by occupying a track circuit and operating a treadle).

On seeing the white light, trains could go over the crossing at a maximum speed of 55mph (89km/h). If there is a fault, such as a power failure, that prevents display of the road signals, the white light fails to flash at the train driver, who would then slow down, stop short of the crossing, and then proceed across cautiously, having checked that the crossing is clear before doing so.

The AOCR system

At Lockington and the other three crossings to the north, the crossing safety system was of the second type, known as automatic open crossing remotely monitored (AOCR). In this case, there was no white flashing light for approaching trains, because correct operation of the equipment was under the supervision of a nearby signalbox, in this case Beverley, a few miles to the south.

A power failure or non-operation of the system

A shock for the train driver

On the bright and sunny morning of 26 July 1986, the 09.30 Bridlington to Hull train had been signalled from Hutton Cranswick, south to Beverley on the up line. It was a four-car diesel multiple unit train, made up of a two-car Cravens-built Class 105 unit, with a driving trailer car leading, coupled to a two-car Class 114 unit built by BR itself. The leading driving trailer, No 54434, weighed just over 24 tons, while its companion motor brake was heavier, at a little over 31 tons. The train left Hutton Cranswick at 09.57 and accelerated away. At about the same time, the signalman there accepted another diesel train, on the down line from Beverley.

The train from Bridlington reached over 60mph (97km/h) as it drew near Lockington crossing. As a train approaches the crossing from the north, the

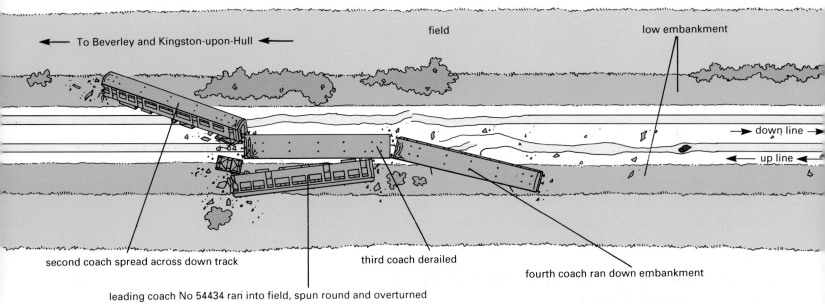

field

low embankment

◄— To Beverley and Kingston-upon-Hull ◄—

→ down line →

◄— up line ◄—

second coach spread across down track

third coach derailed

fourth coach ran down embankment

leading coach No 54434 ran into field, spun round and overturned

view of the right-hand road is obscured by the old station house. To the train driver's horror, he suddenly saw a Ford Escort van emerge on the crossing from the right, from behind the house. He immediately let go of the control handle, which, with its dead man safety feature, applied the brakes, and also made an emergency application of the brakes through his brake valve. But it was too late: the van continued forward and the train was too close for the brakes to take effect.

The left-hand buffer of the leading coach ripped into the side of the van, just behind the passenger seat, and the left-hand lifeguard and leading wheel caught the van's back axle and went as if to climb over it. The van was torn into five sections and thrown to the left, killing the young passenger, and badly injuring the van driver.

However, the train was in even greater trouble: the leading wheels derailed to the left and the whole of the front bogie tilted to the left as it ran diagonally down the side of the low embankment towards a field. The train was now hurtling out of control; the leading coach, No 54434, dived into

the field and the force of the remaining three coaches behind it spun it round from end to end, and tipped it on to its side. Windows shattered, and some passengers were hurled through, being badly injured or killed in the process. The second coach was spreadeagled across the down track, and the damage to the up line caused by the derailment in turn derailed the third coach, and sent the fourth down the embankment, too.

The toll of the accident

Eight passengers on the train and the van passenger were killed, and 59 people – including the train and van drivers – were injured. The train guard escaped injury, having braced himself when he felt shuddering after the collision. He got out and tried to calm the passengers, then realized that a train was due in the other direction. He ran up the line towards the next crossing at Scorborough – this one not an AOCR but operated by the users – and, as he saw the train approaching, gave the hand danger signal of both arms raised. Fortunately, the driver saw his signal and braked to a halt before reaching the wrecked train, avoiding a second collision.

Inexplicable behaviour

How did the van get on to the crossing? Witnesses saw the warning lights flashing before the train approached, and they were still flashing after the accident. The driver was a local man who lived next to the railway. He had got into his van and driven down what used to be the station approach road. He arrived at the junction with the road over the crossing, slowed down, looked to his right and, as there was no traffic coming, turned left and was immediately faced with the flashing red lights. But, instead of stopping, he continued right into the path of the train.

Problems come to light

The inquiry into the accident was conducted by Major Tony King. It soon emerged that some of the local people were dissatisfied with the crossing, and had reported various failures, such as a train approaching without the lights flashing, or the lights flashing with no train approaching. The signal and telecommunications staff could account

▼Ambulances and other rescue and emergency vehicles line up in the field alongside the second, third and fourth cars of the diesel train derailed at Lockington crossing. Fortunately, vehicular access to the scene was unhindered.

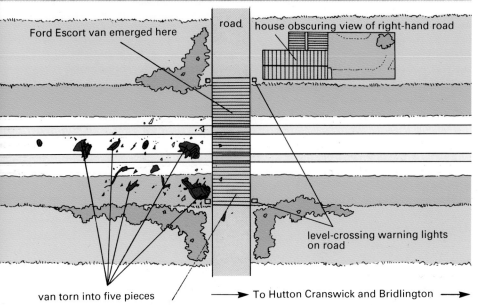

Ford Escort van emerged here   road   house obscuring view of right-hand road

level-crossing warning lights on road

van torn into five pieces   ⟶ To Hutton Cranswick and Bridlington ⟶

Lockington AOCR level-crossing

A moment's inattention

The Ford Escort van turned left out of the old station drive on to the road over the level-crossing just a few yards away. Although the crossing's red lights were flashing to warn of an approaching train, the van went straight on to the crossing, right into the path of the fast-moving train. The train derailed and the leading coach overturned.

Occasional faults on the crossing lights were not reported by local people to British Rail, and sometimes flashing lights were ignored by road users. But on the day of the accident the lights were working correctly.

When questioned, the badly injured van driver could remember nothing.

▲The DMU train was travelling at speed from the right when it hit the van on the level-crossing (out of sight to the top right of this picture). The front car, lying at the foot of the shallow bank with ladders against it, was turned from end to end as it dug into the soft ground, but the second car was thrown across the adjoining track.

for a couple of faults: one a power failure, and the other when a tracked excavator with metal tracks had operated the track circuit in the rails just as a train would, causing the lights to start flashing; but they could not account for a train approaching the crossing without the lights being displayed. In fact, the lights were certainly working properly on the day of the accident.

Major King concluded that the van driver, who had been involved in the talks about the crossing modernization, and was a regular user of the crossing (so must have known about the flashing lights), for some reason had been distracted – possibly by his passenger – as he drove on to the crossing. Presumably he had looked to the right as he joined the road over the crossing, and the flashing light signals were immediately to his left. However, there was evidence that the warning lights were not as bright as they should have been, and that they might have been beamed at a different part of the road.

Lack of care and attention
Of more concern to Major King was that some local residents did not seem to treat the crossing with due respect. They had passed over it when the red lights were flashing in fault conditions, and, on occasions, they had not reported faults to BR. For their part, BR neither recorded all received reports, nor provided explanations to local people on what had caused the unusual occurrences.

The inquiry recommended that two of the four AOCR crossings should be closed, and the remaining two converted to automatic half barriers. Other recommendations included a review of the Highway Code rules to take account of automatic open crossings, and a review of operation during a fault when the lights are flashing without a train being present, both in giving advice to the police if they attend a failure, and to BR mainte-

nance staff to ensure that if the red lights are displayed they are obeyed by road users.

The Lockington disaster, however, brought a much wider-ranging inquiry, by Professor P F Stott, into general open level-crossing safety. He felt that a number of open crossings were potentially dangerous, due to various combinations of factors, ranging from the amount of road and rail traffic passing over the crossing, the train speed, and the methods of monitoring the crossings and reporting faults.

Stott recommended that a table for conditions of suitability should be applied to open crossings, based on a reducing level of road and rail traffic as rail speed increased. Crossings not meeting these conditions should be converted to automatic half barriers, or AOCRs could be converted to AOCLs if within specified criteria since, in any case, train speeds at AOCLs are limited to 55mph (89km/h) and the essential feature is that, in the event of a fault or obstruction of the crossing, the driver himself undertakes the monitoring, and adjusts train speed accordingly, or stops. It was estimated that 42 out of 206 AOCLs, and 32 out of 44 AOCRs would not meet the new guidelines. Since then, a flashing red light is displayed to trains in fault conditions instead of the flashing white light.

Wembley 1984

One evening in October, in the peak hour rush out of Euston, an eight-coach electric multiple unit collided with a Freightliner train crossing in front of it, and three passengers were killed. This was a line with modern signalling and the automatic warning system, so what went wrong?

Just 13km (8 miles) out of Euston, on the West Coast main line, lies the town of Wembley. This north-west London suburb is best known for being the home of Wembley Stadium, where the FA Cup Final is held. Until recent years it also marked the end of a maze of tracks stretching 4km (2½ miles) from Willesden, with extensive marshalling yards and carriage sidings.

By the 1980s these yards and sidings were much less important: there were fewer goods trains, and more running as block loads in a single formation all the way to their destinations; and many West Coast main line long-distance passenger trains, after arriving in Euston, simply formed an outgoing service after quick cleaning and servicing at the platform, and therefore didn't need to run out to the Willesden carriage depot.

Some block goods trains could not run throughout their journeys without intermediate calls – for locomotive changing, for example. Also, some of them combined portions from more than one starting point, and one such train in 1984 was the 16.00 Freightliner service from Willesden to Holyhead. This carried containers brought by road and loaded on to the Freightliner wagon underframes at Willesden Freightliner depot. At Holyhead the containers were lifted off the train and stacked in the ferry for the journey across the Irish Sea to Ireland.

Continental containers

But the 16.00 train did not convey traffic from only the London area; another portion was attached that originated from Felixstowe. This part of the train carried containers arriving across the North Sea from the European mainland – so the containers didn't have to be shipped all the way around the north or south coast of Britain.

The part of the Freightliner train loaded at Willesden started its journey at the Freightliner

▼ Looking along the slow lines towards London on the morning after the accident it can be seen how the Freightliner emerged from the sidings on the left and the side to side collision forced the electric train coaches to the right.

depot on the west side of the West Coast line, between Willesden Junction and Harlesden. The train then ran through the subway under the main line tracks to reach the east side of the line and the marshalling sidings. Here it was joined by the Felixstowe portion, which arrived from the Great Eastern main line through Colchester and Stratford by the North London line to Camden, there joining the West Coast route.

No time to wait

On 11 October the Felixstowe portion was running late for various reasons. The 16.00 train wasn't ready to start until 17.26. At this time it would become tangled up with the evening peak outer suburban trains out of Euston, but because of the connections into the ship at Holyhead, it could not be held back until the commuter rush ended.

In any case, it was electrically hauled from Willesden to Crewe with Class 86 No 86006 at the head; even with a second dead electric locomotive next to 86006 and the 20 Freightliner wagons –

making a total load of 1300 tonnes – it would have no problem in accelerating quickly to 75mph (120km/h), the maximum line speed limit on the slow lines. At this speed, it would not delay following outer suburban electric multiple units making intermediate stops further out between Harrow and Bletchley.

Peak hour evening passenger train departures from Euston were frequent, and there were trains leaving at 17.45, 17.51, 17.54 and 17.56, all booked on the slow line. The key train was the 17.54, which made more stops than the earlier two. The signalbox regulator at Willesden decided to let the Freightliner out on to the slow line between the 17.51 and the 17.54 trains.

The West Coast main line route through Wembley has four main tracks. From the west side, these are the down fast, up fast, down slow and up slow. A fifth track on the east side, the up and down reversible goods line, provides access between the main running lines and the marshalling sidings. (There are other connections to

▼ Some of the containers were thrown off the Freightliner wagons as fastenings were dislodged when the electric train on the right tried to share the track with the Freightliner. Workmen are preparing to lift a Freightliner wagon in order to replace the bogies. The pantograph has been removed from the motor coach in the centre of the picture.

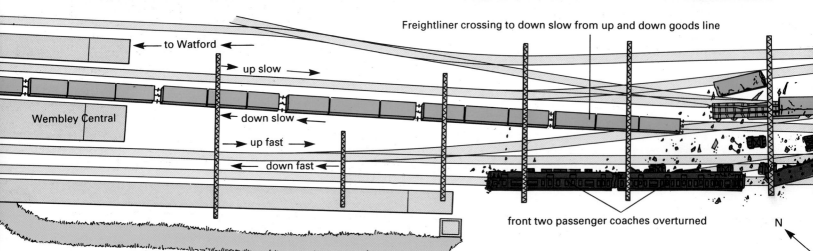

Freightliner crossing to down slow from up and down goods line

to Watford ←

→ up slow →

Wembley Central

← down slow ←

→ up fast →

← down fast ←

front two passenger coaches overturned

N

at about 17.30 and, after a few minutes, its driver used the signalpost telephone to call up the signal-box, asking when he was to be let out. The signalman told him that two more outer suburban trains would go past, then it would be the Freightliner's turn. The fast lines were also busy with long-distance express services.

Approaching Wembley from Willesden there were three signals, unevenly spaced but giving adequate braking distance. First came signal WN211, followed 615m (674yd) further on by signal WN46 and a further 1364m (1492yd) on by signal WN27. All were four aspect signals, normally operating for trains on the down slow in automatic mode. With the impending move of the Freightliner from the up and down goods line to the down slow, the signalman had to restore the manual mode, which he did after the passage of the 17.45 train.

Signal showing red

The signalman set the route for signal 27 onwards along the down slow for the 17.51 and, after it passed, reset the route from signal 26 from the up and down goods line to the down slow ready for the Freightliner to leave. This meant signal 27 was showing red, signal 46 single yellow and signal 211 double yellow for the 17.54 from Euston.

When the Freightliner started to move, at about 18.00, the 17.54 train was about 3km (2 miles) away. It was travelling at over 70mph (113km/h), with plenty of room to stop at signal 27, which

▲ The motor coach, left, of the leading unit of the 17.54 from Euston collided with some of the Freightliner train as it derailed. A container, on the right, leans on its derailed wagon. By the time this picture was taken, on the morning after the accident, the second coach of the electric train, in the background, had been pulled upright.

the carriage servicing depot but they aren't relevant.) All are electrified on the 25kV system with overhead catenary, and all are controlled from an entrance-exit panel by push buttons on a track diagram in Willesden signalling centre.

Colour signals are used throughout; four aspect on the fast and slow lines, three aspect on the goods line. The whole area is track circuited and the fast and slow line signals have automatic warning system (AWS) magnets 183m (200yd) before the signals to which they apply. It was all commissioned in 1965, just before the completion of electrification the following year. To complete the picture, there are two other tracks for inner suburban services to Watford, electrified on the DC third and fourth rail system to the west of the main lines, but they are totally segregated and played no part in the accident.

Freightliner waits its turn

The Willesden signalman set the route for the late-running Freightliner from the sidings to wait at the exit signal on the up and down goods line. Here it would be ready for the move on to the down slow line through the single crossovers over the up slow line. The Freightliner arrived at exit signal WN26

Key

■ 17.54 Euston – Bletchley passenger train

□ 16.00 Willesden – Holyhead Freightliner (running late)

A passing spasm

During a busy period in the evening commuter rush at Wembley on the West Coast main line, the signalman set the route for a late-running Freightliner train to run out on to the down slow line between the passage of two outer suburban electric trains. Although the signals for an approaching electric train were at caution and danger, and its driver had been fully alert, somehow he did not react to two vital signals, the second caution aspect and the red danger signal; he must have unknowingly cancelled the AWS warning at the caution signal.

The train ran past the danger signal and hit the Freightliner side-on, derailing seven of the eight coaches of the electric train and resulting in three deaths. Investigations showed that the driver had probably suffered a short period of amnesia caused by a disturbance of the blood flow to the brain – a rare but recognized medical condition.

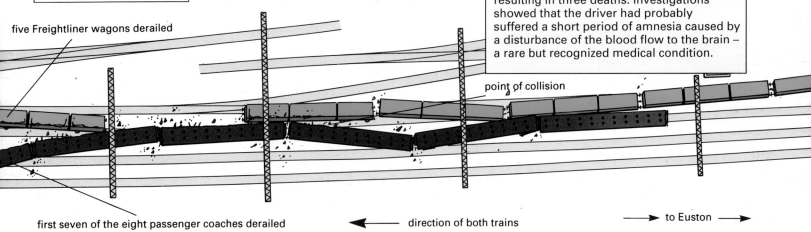

five Freightliner wagons derailed

point of collision

first seven of the eight passenger coaches derailed ⟵ direction of both trains ⟶ to Euston ⟶

▲ The glare of floodlights highlights the eery scene at Wembley Central on the evening of the accident. The front two coaches of the electric train lie on their sides on the down fast line as rescuers check for more casualties. Other coaches lie derailed in the background and the wreckage of the Freightliner is in the left background.

Automatic protection
By the late 1980s, inspecting officers were recommending the development of automatic train protection (ATP). This feature, with much more sophisticated track to train communication than simple AWS, would not only override the driver's action (or inaction) if he failed to slow down when required at caution signals or stop at a danger signal, but would keep an automatic overall check on the running of the train at all times. But ATP development may well be held back for a Europe-wide system.

was about 365m (400yd) short of the crossover being used by the emerging Freightliner. The signalman and regulator expected to stop the 17.54 train for no more than a few minutes, allowing the Freightliner to get away and cause no further delay to this and following services.

The Freightliner locomotive 86006 was partly through Wembley Central station when its driver felt a pull on the train and it came to a stop. The 17.54 train, formed of two four-coach Class 310 electric multiple units, instead of slowing down and stopping at signal 27, had run past it at full speed. Although its driver made an emergency brake application, the train was still travelling at about 60mph (100km/h) when it hit the eleventh Freightliner wagon side to side.

The 17.54 was deflected to the left and all coaches except the last derailed. The leading two coaches overturned and finished up on the down fast line, with the rest of the train weaving between the down fast, the up fast and the down slow lines. Five Freightliner wagons were derailed. Although the coaches were not destroyed, the damage was bad, and three passengers were killed. Another 17 passengers, plus the driver, were injured (although only two people had to be kept in hospital).

Quick thinking saves lives
The uninjured staff on the 17.54 and one of the passengers (the editor of a railway journal) realized that there was imminent danger from a further collision if a train approached on the up or down fast lines, and acted quickly to avert another collision by putting track circuit clips across the rails of the fast lines, to set the signals to danger. In addition, the signalman and regulator at Willesden signalbox had seen an array of red track circuit lights switch on at Wembley. They had assumed something was wrong and put the signals on other lines to danger. But what had caused the accident

on a line with modern signalling, and AWS on both track and trains?

Checks on the signalling and on the brakes of the 17.54 revealed no faults. Time checks proved that the signalman could not have changed his mind by giving the 17.54 clear signals and then putting them back to danger. It all came down to the actions of the 17.54's driver.

He explained to Major C F Rose, the inspecting officer at the inquiry, that, after having green signals from South Hampstead, he remembered seeing the double yellow aspect on signal 211 and had acknowledged the horn warning of the AWS and shut off power. The line was straight and he saw the single yellow of signal 46 ahead. After that he remembered nothing until hearing the AWS horn as the train approached signal 27, still travelling fast. He did not see the signal aspect but made an emergency brake application and released the dead man's handle. He saw the Freightliner coming on to the down slow ahead of him and realized his train was going to hit it.

The benefit of the doubt
The authorities planned initially to prosecute the driver, but it emerged that a medical condition might have accounted for his lapse. Investigations by the inspecting officer and a panel of eminent doctors, including two consultant neurologists, suggested that the driver suffered a short period of amnesia caused by a momentary disturbance of the blood supply to the brain. The driver had fallen from a ladder some months before and was badly bruised, but did not think he had been unconscious. He also suffered from a form of migraine. The inspecting officer did not think it was possible to ascertain the exact cause of the accident, but felt that the driver should be given the benefit of the doubt, saying that his lack of reaction to the caution and stop signals was a result of a passing medical condition.

Recommendations
As the medical condition that appeared to have been behind this accident was rare, the inspecting officer, Major Rose, didn't think there was a great risk of it happening to other drivers.

The 17.54's driver had several weeks' absence after his fall. Despite that, he hadn't been seen by a railway doctor on his return to work. Major Rose thought that a medical check after four weeks' absence ought to be mandatory. British Rail's chief medical officer was to look at the measures needed to reduce the chance of a similar short spell of amnesia occurring in drivers.

There had been the failure of two technical devices that should have prevented the accident: the dead man's handle, which had remained depressed until the train approached signal 27, and the AWS. Major Rose recommended the adoption of a vigilance device to ensure that the driver was alert, and also recommended more effective AWS.

Polmont 1984

George Stephenson, when asked what would happen if a train hit a cow, replied, 'It would be awkward for the coo'. On just such an occasion at Polmont, not only was the cow killed, but so were 13 passengers when a train travelling at 85mph (137km/h) was badly derailed.

Late on the afternoon of Monday 30 July 1984, with the weather fine and clear, trains on the Edinburgh – Glasgow main line were running normally. This line carries frequent trains between the two major Scottish cities, and serves some of the towns along the way in the important Forth – Clyde corridor.

Push-pull operation

In 1984, express trains were scheduled every half an hour, running the 47 miles (76km) between the Scottish capital and Glasgow in 42-48 minutes, and making one to three intermediate stops en route. The trains were unusual in that they operated push-pull, with a Class 47 diesel locomotive at one end of the normal six-coach formation, the sixth coach at the opposite end being equipped with a driver's cab and controls to operate the locomotive remotely. The locomotive was therefore not uncoupled from the train during its normal day's work; it pushed the train in one direction, normally from Edinburgh to Glasgow, and then pulled it in the other. This push-pull working was often used in steam days on local or on branch trains, normally with no more than two or three coaches and usually at fairly low speeds of about 40-50mph (65-80km/h).

However, in the 1970s push-pull operation for express services was being tried out on quite a few routes. It had first been seen in 1967, on Southern Region express electric trains running between Waterloo and Bournemouth, with a four-coach powered electric unit coupled to four or eight unpowered coaches, and running at speeds of up to an official limit of 90mph (145km/h) and occasionally just touching 100mph (160km/h). The Scottish Region Edinburgh – Glasgow service was the first to use diesel locomotives in regular high-speed push-pull operation, at speeds of up to 100mph (160km/h).

The 17.30 Edinburgh – Glasgow train on the evening of 30 July 1984 was formed from one of the push-pull trains, with locomotive No 47707 at the Edinburgh end, and five Mark III coaches between the locomotive and the leading Mark II driving trailer brake second at the Glasgow end. Like all express trains on this service, the 17.30 called at Haymarket soon after leaving Edinburgh

▶ This aerial shot shows the six-coach Edinburgh – Glasgow express after hitting a cow. The leading driving trailer coach is on the right, and the second coach is on the left, completely derailed. Thirteen passengers died and 17 were seriously injured.

Waverley, but being a commuter train it also made a call at Linlithgow, which most other express trains avoided, before running fast to Falkirk High and then Glasgow Queen Street.

An unexpected obstacle

Just west of Polmont station, the line to Falkirk Grahamston and Stirling diverged to the right; the 17.30 continued straight on the line to Falkirk High. The train would have reached a speed of about 85mph (137km/h) by this point, with the driver just starting to prepare for the stop at Falkirk High, five kilometres (three miles) ahead. The 17.30 was still travelling at over 80mph (130km/h) as it entered a gentle right-hand curve about 2.5km (1½ miles) beyond Polmont when – to the driver's horror – he saw a cow standing on the line ahead.

Normally, cattle or sheep on the line are killed instantly if hit by a train; there is rarely much damage to the train. But the 17.30 driver's instinct on seeing the animal ahead was to make an emergency brake application, though he had no chance of stopping in time. It was only a matter of seconds before the unfortunate animal was hit, and this time the effect on the train was different. Parts of the animal went under the leading bogie of the

driving trailer and, despite the 33½ tonnes weight of the coach, and an axle loading of about eight tonnes, the leading wheels were lifted on top of the left-hand rail and dropped on to the left side, derailing the front bogie. The right-hand wheels ran on top of the sleepers between the two rails until the front of the coach, still travelling at speed – despite the emergency brake application – veered so far to the left that the right-hand wheels hit the left-hand rail, overturning and breaking it, so causing a general derailment.

The train was now hurtling into disaster at high speed. The leading coach ran derailed for almost 220yd (200m), all the while veering further to the left. The line here was in a cutting, and the weight of the five coaches and the locomotive behind propelled the leading coach onwards and to the left, until it could go no further without running up the cutting side. It reached the top and cut a swathe of wreckage through the boundary wall, fence and lineside trees for over 110yd (100m). When it stopped it was turned end to end, with the driver's cab facing back towards Edinburgh, and the coach lying on its side diagonally down the cutting bank. One of its bogies was found in a tree 110yd (100m) back towards where the coach had first been pushed to the top of the cutting.

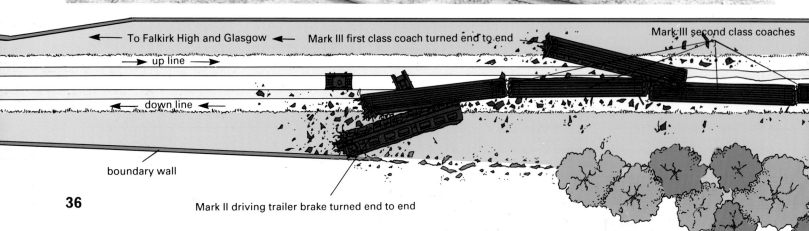

To Falkirk High and Glasgow ← — Mark III first class coach turned end to end — Mark III second class coaches

→ up line →

← down line ←

boundary wall

Mark II driving trailer brake turned end to end

▲This shot is taken looking on to the leading end of the third coach. The second coach is on the left, turned end to end by the derailment. Rescue workers can be seen searching the wreckage for injured passengers.

◄ In the foreground is the derailed rear bogie from the overturned driving trailer coach, seen on its side on the cutting bank. The coach at the bottom of the bank is the third coach.

The wreckage continued as the energy in the speeding train was expended, for the second coach, a Mark III first class coach, was totally derailed and turned end to end on the opposite line by two of the other four Mark III second class coaches, as they overtook it before coming to a stop, damaged and derailed.

A fast reaction averts a second crash

The drama was not quite over: a second disaster was only just averted by the vigilance of the train driver of the 17.30 Glasgow – Edinburgh push-pull train, which was accelerating away rapidly from its booked stop at Falkirk High. The train had reached about 65mph (105km/h) when the driver passed a signal showing double yellow, meaning that he might have to stop at the second signal ahead. Almost simultaneously he saw the derailment, and a coach somersaulting through the air a little way ahead of him. He made an emergency brake application and his locomotive stopped just 179yd (164m) from the derailed train. It had been a near thing.

Undoubtedly, the number of casualties would have been higher if the second train had run into the wreckage of the first, but it was bad enough with the derailment of just one train: 13 passengers were killed and 14 passengers and three railway staff were seriously injured, including the driver.

Trying to unravel the circumstances

How had the cow got on to the line, and why was the outcome so terrible? The train driver was so badly injured that he was unable to recall the details. The guard, who was travelling in the leading driving trailer coach just after completing a round of ticket inspection, was unfit for interview until five months after the accident. He and another railwayman then confirmed that an emergency brake application had been made just before they felt a thud, which must have been the moment when the train hit the cow. They were badly injured and lucky not to have been killed.

The first sighting of the cow was by the driver of the 17.15 Glasgow – Edinburgh train. He saw it on the cutting slope near the down line (that is, towards Glasgow), but it was not on the track, and he decided to report it on reaching his next stop at Polmont, 2.5 kilometres (1¹/₂ miles) ahead. His assistant was just telling the station staff about the cow when the 17.30 Edinburgh – Glasgow sped past in the opposite direction. The 17.15's driver told the inquiry inspecting officer, Major A G B King, that had he seen the cow on the track, or had he seen a herd of cattle, he would have stopped at the nearest signal, put down detonators, set a track circuit clip to put signals to danger and telephoned the signalman.

Fencing near an abandoned road level crossing, about 260m (285yd) towards Glasgow from the

---

The dreadful consequences

When the 17.30 Edinburgh – Glasgow high speed push-pull train hit a cow at about 85mph (137km/h), the animal's remains went under the leading bogie of the driving trailer coach and lifted the leading wheels right off the track. Despite an emergency brake application, the energy in the train catapulted the leading coach up the left-hand cutting bank, where it demolished trees and the boundary wall for over 110yd (100m) before being turned end to end and finishing on its side. The second coach was also thrown front to back. An engineer estimated that the stored energy in a train travelling at that speed was enough to throw two coaches to the top of the Eiffel Tower.

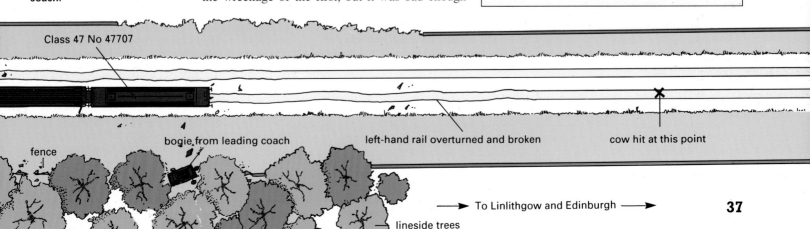

Class 47 No 47707

fence

bogie from leading coach

left-hand rail overturned and broken

cow hit at this point

lineside trees

To Linlithgow and Edinburgh ⟶

▲ Locomotive No 47707 was left derailed, and sitting on top of an overturned rail. The driver was seriously injured, and the toll of 13 dead would have been greatly increased had not the driver of the 17.30 Glasgow – Edinburgh train reacted so promptly to the derailment ahead.

Push-pull

Push-pull operation was introduced on the Edinburgh – Glasgow service in 1979, using Class 47/7 locomotives that had been modified for this purpose, Mark III coaches, and Mark II brake seconds converted to driving trailers (DBSO). Existing lighting circuits were used to transmit the control signals from the DBSO to the locomotive, which was always at the Edinburgh end of the train.

The next major introduction of push-pull operation was in 1984, on the Gatwick Express, where 77 locomotive-hauled coaches have been modified into permanently coupled two- and three-car units.

final resting place of the 17.30 train, had been vandalized: this was probably the access point for the cow, which must have wandered along the line and the cutting banks looking for grass. The inspecting officer was told by permanent way staff that the fencing in the area was difficult to maintain because of frequent vandalism, and although repairs were carried out quickly, further damage was soon caused. Ways of improving both the reporting of damage and of making repairs were under examination.

In the five years leading up to this accident there had been seven occasions when cattle had broken through to the line between Glasgow and Polmont and been hit by trains. In three instances a driving trailer coach of a push-pull train had hit the animal, while in the other instances a locomotive or diesel multiple unit train had been involved. In no cases had a derailment been the result. In fact, on the whole of British Rail, in the 11 years from 1974 to 1984, there had been 1096 collisions with animals, but only 24 had resulted in derailments, with no casualties.

Should light coaches be used?

Much of the inquiry centred on the comparison of push-pull operation with a relatively light coach at the front, as against push-pull with a heavy locomotive. Engineers described the many trials carried out with high speed diesel and electric push-pull trains before the introduction of this type of working between Waterloo and Bournemouth in 1967 and between Edinburgh and Glasgow in 1979. However, reasonably enough, the trials were not conducted with a view to finding out what happened if a train hit an animal. After the Polmont accident a search was made of the records, but there had been no previous instance where an animal strike had resulted in human

deaths. The trials for high speed push-pull operation had been concerned largely with traction and braking forces, and the riding of stock when the locomotive or power unit was at the back of the train. Engineers pointed out to Major King that the driving trailer coach at the front of a push-pull train was little different from a diesel or electric multiple unit driving trailer, which had been in operation for many years. All these driving coaches had guard irons, or lifeguards. These usually consisted of angle-iron projections extending down from the bogie frame, in front of the leading wheels, to within five centimetres (two inches) of the rail. Lifeguards would normally sweep away any small obstructions.

The Continental solution

A study was also made of the Continental practice, where express push-pull trains were operated with no problems on lines that often had no fencing. Only in Great Britain are railways required to fence lines (with a few local exceptions) to keep out animals and trespassers. In mainland Europe it is the farmers' responsibility to fence their fields to keep in animals.

Some Continental railways are fitting their trains with snow ploughs, which do sweep away other light obstructions. But a snow plough is not designed to withstand a heavy impact and could break off, going under the wheels and causing as much damage as an obstruction. But some form of deflector, akin to the cowcatcher of American and other locomotives, seemed to be desirable.

Recommendations

Although there had been no recorded instances of passengers being killed in a train crash caused by striking an animal, the inspecting officer recommended alterations to the rule book so that any animal within the railway fences should be treated as an immediate potential danger to trains, and must be reported and the lines protected.

The inspector also recommended improved reporting of damage to fences near fields where animals graze and a higher priority to stopping trespass and vandalism; the introduction of train-to-signalbox radio to speed emergency messages (this is now standard on many routes); and the adoption of derailment resistance measures such as deflectors in front of the bogies of driving coaches.

Finally, Major King said that there should be a study of the derailment potential where speeds over 100mph (160km/h) are contemplated using driving trailer coaches at the front, instead of a locomotive or a heavy power car such as an InterCity 125 unit. Adding ballast weight to increase axle-loading was impracticable, but deflectors attached to driving coaches that would sweep obstructions out of the way should be developed. Today, driving van trailers are used on electric push-pull trains travelling at over 100mph (160km/h) on both East and West Coast routes from London.

Seer Green 1981

**The driver of an empty DMU had stopped in heavy snow
to remove a tree branch which was blocking the line. As he did
so the following passenger train smashed into the back of the
stationary train, killing three people.**

December 1981 was one of the rare winter months in southern England when it snowed before Christmas. As early as the second week of December, freezing temperatures and snow falls were already affecting parts of the South East, particularly on higher ground such as the Chiltern Hills.

In the deep cuttings of the Marylebone to High Wycombe line, between Gerrards Cross and High Wycombe, the trees had grown quite large and the branches extended out over the running lines. When it first snowed heavily on Tuesday 8 December, overhanging branches began to sag from the weight of snow and started to brush the trains.

By dawn on 11 December, the trees had bent right down with the weight of the snow on them. An early train was reported as having hit some branches as it went through a cutting between Gerrards Cross and Seer Green. It was about 7am, and at that time the signalboxes open were West Ruislip and High Wycombe. Gerrards Cross, between them, was closed and the block signalling equipment was switched through to the boxes on each side.

The signalling between Gerrards Cross and High Wycombe was unusual, since it had been rationalized on a piecemeal basis from former times when each station had its own signalbox. The line beyond the Gerrards Cross down starting signal was track circuited for nearly six miles to a point just on the High Wycombe side of Whitehouse Tunnel. There were three colour light stop signals, sited at Seer Green and Beaconsfield stations and just beyond Whitehouse Tunnel.

The signal at Seer Green could be controlled by the Gerrards Cross signalman, and that at Beaconsfield worked automatically. The one near Whitehouse Tunnel was what was called an intermediate block home signal and was also controlled by Gerrards Cross. The normal block section ran from this signal to the first of High Wycombe's signals. Therefore the Gerrards Cross signalman did not have to offer trains to High Wycombe on the block system until they were at least at Beaconsfield and heading towards Whitehouse intermediate block signal.

The next train down the line was the 7.25

▶ The four casualties were in the front coach of the passenger train which telescoped into the last coach of the empty train. The second train should have been driven more slowly and the first ought to have been protected by detonators, but the accident would probably have occurred anyway.

empty train from Marylebone to Princes Risborough. This was a four-car Class 115 diesel multiple unit (DMU). These sets worked all of the passenger trains on the route from Marylebone to High Wycombe and Princes Risborough. They consisted of a driving power car at either end, with two trailer cars between them.

The 7.25 empty train was brought to a stop at West Ruislip, where the signalman told the driver that trees had been reported down near Gerrards Cross and that he was to run at extreme caution. The train continued towards Gerrards Cross, but meanwhile the Gerrards Cross signalman had arrived on duty rather late. It was snowing hard and the signalman, who lived in Aylesbury, 24 miles away, had tried to get to work by motor cycle but he didn't get very far as the conditions were too bad, but he managed to get on a goods train from Aylesbury which was routed through Gerrards Cross and arrived to open the signalbox at 7.50am.

The empty DMU was already in the section from West Ruislip. When it arrived at Gerrards Cross the signalman, who had been told about the fallen trees, stopped it and told the driver again to proceed with caution to Seer Green and to look out for the trees. The signalman cleared the starting signal, but the lever was very stiff and hard to pull. The empty DMU went on and the signalman saw from the red lights on his track diagram that the train was in the section towards Seer Green. He put

the starting signal back to danger.

After giving the train out of section bell signal to West Ruislip for the empty train, he was offered a down passenger train, the 7.31 Marylebone to Banbury DMU, also Class 115, which he accepted. He signalled it into the platform loop but left the signal at the departure end of the platform, called the down home signal, at danger. The signalbox was between this signal and the points where the loop line rejoined the main line. Another 325yd beyond that was the starting signal leading into the section ahead. The signalman cleared the home signal, but showed a red flag to the driver, meaning that he was to stop at the signalbox. The train stopped with the front cab alongside the signalbox so that the driver could hear the signalman's instructions.

The Gerrards Cross signalman had only to keep an eye on the track diagram to see where the trains were. When he had stopped the passenger train, he told the driver that there might be trees down and that he should drive on cautiously. The signalman then tried to pull the lever for the starting signal, but it was held locked at danger. His first thought was that the signal and wires had frozen since the lever had been hard

▲The dreadful weather of 11 December hindered rescue work, with firemen and other rescuers having to be lowered from the bridge beyond the crashed trains. Fortunately the wreckage had not fouled the up line and another train was brought alongside to evacuate the passengers.

Key	
■	7.31 Marylebone – Banbury DMU
▨	7.25 Marylebone – Princes Risborough empty DMU

To Gerrards Cross

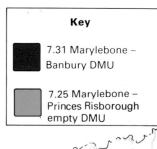

to pull for the previous train. He glanced at the track diagram and thought he saw the track circuit lights were lit for the section between Seer Green and Beaconsfield, meaning that the empty train was on its way forward in the next automatic signalling section. He noticed that the track circuit lights were still on in the section between his starting signal and Seer Green, but thought that it was a track circuit failure, caused perhaps by a tree lying across the line.

A fatal mistake

The signalman told the driver of the 7.31 train that there was a track circuit failure and to pass his starting signal at danger and proceed at caution. But the driver seemed irritated at being told to run at caution. He set off but as the signalman closed the signalbox window and looked at the diagram he saw that while the lights were still on for the section between Gerrards Cross and Seer Green, there were no lights for the track circuit on to Beaconsfield or anywhere towards the Whitehouse intermediate block signal. The signalman realized that the empty train had not reached Seer Green and was still in the section into which he had just sent the 7.31 passenger train. He ran back to the window and shouted as the train gathered speed, but no-one heard him. The guard had been looking out from the back coach while it was stopped at the signalbox but did not see the signalman again after the train started.

The 7.31 accelerated away from Gerrards Cross. Snow was falling heavily and visibility in the early daylight was little more than 200yd. Witnesses afterwards thought that the train was

travelling at 25 to 30mph, but one thought that it was going at the usual speed. But whatever the speed, the empty DMU was standing 1¾ miles ahead. The driver of the 7.31 had little chance of seeing it in the heavily falling snow and, although he made an emergency brake application which slowed the train down, it struck the back of the standing train at a speed of at least 20mph.

The front coach of the 7.31 train and the back coach of the empty train telescoped as they smashed together and parts of the body sides and roof burst open. The front part of the 7.31's leading coach was crushed, killing the driver and three passengers – a teenager and two schoolboys. Other passengers were trapped. The deep cutting and the weather made rescue difficult. Although there was an overbridge ahead, ropes had to be used to get firemen and ambulancemen down on to the track. It was clearly going to be too difficult to get the injured out that way, so another train was brought up alongside on the up line. Passengers who could walk and those who had been injured were ferried to Seer Green station where ambulances were waiting.

The inquiry into the accident was held by

▼The separate chassis and body construction of modernization plan era coaches has the drawback that telescoping may occur during collisions. Here the heavy chassis of the passenger train has ridden up over that of the stationary train destroying the relatively lightly built bodywork of both.

A combination of errors

The inexperienced signalman at Gerrards Cross sent an empty train on towards Seer Green. When he later tried to clear his starting signal for a passenger train, which was waiting at his signalbox, he found that he was unable to pull the lever back. Therefore he told the driver of the passenger train to pass the signal and to drive at caution.

Too late the signalman realized from the track circuit diagram that the signal was locked at danger because the earlier empty train was still in the section. The train driver made the accident worse by driving too fast for the conditions.

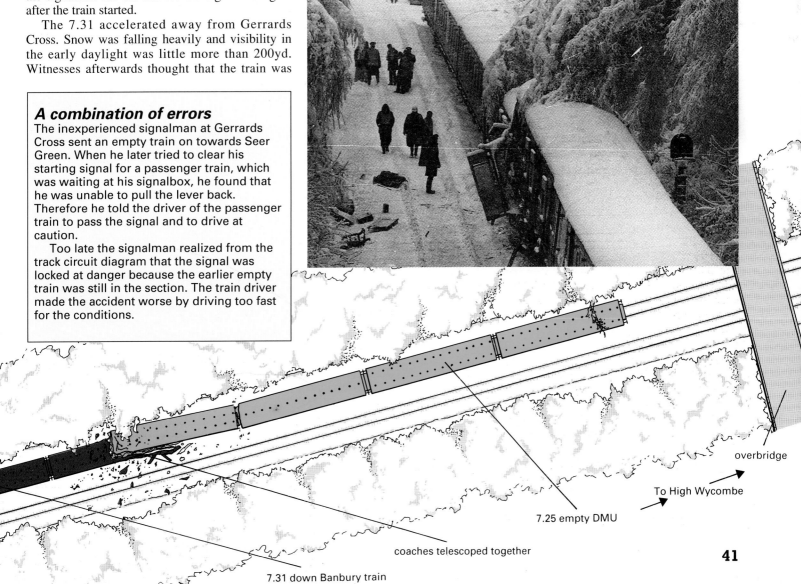

overbridge

To High Wycombe

7.25 empty DMU

coaches telescoped together

7.31 down Banbury train

Major C F Rose. Because the signalman had only been passed out a month before the accident, the enquiry reviewed the training that he had been given. This had lasted five months and included working Gerrards Cross signalbox under instruction. But after examining all the factors Major Rose concluded that, for allowing the 7.31 train to enter the section to Seer Green, already occupied by the empty train, the signalman had to accept the main responsibility for the accident. But there were other factors. The weather was exceptionally bad with heavy falling snow and poor visibility. Once he had told the driver of the 7.31 to pass the starting signal at danger and proceed at caution, the signalman realized his mistake and shouted to the train as it moved off.

What went wrong?

The guard of the 7.31 train told Major Rose that the starting signal was clear, yet the only way he could have seen it was to have kept looking out of the train window for 350yd beyond the signalbox, but he had already said that he closed the window as the train passed the signalbox. Had he been looking out he could not have failed to hear the signalman's shouts, which were heard by a passenger on the up platform. The signal was, in fact, locked at danger by the track circuits.

The driver of the empty DMU had rung High Wycombe signalbox from a telephone on the signal post to say that he had stopped because there was a branch across the track and that it would take him a few minutes to move it. Should the High Wycombe signalman have passed this information on to his colleague at Gerrards Cross? How was the passenger train driven after leaving Gerrards Cross under caution? The witnesses estimated the train's speed at about 35mph as it entered Seer Green cutting – far too fast for the conditions. Had it been driven more slowly the collision might have been avoided or lessened.

The empty train had been standing there for only a few minutes. Normally the rules say that if a train has stopped in an emergency it must be protected by detonators. To provide full protection means that the guard must walk back for a whole mile putting one down at a quarter of a mile, one at half a mile and three 20yd apart at one mile. This would take at least 15 to 20 minutes in good weather. In such heavy snow the guard would probably not have gone back more than 200yd before the passenger train approached. As the driver thought that he could move the branch in five minutes, the crew never thought of protecting the train because the line was track circuited.

It was a tragic accident involving a mixture of old semaphore and modern colour light signals and track circuits. Major Rose said that it arose from a combination of errors and misjudgements. Although at the time no major resignalling was proposed, he welcomed moves to install full modern signalling, controlled locally, between West Ruislip and High Wycombe. In the event, this did not happen because the entire line from Marylebone to Banbury was resignalled in 1991, and is now directed by integrated electronic control.

Recommendations

The main responsibility for the accident was placed on the Gerrards Cross signalman for telling the driver of the 7.31 train to pass the starting signal at danger while the section ahead was occupied by the empty DMU. The signalman had misread the track circuit diagram.

The driver of the 7.31 train, having been told to pass the signal at danger and proceed at caution, then drove too quickly. According to the rules the standing train ought to have been protected by detonators, but Major Rose suggested some relaxation in the rules, since it would often be quicker to remove a small obstruction than it would be to carry out protection.

Radio links between trains and signalboxes rather than trackside telephones were suggested, along with brighter red tail lamps for new trains. Full modern signalling was also recommended.

Bushey 1980

An electrically hauled express train travelling at almost 100mph was derailed when a rail was displaced after a welded joint had broken. It was a recipe for disaster, yet not a single passenger was killed in the accident on the West Coast main line at Bushey in 1980.

On the evening of 16 February 1980 the 20.25 train from Euston to Manchester left the London terminus just as many other electric trains on the West Coast route have done ever since modernization was completed in 1966.

It consisted of nine carriages: a Mark 2E open second, followed by four Mark 3A open seconds, a Mark 1 Restaurant Buffet car, a Mark 3A open first, a Mark 2F open first and a Mark 1 full brake. Class 87 electric locomotive No 87007 *City of Manchester* headed the train. The line was electrified on the 25kV AC system with overhead catenary – the wires are supported from lattice structures spanning across the four tracks of the main line.

Once clear of the inner suburbs at Willesden trains can soon reach the line speed of 100mph (160km/h). The 24 mile climb from Wembley to Tring summit, on gradients no steeper than 1 in 335, presents no problem for today's electrics, although in steam days locomotives hauling heavy expresses often found it hard going.

The 20.25 train that evening was quickly through Harrow and was approaching Bushey five miles further north only 15 minutes after leaving Euston. The express was travelling at about 96mph, just less than the line speed, when it derailed. The locomotive stayed on the track but all of the carriages left the rails at high speed just as the train was entering Bushey station. The carriages bounced and slid along the sleepers and ballast, bogies were torn off and the third, fourth and fifth, all mark 3A vehicles, turned over. The others, although derailed, stayed upright.

The platform faces helped to contain the movements of the first three carriages, although the third came to rest on its side between the up and down platforms, while the fourth and fifth slewed at an angle on to the adjoining local DC electric lines. Although derailed the rest of the train ended up almost upright between the down fast line, on which it had been running, and the up DC local electric line. As the snaking carriages hurtled out of control they brought down several of the lattice

▼The buck-eye coupling of one of the overturned carriages can be seen here. Although such couplings have usually prevented carriages turning over, in this case vertical movement let them disengage. The inspecting officer recommended that the design be altered to prevent this.

▲Torn from its bogies, one of the carriages turned over and slid right across on to the DC local lines. Had any other trains been passing Bushey as the 20.25 Manchester express left the tracks, then the crash would certainly have been far worse, possibly involving fatalities.

arm rests bent. More remarkably only seven outer and two inner panes of glass in the double glazed windows were broken. The following three Mark 3A carriages which had fallen on to their sides were more extensively damaged as they had struck the overhead catenary structures. But they remained intact and again just two inner panes of glass between the three of them were broken.

It was the strength of the Mark 3 carriage design, in which the body is a self-supporting structure, which saved the passengers. The fact that so few windows were broken had stopped passengers from being flung out. Of course there were casualties. Of the 150 people on the train, 48 were injured. Most of them suffered cuts and bruises, but 19 were more seriously hurt and were kept in hospital for treatment. However, considering the speed of the derailment and the way in which the carriages overturned it was remarkable that no-one was killed.

What went wrong?

But what had caused the derailment? The investigators soon found a broken rail and realized that the welded joint between two rails on the left side of the track had fractured. As the locomotive passed over the break, the rail was bent towards the centre of the track and then struck by the

overhead catenary support structures.

The wreckage was spread over four tracks. The potential was there for appalling disaster involving several trains. Fortunately no trains were due either on the up fast line or on the local electric lines. The signalman at Watford signalling centre knew that something was wrong and set the signals to danger to stop any other trains approaching.

When the rescue services arrived and saw the carriages spreadeagled along the track they were full of foreboding at the carnage they expected to find. But when they reached the carriages they found to their surprise that passengers were beginning to climb out through the doors of carriages which were remarkably intact.

The leading carriage had no interior damage. The second was tilted over to the side and badly damaged underneath, with bogies displaced and equipment ripped off. Inside it was only slightly damaged with two tables moved and eight seat

---

Welded rail

Welded rails simplify maintenance and overcome the potential danger from a rail break.

One of the disadvantages of welded track is that signalling track circuits do not always match the welded lengths and the rail has to be cut for an insulated joint to be put in. To overcome this problem jointless track circuits were devised – but they are unsuitable for electrified lines.

Welded rails still break but at about half the rate of rail breaks in jointed track. In 1990 for example there were 27 breaks for every 1000 miles of jointed track, but only 16 broken welds in every 1000 miles of welded track. None caused major disasters, due to early detection.

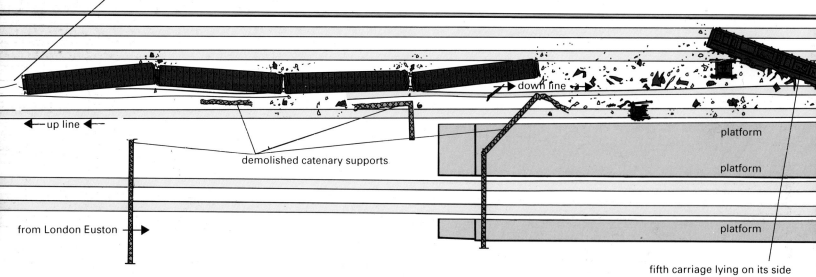

point of derailment

← up line ←

down line

demolished catenary supports

platform

platform

from London Euston →

platform

fifth carriage lying on its side

wheels of the following carriages. They then jumped the track, breaking up the concrete sleepers as they continued forward. The rail was left unsupported and was ripped from its fastenings, derailing the entire train. Close examination of the weld showed that it had not been a perfect joint and the rail foot had not been welded properly.

It was clear that the first of the broken sleepers had been broken before the derailment. This gave a clue to the sequence of events. The weld was certainly unbroken ten hours before the derailment because the track patrolman walking the line had not noticed anything wrong. But witnesses on trains passing three quarters of an hour before the derailment said they had heard and felt a bump at that point although it was not bad enough to warrant stopping the train to report it. The welded joint had clearly fractured by then and the two rails were no longer joined or supported at the gap. All the weight of a train was being taken by the first sleeper as the wheels ran off one rail on to the next, deforming the rail downwards so the sleeper gradually disintegrated.

When the 20.25 train ran over the join, the rail was no longer supported by the first sleeper of the running-on length and the rail moved laterally just after the locomotive passed over it, starting the derailment of the carriages. As each set of wheels pounded over the rail it was torn from its fastenings on the following sleepers and was pushed right out of line beneath the derailed carriages.

The welded joint was made by the SkV Alumino-Thermic process in which moulds are clamped round the rails to be welded and a crucible and burners attached above. The welding material, including iron oxides, aluminium and alloying material to match the rail steel, is then placed in the crucible and heated. The moulds and rail ends are also heated by the gas jets and after a specified time the molten metal is released from the crucible into the moulds surrounding the adjoining rail ends. At about 2000°C (3630°F) the heat melts the rail ends so that they blend with the weld material to form an unbroken rail. The process relied on the welders following a set procedure including ensuring a minimum gap of 22mm ($^7/_8$in) between the rail ends before welding.

Examination of the broken weld showed that it had not been made correctly. The moulds had not been upright so that parts of the adjoining rails had not fused together. The rails to be welded were at least 8mm ($^5/_{16}$in) closer than specified so there may not have been enough room for the weld material to flow into the join and fuse with the rail ends. The aluminium content in the weld material was higher than usual which could have arisen from a number of causes, such as poor cleaning of

▲Although battered by the force of the high speed derailment the strength of the Mark 2 and Mark 3 (above) carriages was such that their bodies stayed intact protecting the passengers. Rescuers who saw the wreckage in the dark feared the worst, but were amazed to see passengers climbing out unassisted.

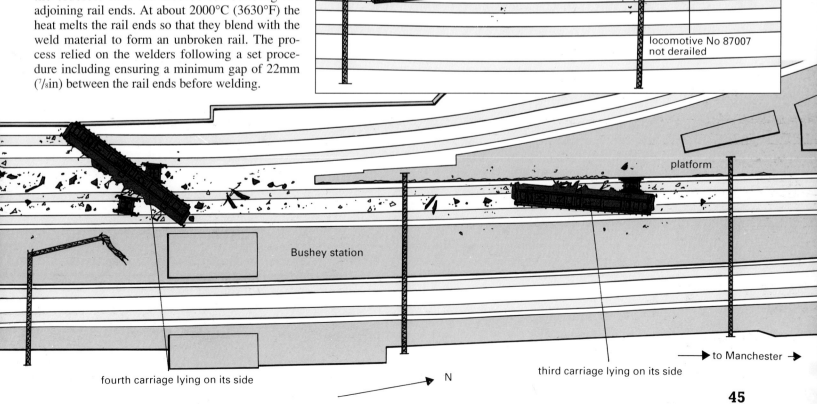

700yd from point of derailment

locomotive No 87007 not derailed

platform

Bushey station

N

fourth carriage lying on its side

third carriage lying on its side

→ to Manchester →

▲Two breakdown trains with cranes work to clear the wreckage of the derailed London to Manchester express. To the left of the nearer breakdown train are the last four carriages which stayed coupled together and so did not turn over. To its right can be seen fragments of the overhead catenary supports brought down by the train.

the crucible.

At the subsequent inquiry, chaired by inspecting officer Lt Col A G Townsend-Rose, the organization, training and supervision of welders was criticized and their equipment was found to be in need of improvement.

Lt Col Townsend-Rose described the storage conditions at Watford, where welding equipment and materials were kept, as deplorable. There had been little or no quality control of welders' work other than half-yearly visits by welding supervisors. The permanent way supervisors had not had any instruction in welding and the supervisor covering the Bushey area felt it was not his job to supervise the welders.

The welders themselves had no way of checking whether the weld was good or bad although, had they followed the instructions, there was no reason to suppose that the weld would be unsatisfactory.

Lt Col Townsend-Rose recommended that the organization of the welding teams should be strengthened with more supervisors, better arrangements for ordering and keeping materials, and improved record keeping. There should be better uniform training standards, and supervisors and technical staff involved with track work should be given courses on welding so that they would know what was involved even though they were not doing the job. This would stop them pressuring welders to hurry their work by taking short cuts which might result in dangerously weak welds.

Undetected break

The failure of the signalling track circuits to detect the broken weld was also most alarming. With normal double rail track circuits an electric current is passed through both rails of insulated sections of track and shorted out by the presence of a train which puts the protecting signals at danger. A broken rail or welded join would also interrupt the electric current, automatically setting the signals to danger.

But at Bushey on the West Coast electrified route only one of the rails was divided into sections for signalling purposes. The other one was electrically continuous to carry the return traction supply from the wheels. It was unfortunate that it was the continuous rail carrying the traction return current that broke, so it was not detected by the signalling track circuits.

It was possible for both rails to be insulated for signalling purposes but special impedance bonds would be needed where adjacent track circuits met to allow the traction current to pass through, but not the signalling circuit.

Lt Col Townsend-Rose said that providing such equipment would be costly in terms of both money and the time of railway and industry staff spent in providing it. Impedance bonds had been used on the DC electric lines of the Southern Region for many years but the problems with high voltage AC were greater. Nevertheless he recommended that ways should be examined to find an automatic detection system which would show up a total rail or weld break. Even so, Bushey was a remarkable demonstration of a disaster by no means as bad in terms of casualties as it might have been.

Recommendations

Lt Col Townsend-Rose recommended that means should be found to prevent the vertical disengagement of buck-eye couplings which had led to some of the carriages at Bushey turning over.

The accident was caused by a broken weld found to be sound less than eleven hours earlier by a track patrolman. The weld was poorly made, being 8mm too narrow and not properly vertical. The inquiry put this down to inadequate supervision of track welding teams. In response to the recommendations, British Rail gave welding supervisors clerical support, so that they could spend more time out on the line to supervise welding, rather than spending time on paperwork.

Invergowrie 1979

Almost exactly a century after the terrible Tay Bridge disaster of 1879, another train was thrown into the River Tay. This accident was along the north shore, and four people died – all because a signal failed to show a proper danger indication.

For much of their lives, the Tayside railways have owed their existence as much to the politics of Scottish railway history as to planned needs. In this part of Scotland, the two main rival companies – the Caledonian Railway (CR) and the North British Railway (NBR) – competed for the traffic between the Forth and Clyde valley and the north-east port of Aberdeen. The CR worked the west coast route from Euston, while the NBR was one of the east coast partners from King's Cross. The Caledonian route from Glasgow approached the area through Stirling and Perth, and continued north-eastwards through Coupar Angus and Forfar to Kinnaber Junction, where it was joined by the NB route from Edinburgh via the Forth and Tay bridges and Dundee.

Modernization brings re-routing

Closures and rationalization in the 1960s brought radical changes, and the Glasgow – Aberdeen services from Perth were re-routed through Dundee and the former NBR coastal route to Kinnaber Junction (now no longer a junction) on their way to Aberdeen. Between Perth and Dundee, what was now a principal route ran along the north shore of the River Tay from Longforgan to Invergowrie and on to Buckingham Junction at Dundee.

Old-fashioned signalling

The signalboxes concerned in this accident were at Longforgan and Buckingham Junction. The block section between them was about 5½ miles (9km) long, and in the late 1970s still relied on mechanical signalling. Longforgan box had British Rail (BR) pattern block instruments, which were interlocked with signals so that the down section signal (formerly called the starting signal) at Longforgan could be pulled to clear only when 'line clear' was displayed on the block instrument for the section to Buckingham Junction, and then for one pull only. When the signal had been returned to danger, it could not be pulled to clear a second time until the block instrument for the forward section had gone through the normal procedures, and 'line clear' displayed a second time. Longforgan could not give 'line clear' to the Inchture signalbox – its rear section – unless the home signal was at danger and the colour-light distant signal was showing caution.

There were no track circuits at Longforgan, so there was not full Welwyn control (the sequential locking system instituted after the 1935 Welwyn Garden City accident) on the block instruments,

nor signals to prove that a train had passed correctly through the section and been properly signalled, although Welwyn control was fitted at Buckingham Junction. Furthermore, the down section signal wire was not equipped with a slack adjuster to allow the signalman to tense or slacken the wire in hot or cold weather, although the signal engineering staff could alter the wire connection to the lever if the signalmen reported that the signal was not working properly.

▼This aerial shot shows the disposition of the two trains a short while after the accident. On the right-hand side of the picture can be seen the corridor brake first and one second-class coach of the 08.44, which were thrown over the wall on to the muddy shore. All but the crushed cab and two coaches of the 09.35 (left-hand side) have been removed.

Between Longforgan and Dundee was Invergowrie station, about two miles (three kilometres) from Longforgan, unstaffed and without a signalbox. Normally only a few local trains called there, and it was not served by expresses.

A faulty engine

On the morning of 22 October 1979, the 08.44 Glasgow to Dundee train made its booked call at Invergowrie, but all was not well with its Class 25 locomotive. Although it had only a light load, comprising four open second-class coaches with a corridor brake first at the back, it was already 25 minutes late, having lost time between Glasgow and Perth because of faults in the traction power. On two occasions power had been lost for a moment or so, and approaching Perth was lost totally, the train coming to an unscheduled stop just outside Perth station. There seemed to be an electrical short circuit to earth, but after the driver had isolated the earth fault switch he found he could restart the locomotive. A fitter attended the locomotive at Perth, and said it could continue to Dundee. But on leaving Invergowrie, the driver felt the train was dragging, and after stopping again it seemed to him that the locomotive brakes were binding. He restarted the train, hoping to cover the remaining three miles (five kilometres) to Dundee, but his assistant called out to say that one of the traction motors was on fire. They decided the locomotive could go no further. The assistant started to walk back to tell the guard that they needed help, and to arrange protection for the line.

▲Almost one hundred years after the Tay Bridge disaster of 1879, rescue workers were once more at work in the river. The second and third coaches of the 08.44 were thrown on top of the wall.

The inspecting officer's conclusions

Major Rose said that the direct cause of the accident was the passing of the Longforgan section signal at danger by the 09.35 train. But the evidence suggested that the arm was not horizontal, instead being raised by at least 6° and (probably) not more than 10°. It was also possible that the arm had been more inclined when the train passed it. By the time the arm was examined, later in the day, the temperature had risen slightly from the time of the accident, and might have expanded the wire just enough to allow the arm to lower slightly. Even so, the signal engineers did not think the arm could have been more than 10° above horizontal when the driver saw it. The inspecting officer himself saw the apparent difference in the position of the arm when set at 6° above horizontal and viewed from different locations.

Key to trains

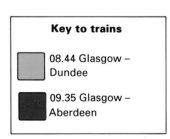

08.44 Glasgow – Dundee

09.35 Glasgow – Aberdeen

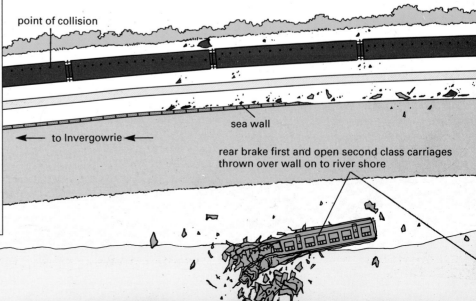

point of collision

to Invergowrie

sea wall

rear brake first and open second class carriages thrown over wall on to river shore

The next train approaches

Meanwhile, the following 09.35 Glasgow – Aberdeen express was catching up on the 08.44. The 09.35 had a more powerful locomotive – a Class 47 No 47208 – at the head of its seven vacuum-braked coaches. As it approached Longforgan, the colour-light distant signal was showing a yellow light for caution, and the train slowed to a crawl as it approached the home signal, at danger. As the locomotive came close to the signal, the signalman pulled the lever to move the arm from danger to clear, allowing the train to run forward towards the section signal, which the signalman had put back to danger after the 08.44 train had passed. However, the 08.44 had not cleared the section to Buckingham Junction, so the block indicator was still showing 'train on line' and the Longforgan signalman could not have pulled the lever to clear the section signal. For whatever reason, the 09.35 train did not stop at the section signal, but – to the signalman's horror – accelerated past the signal as though it had been clear.

The 09.35 express had reached about 70mph (113km/h) on arrival at Invergowrie. The line here was on a right-hand curve alongside the River Tay, and just after the train passed the platform the 09.35's driver must have seen the standing 08.44 train only a few hundred yards ahead. He made an emergency brake application, and speed was reduced, but not enough to avoid a violent collision in which the heavy Class 47 ploughed into the back of the 08.44 train, with such force that the rear brake first and open second class coaches were hurled to the right over the sea wall and on to the muddy shore of the river. The second and third coaches of the 08.44 landed on the top of the wall, while the first coach, still coupled to the Class 25 locomotive, was thrown towards the wall. The Class 47 of the 09.35 train was badly damaged, and the cab crushed, killing the driver and his assistant. Two passengers in the rear brake first of the 08.44 also died.

How did the 09.35 train come to be in the same section as the standing 08.44? The 08.44's crew did not have time to go back with detonators and flags to protect their train, for it had been there only two or three minutes before the 09.35 approached at speed. The key to this accident lay in the indication displayed by the arm of Longforgan's section signal. Was it at danger, clear, or half-way between? This puzzle confronted the inspecting officer, Major C F Rose.

An awkward signal

The Longforgan signalman was certain that he had seen his section signal arm go back to danger after the 08.44 train had passed. Both the regular signalmen and the relief signalman, who was on duty at the time of the accident, and who had previously been on the regular staff there, knew that the section signal – 522yd (477m) from the signalbox – needed to be treated firmly, particularly when being restored to danger, by a good push of the lever to its normal position in the frame; indeed, almost throwing it back to ensure that the wire to the signal did not bind.

This was an upper quadrant signal, meaning that the arm was horizontal for danger, and raised at 45° for clear. When the lever was put back, gravity should make the arm drop to the horizontal position. But if the wire was tight, perhaps

▼This picture shows the brake first coach from the 08.44 lying on its side on the muddy shore of the River Tay. The 09.35's driver had only a few hundred yards in which to reduce his speed when he saw the 08.44 in front of him. Since he was slowing down from 70mph (113km/h), the force of the collision was considerable.

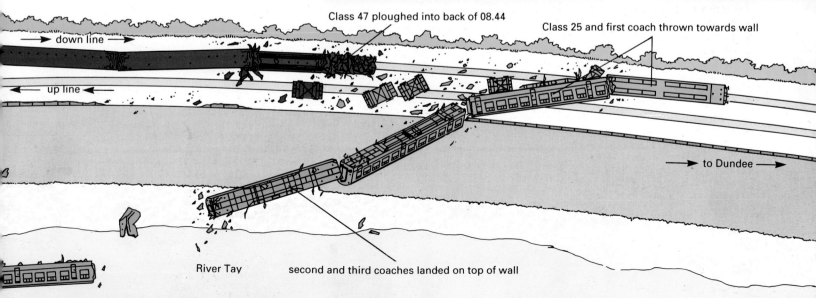

Class 47 ploughed into back of 08.44

Class 25 and first coach thrown towards wall

→ down line →

← up line ←

→ to Dundee →

River Tay

second and third coaches landed on top of wall

▲In the Tay Bridge disaster of 1879, when the bridge was destroyed in a gale, over 70 people died. In that instance, a combination of poor design, shoddy construction and inadequate maintenance was to blame. In 1979 a mis-read signal caused the catastrophe.

The crucial angle
The diagram demonstrates the difference between what the 09.35's driver saw, and the minimum angle above horizontal that may be taken as a clear signal. The evidence suggests that the driver saw the arm at between 6-10° above the horizontal, way below the required 'clear signal' minimum of 37½°. His mistake caused four people to die.

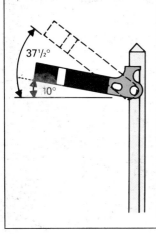

because of cold weather making it contract, the arm might remain slightly pulled, and thus raised slightly, but not so far as to give a good, clear indication. Provided with a slack adjuster, the signalman could adjust the wire to allow for variations, but Longforgan had no such equipment on this signal. Nor did it have a signal repeater in the signalbox (an electrical device attached to the arm of the signal, showing whether it is at danger, clear or wrong). Instead, the Longforgan signalman had to look over the ¼ mile (400m) or so distance to the signal, and judge for himself whether it was in the correct position.

Was the signal at clear or at danger?
After the 08.44 train had passed Longforgan that morning, the signalman believed the signal to have returned to danger. In fact, the locking between levers meant that the section signal lever *had* to be at danger before the home signal lever could be pulled for the 09.35 train to draw past the home signal and go towards the section signal.

As the 09.35 train passed the signalbox, the signalman gestured to the driver with what seemed to be a wave – could this have been a contributory factor? In whatever way the driver might have interpreted this gesture, he went on slowly, and then opened up his power controller to accelerate, travelling past the section signal towards Invergowrie. The train guard saw the signalman, and shook his fist in fun as he went past, the signalman waving back. But the guard then went to the other side of the train to look out at a spot where stones had been thrown at a train on an earlier journey. Then he went back to the left-hand side window and saw the section signal as his coach went by.

When he saw the signal it was partly raised, neither giving a full clear indication, nor being horizontal. He did not consider whether the signal

was just returning to danger, or had been at full clear when the driver saw it – he said that his driver was experienced and competent, and would not have passed a signal without a full clear indication. At the subsequent inquiry, the guard placed the arm of a model at just over 7° above horizontal to show what he had seen.

Experimenting with the signal
After the accident, various operating and engineering staff went to the site, and several of them examined the arm in a partly raised position. An operating inspector told the inquiry that the arm appeared to be at different angles when seen from different viewpoints: from the signalbox, it appeared to be at danger; from the north side of the line, about 12° above horizontal; and from the shore side, as much as 17° up. Other onlookers estimated anything between 6° and 10°. One of the regular signalmen said that on several occasions the signal could not be made to give a good clear or danger indication, and he had adjusted the wire connection to the lever. A bracket at the base of the signal carrying the signal wire fittings was found to be bent, and this could have been binding on the wire.

Major Rose concluded that the driver of the 09.35 train had gone past the section signal at danger. The evidence suggested strongly that the arm at the time was raised above horizontal by 6-10° and was therefore not a clear signal. As such, it should have been treated as a danger signal. Although a clear signal is normally at 45° above horizontal, some latitude is allowed as to what can be taken as a proper signal, with the clear angle of the arm considered as being anything between 37½° and 65° above horizontal. But 10° could in no sense be taken as anything other than a danger signal. Major Rose discounted the signalman's wave of the arm as being a signal to the driver to proceed.

The signalmen said that they had asked for wire adjusters, but had not made strong representations, and the management were unaware that signalmen had tampered with the wire connections. However, the accident instigated a thorough review of the need for adjusters and signal repeaters right through BR.

Recommendations
Although the signalmen had mentioned the need for a slack adjuster, they had made no formal complaint on the working of the signal and the lack of adjustment. The management, therefore, had not made the improvement of this equipment a high priority.

After the accident, a review was undertaken on signals sited 400yd (366m) or more from their controlling signalboxes right through the Scottish Region (and later on the whole of British Rail) to assess the need for fitting adjusters and repeaters to those signals without them, and, indeed, to consider whether the signals were still needed in their present positions at all.

Paisley 1979

On Easter Monday 1979, day trippers who had spent the day at the seaside along the Ayrshire coast were returning to Glasgow in special trains. One train passed a signal at danger at Paisley, and the day turned to tragedy when it hit an electric train head on, killing seven people.

Paisley Gilmour Street station is an important junction on the line from Glasgow Central to the Clyde and Ayrshire coastal resorts. Between Glasgow and Paisley the line had four tracks: from north to south they were the up slow, down slow, up fast and down fast. In the station the slow lines became the double track route to Wemyss Bay and the fast lines the route to Largs, Ardrossan and Ayr. The history of the railways in this area is complicated, but both the Caledonian (CR) and the Glasgow & South Western (GSW) companies were involved in ownership before the 1923 Grouping.

The line between Paisley and Glasgow was originally jointly owned by both the CR and the GSW, with access from both Glasgow Central (CR) and Glasgow St Enoch (GSW). The Wemyss Bay line was owned by the CR, but the Largs/Ayr route was the property of the GSW. Having connections further south around Ardrossan, providing through routes to Kilmarnock and on to Carlisle, the GSW lines south-west from Paisley followed the usual designation of up towards London and down towards the north. For this reason, what was the down line from Ardrossan arriving in platform 2 at Paisley Gilmour Street continued forward as the up fast towards Glasgow.

A mix of old and new

In 1979 past history was still partly in evidence, with this track designation continuing even after closures of some of the linking lines and of Glasgow St Enoch. The whole area had been re-signalled in 1966-67 as part of the electrification of the Gourock and Wemyss Bay lines on the 25kV overhead system. By 1979, the signalling at

▼ **An Ayr – Glasgow special started away from the platform at Paisley when the starting signal was still at danger. The leading DMU car rode up and over the electric train in the collision, as seen here, crushing the leading EMU car, and demolishing both drivers' cabs.**

▲ The scene after the leading DMU car was lifted away from the remains of the front EMU car (on the right). Right of the nearest crane is the switch diamond crossing. The left-hand switch can be seen with the blades after they had been run through by the DMU, which was diverted to the right by the right-hand switch.

Paisley and its approaches was under the control of Paisley signalbox, equipped with an entrance-exit type push-button control panel, with the buttons arranged along the track diagram alongside their respective signal sections.

Just east of Paisley station the four tracks were linked by two sets of parallel crossovers, known as Wallneuk Junction. This junction allowed trains on the fast lines to run to and from the Wemyss Bay/Gourock route, and those on the slow lines to run to and from the Largs/Ardrossan/Ayr line. The intermediate diamond crossings of the crossovers were equipped with switch diamonds (a form of point blade) to eliminate the gaps between some of the rails of the crossings at the point where trains went straight across the intervening track.

In the early evening of Monday 16 April 1979 a number of extra trains were running from the coastal resorts to Glasgow carrying returning day-trippers to the city. Many passengers had spent a fine Easter Monday relaxing on the beach, or cruising on the Clyde Estuary from one of the several piers served by the Clyde steamers. There were additional electric multiple units (EMUs) laid on from Wemyss Bay and Gourock, and special diesel multiple units (DMUs) from the Ayrshire coast resorts on the then non-electrified GSW route.

The Ayr – Glasgow special

One of the special DMUs was the 18.58 train from Ayr to Glasgow. It was formed of what were called intercity units (no relation to today's InterCity 125 trains), which were three-car diesel trains with through corridors, toilets and main line type seating, with two seats on each side of the central passageway rather than the usual 2+3 of

Key to trains

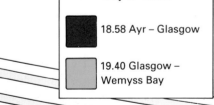

- 18.58 Ayr – Glasgow
- 19.40 Glasgow – Wemyss Bay

← to Wemyss Bay ←

switch diamonds

← to Largs, Ardrossan and Ayr ←

switch diamonds

short distance DMUs. The 18.58 train had two of these three-car units coupled together.

The 18.58 train arrived on the down line at Paisley's platform 2, having passed the colour light signal P35 on the approach to the station. This was showing a single yellow aspect. The platform starting signal, a four-aspect colour light, P31, was at red. The driver would have had to acknowledge the warning from its automatic warning system magnet as the train entered the platform.

When he signalled the DMU into the station, the signalman had not decided in which order he was going to send this and another train through Wallneuk Junction at the east end of the station. The second train was the 19.40 electric train from Glasgow to Wemyss Bay. It comprised two three-car EMUs of Class 303, and at that moment was travelling on the down fast line near Hillington between Glasgow and Paisley. The 19.40 would need to cross over from the down fast to down Wemyss Bay line across the path of the 18.58 from Ayr. In the event, the signalman decided to clear the signals for this train while the 18.58 from Ayr was completing station work at platform 2.

A third train arrives

The Paisley signalman therefore pressed the route setting buttons to set the route and clear the signals from the down fast line, over the crossover, to the down Wemyss Bay line for the 19.40 electric train. Just then another special train, this time an electric train from Wemyss Bay to Glasgow, arrived at platform 4. The signalman was just operating the route buttons to signal this train along the up slow line, and noting that the 19.40 from Glasgow was showing up on the track circuits as approaching the crossover, when he heard a loud bang. He looked out of the signalbox and saw that there had

▲ Rescue services are seen here sifting through the wreckage of the electric train. No one knew why the DMU driver had set off against a red signal – it was assumed that he had heard the ready to start signal from the guard and omitted to check the signals for himself.

been a collision. The 18.58 special DMU had started away from platform 2 towards the up fast line, and just 127yd (116m) beyond the platform starting signal had hit the approaching 19.40 EMU from Glasgow head-on as it swung over the crossover from the down fast across the up fast to the down Wemyss Bay line.

The electric train had been travelling at about 20mph (32km/h) and the DMU could not have gained much speed in the 180yd (165m) or so from a standing start, but the impact was sufficient to throw the leading DMU car on top of the front car of the EMU, demolishing both drivers' cabs and severely damaging the rest of the front electric car. Both drivers were killed, as were five passengers, while 67 further passengers and the EMU guard needed hospital treatment.

The signals were clear for the electric train and tests showed that the platform starting signal was red against the 18.58 from Ayr. The interlocking would not have allowed any other

Ding-ding and away

The Paisley accident was caused when a special DMU started away from platform 2 after the driver received the ready to start buzzer signal from the guard. The platform starting signal was at danger, and just 127yd (116m) ahead the DMU hit an EMU head on when the two trains reached a diamond crossing simultaneously. The leading DMU car rode up and over the front of the EMU, killing the two drivers and five passengers.

There was no firm evidence as to why the DMU had started against the danger signal. The driver had not been taken ill, nor was he under the influence of alcohol. The Inspecting Officer concluded that the buzzer ready to start signal had overridden further thought on the signal aspect and the driver had not checked before restarting.

Walneuk Junction

to Glasgow

up slow

down slow

up fast

down fast

point of impact

leading DMU car thrown on top of front EMU car

53

▲ Having separated the front car of the DMU and the wrecked EMU (on the right), repair gangs and rescue services continued with the clearing-up operation. After this accident, the rules were changed so that platform staff and guards were also responsible for checking signals.

At Paisley that evening, the guard of the 18.58 had been given the right away by the platform staff, and he transmitted the two buzzes 'train ready to start' signal to the driver, which the driver acknowledged by repeating the buzzer signal back to the guard: the train moved away. At some point the guard saw the platform starting signal at danger. His evidence to the inquiry, chaired by Major P M Olver, the Inspecting Officer, was inconsistent, and it was not clear at what point he saw the signal at danger, and what he did or did not do as a result. Whatever he did, it was too late, and the diesel train accelerated to collide head on with the electric train on the diamond crossing beyond.

Was the old system better?
Major Olver concluded that the accident was caused when the DMU driver started his train against the danger aspect of the platform starting signal. But the accident reopened the discussion of what interpretation was to be placed on the guard's ready to start signal, and when it should be given.

Early in 1980 the rules were changed again, and once more it was decided that the guard should give the ready to start signal to the driver only after he had checked that the lineside signals were clear. At many stations this was no problem, but at some – because of curvature or overbridges, station roofs or other obstructions – it was not always possible for guards to see platform starting signals. It was agreed that at certain stations, where there was a risk of accident if a train started against a danger signal because of a junction or other hazard ahead, repeater signals would be provided, or the main starting signals repositioned, so that the guard could see them and thus comply with the new rules.

aspect to have been shown, while further calculations proved that the signalman could not have changed his mind about which train to signal first. Thus, both while the 18.58 approached platform 2, and all the time it stood there, the platform starting signal had been showing a red danger signal: why had it moved on?

A weakness in the new rules
The other prime consideration was the way in which the right away signal was given to the driver from the platform staff and guard. Until the 1970s (and right from the early days of railways) train guards were expected to look at the main signals, particularly at stations and junctions, as part of their duty to keep a good look out. At stations, guards could give the right away signal to the driver after satisfying themselves that 'all was right for the train to proceed', meaning that the signals were clear. However, in 1972 the rules were altered, and the guard's signal to start was reworded so that it was up to him to indicate that station work was complete, and it was entirely the driver's responsibility to ensure that signals were clear for the train to proceed. This was still the situation in 1979.

In the intervening seven years since the rule change there had been an increase in the number of signals passed at danger when starting from stations, after drivers had been given the ready to start signal from the guard. Some of these incidents had resulted in accidents, although most were minor. In the case of diesel and electric trains equipped with bells (or, in the case of DMUs, buzzers) between guard and driver, the ready to start indication was given by two rings on the bell, rather than by the guard standing on the platform waving a green flag (as on locomotive-hauled trains). This gave rise to the 'ding-ding and away' syndrome, in which drivers moved away on the bell starting signal, rather than looking at the lineside signals to ensure they were clear.

Taunton 1978

**As the overnight train from Penzance to London sped
through the night, passengers in sleeping car B slept on – unaware
of the disaster about to strike. Piles of bed linen placed near
a heater caught fire and quickly filled the car with flames
and toxic fumes, killing passengers in their beds.**

On the evening of 5 July 1978, the 21.30 overnight sleeper for Paddington left Penzance with its usual heavy formation of six sleeping cars, followed by two ordinary passenger coaches, a full guard's and luggage van, two more passenger coaches and another parcels and luggage van.

Three more coaches waited at the platform of Plymouth station from about 22.30, so that passengers could board and get to bed before the arrival of the main Penzance part of the train at 23.50. There was a guard's and luggage van (known as a brake van) and two sleeping cars – W2437 (car B) and W2423 (car C) – placed in position by the locomotive, a Brush diesel No 47498, which was to take the train on to London.

Each compartment of car B was occupied, although the first two second class two-berth compartments at the front of the carriage had only one passenger in each.

The sleeping car attendant locked all the platform-side doors of the two sleeping cars – except for the one alongside his pantry at the front of car C – so that he could check in the passengers. He did not unlock the doors before the train departed.

Two piles of linen bags were stacked inside the leading vestibule of car B: one pile consisted of soiled linen from the previous night's trip and the other comprised bags of clean linen. They were stacked against an electric heater.

Although it was midsummer, the electric train heating was turned on from the locomotive generator. The hot air fan of the pressure ventilation system was switched off in car B and only the cold air fan was working, but the convector heater to the leading vestibule, on the partition with the unused sleeping car attendant's pantry, had been left switched on.

▼Firemen gesture to a colleague inside berth 9/10 as they bring the blaze under control. Most of the fatalities occurred in this berth and those on either side. Toxic fumes entered ventilation ducts at the source of the fire (above the Inter-City logo) and probably asphyxiated passengers even before the full force of the fire reached them via the ceiling and corridor.

Fire!

Once the main part of the train from Penzance had arrived and been coupled up behind the waiting coaches, the complete rake left Plymouth on time – at half-past midnight – and made its booked calls at Newton Abbot and Exeter.

Here a carriage and wagon examiner looked at each coach from the track and saw nothing wrong. On the platform, rail staff unloaded mailbags from the front full brake van next to car B. They did not see anything unusual either – yet 45 minutes later the train came to an emergency stop, just before reaching Taunton, with car B on fire and 11 passengers dead. Most were poisoned by deadly fumes given off by burning materials which may have been drawn through the pressure ventilation system. One passenger died later.

Six passengers managed to escape from the burning coach by crawling along the corridor floor, surrounded by smoke and with flames consuming the front end of the coach. Although no one really knew which way to go, the passengers made their way as best they could towards the door by which they had joined the train at Plymouth – the leading door of car C. Tragically, after escaping from the train, one passenger died outside from a heart attack.

One or two of the survivors recalled that the train was travelling fairly fast when they first became aware of the smell of burning and smoke. When they investigated the source of the smell by entering the corridor, they were overcome by thick constricting smoke.

The sleeping car attendant looking after the following two cars, D and E, smelt burning as the train passed through Whiteball Tunnel on the Devon/Somerset border, about 10 miles before Taunton. As the train speeded up on the descent through Wellington, he checked the rear sleeping cars first and then went forward and found thick smoke in car C. He went to his pantry in car D and pulled the alarm signal and returned to car C to alert passengers, but smoke from car B beat him back. As the train stopped, he found the attendant for cars B and C lying in the corridor of car C. He assisted the attendant out of the train, where he recovered consciousness.

The police and fire brigade were quick to arrive on the scene. It was fortunate that the train had stopped just opposite a lineside telephone by a shunting lever frame in the sidings, so that the driver could ring Taunton station office. They in turn made an emergency call to the local rescue services.

At first the police and firemen could not get into the burning coach because the doors were locked, but they obtained the keys from the sleep-

▶ The gutted remains of a compartment in car B is proof of the ferocity of the fire. Originally, firemen suspected it had been started by a smoker on the top bunk. Only after the inquiry was it proved that the fire had begun in the front vestibule and spread from there into the compartments.

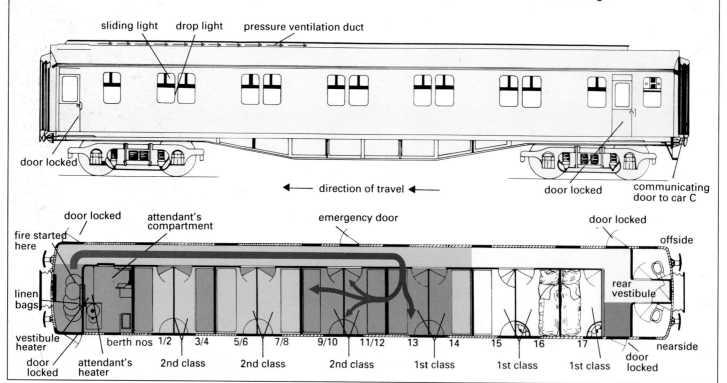

Avenues to disaster

The fire started in the leading vestibule, spread down the corridor and into berth 13 which had its door open. It then burnt through the bulkhead back into berths 11/12 and 9/10. A foam mattress in berth 13 burned particularly fiercely, accelerating the spread of the fire into berth 12. Some occupants may have died before the fire reached them, as a result of inhaling toxic fumes which spread via air ventilation ducts.

▼The heavy red arrow shows the main path of the fire through car B. The darker shades of orange represent those areas worst affected by fire damage.

sliding light   drop light   pressure ventilation duct

door locked

← direction of travel ←

door locked

communicating door to car C

door locked   attendant's compartment   emergency door   door locked

fire started here   offside

linen bags

rear vestibule

vestibule heater   berth nos 1/2   3/4   5/6   7/8   9/10   11/12   13   14   15   16   17   nearside

door locked   attendant's heater   2nd class   2nd class   2nd class   1st class   1st class   1st class   door locked

ing car attendants and gained entry. Then they were driven back by the dense smoke and heat.

Even firemen with breathing apparatus were held back by the profound heat until the coach had been hosed down inside. When they eventually got into the leading vestibule of car B, the firemen found a pile of blazing bed linen in nylon bags and the partition with the attendant's pantry had burnt through. The centre compartments were the last to be reached, and it was here that the bodies of those who had died were found.

Once the fire was out and 16 injured passengers had been taken to hospital, the Penzance part of the train was uncoupled, drawn back and shunted into Taunton station. The remaining passengers were given refreshments, and facilities to advise relatives that they were safe were provided.

The locomotive and the two fire-damaged sleeping cars were shunted into the yard at Taunton for forensic examination.

Investigation

Forensic tests after the fire confirmed that there was no fault in the electrical circuits or the gas equipment in the pantry of car B. All the evidence pointed to the fire starting in the bags of bed linen which had been leaning against the electric convector heater in the front vestibule. Although static tests on similar bags showed a lengthy time before smouldering started, the draught around the bags on the train, caused by the train movement, would have fanned any smouldering into a fire.

Fire retardant materials were used inside the sleeping car for partitions, ceiling panels and the like, but some of the laminated panels within the all-steel body had been replaced during overhauls with other materials which were not fire retardant. Some had even been painted with non-fire retardant paint.

Bedding was not fire retardant and one of the mattresses included polyurethane foam, commonly used at that time in furnishings but which has since been proved to be dangerous in a fire because of the toxic fumes it gives off.

The fire had started in the bags of linen and then spread into the partitions and ceiling panels; some of the materials gave off toxic fumes as they burned – including the adhesives in the laminated sheets and the paint – and the cooling fans had drawn the fumes into the ventilation system and into the compartments where the ventilation controls were open.

The pathologist at Taunton hospital established that most of those who had died had inhaled large amounts of cyanide and carbon monoxide. There were also signs, such as blistering in the throat, that some victims had inhaled very hot gases.

▼A fireman picks his way through the burnt-out corridor of sleeping car B after the fire had been extinguished. Thick, noxious smoke had filled the corridor as the fire took hold, making it very difficult for escaping passengers to crawl towards the only unlocked door.

Sleeping cars on BR

By the time of the Taunton fire, sleeping cars had been in use in Britain for just over 100 years. The basic design consisted of coaches with narrow compartments off the corridor, with a bed, or berth as it used to be called, across the coach from the corridor to the window. Each compartment had a wash basin in one corner, but passengers had to walk down the corridor for the toilet compartment.

Originally, only first class sleeping compartments were provided, with single berths, but from 1928 third class cars were introduced with four bunks per compartment – two upper and two lower. They were equipped with just rugs and pillows.

From 1952 new two-berth third (later second) class compartments with full bedding were introduced. The cars involved at Taunton were the BR standard version of this arrangement, dating from 1960, with the berths fitted one above the other. Some cars were composites, with six second class and five first class compartments (car B of the Taunton train was a composite), while others were

either all first or all second class.

On most services, each pair of cars was served by one attendant who checked in passengers from his booking chart, dealt with any queries, patrolled at night to make sure all was well, made sure passengers were roused if any were leaving at intermediate stations and served morning tea.

Communication bells from each compartment would ring in the pantry in the same coach. If this was not occupied by the attendant, the bell circuit should have been coupled to the adjoining car where it would ring in the staffed pantry. In the cars involved at Taunton, the bell had been disconnected because of a fault.

The BR sleeping cars had pressure ventilation through ducts in the roof. One duct carried warm air if the heating equipment was on. Air was drawn into the system from the vestibule and from outside. In the compartments, passengers could select warm (when on) or cold air, or they could close the ventilator altogether. There was also a side sliding ventilator external window and below it a drop window.

What went wrong?

The inspecting officer, Major Tony King, was critical of many aspects brought out by the fire:

The bell communication between the compartments and the staffed pantry in each pair of sleeping cars was not coupled properly anywhere on the train so that passengers in car B were unable to call the attendant in car C.

Supervision of sleeping car staff was inadequate. New staff were not supervised by qualified training staff; instead they gained their knowledge (good and bad) from working with existing staff. The sleeping car attendant in car C might even have been asleep before he became aware of the fire, said the report.

There was no fire detection equipment or any means of raising the alarm, no fire instructions to passengers, or clearly marked exits.

The placing of bags of linen in the vestibule had been authorized some years earlier, before the adoption of electric heating. But lessons had not been learned from a similar fire on a Glasgow to Euston sleeping car train in 1973, when linen placed against a heater started to smoulder but was quickly put out with a portable fire extinguisher. There was also a case at Rugby in 1977 when a small fire was discovered among bags of Post Office mail resting against a convector heater which had no protective guard.

Most sleeping car external doors were locked and drop windows in the compartments were stiff and would not work. Major King did not think that

the locked doors caused any of the casualties, but there was no direction to the emergency door in the middle of the corridor, which could be opened by pulling a tear-off strip at the top and working the release handle. The long standing practice of locking internal doors and the corridor door to the ordinary seating coaches kept sleeping car passengers free of rowdy intrusions at intermediate stations, but had been banned in the standing instructions.

▲Class 47 No 47498 has been disconnected as firemen conclude their rescue operation soon after the disaster. The white debris on the ground to the left of the group of firemen is the remains of the bed linen which ignited after being piled against an electric heater in the leading vestibule of the second coach.

Recommendations

Several recommendations were immediately introduced as a temporary measure for the existing BR Mark 1 sleeping cars. But because new Mark 3 sleeping cars were already being designed to replace the Mark 1 coaches early in the 1980s, more far-reaching recommendations were added which entailed redesigning the Mark 3 details to provide built-in safety features.

The recommendations were wide ranging; the introduction of new rail safety measures brought fire precautions on sleeping cars in line with the standards required for hotels and offices.

The immediate precautions:
● All drop windows to be checked to ensure they work

● Communication bell systems must work and be tested on every trip

● Portable warning horns to be issued to attendants

● All attendants to be instructed in their duties

● No obstructions permitted in corridors

● Luggage and linen bags to be placed only in brake vans

● Hammers to be available in compartments to break windows

● Vestibule air intake to ventilation system to be sealed, relying only on external air thereafter

● Vestibule heater to be removed

● Proper fuses to be used – some found on the Taunton train were the wrong rating

● One fire extinguisher to be sited at each end of the coach, not two at the same end, as was previously the case

● Centre emergency corridor door to be converted to ordinary door

● Fire precautions notices in each compartment and exit signs to be provided

● Polyurethane mattresses to be removed and fire retardant bed linen used

● Warning notices to be displayed by all heaters regarding danger of obstruction

● Closer supervision of sleeping car attendants by inspectors

● New training syllabus for attendants, including fire fighting

Long term recommendations:
● The air-conditioned Mark 3 sleeping cars with fixed double-glazed windows to have an ejecting frame with an emergency handle

● Maintenance levels to be improved to ensure that materials with a lower fire rating are not used for repairs

● Lining and furnishing materials to be of at least Class 2 fire rating

● Artificial materials not to be used – wool carpets resisted the Taunton fire

● Smoke detectors or fire alarm system to be provided

● The Mark 3 corridors to be divided into three by swing doors fitted with electro-magnetic catches which release automatically in a fire

● Proper patrolling by attendants with time clocks and keys

● Proper fire drill to be instituted

● Better train to signalbox communication, with more telephones and direct-dialled emergency calls. Train to signalbox radio also to be developed on a wider scale. (This has been in hand now for some years and gradually InterCity trains can call up signalboxes by radio)

Nuneaton 1975

The driver of an overnight sleeper from Euston to Glasgow, speeding through the dark at 80mph, missed an unlit 20mph speed restriction warning board for a temporary length of curved track at Nuneaton station. The train derailed resulting in six fatalities and 38 injuries.

On the night of Thursday 5 June 1975, signalman Young and regulator Marlow were on duty in Nuneaton signalbox. Just before two in the morning, the late running 23.30 Euston to Glasgow sleeping car train approached their control area. All the signals were at green, and Marlow followed the train's approach on the signalbox's illuminated diagram. He felt that the train was approaching somewhat faster than usual, considering the temporary 20mph speed restriction that was in operation due to engineering works, but he had no way of judging the speed exactly.

As the train sped past the signalbox at 80mph, Marlow and Young realized with horror that disaster was imminent. Seconds later they saw flashes from the overhead lines and heard a tremendous noise, and suddenly the track circuits on their control panel showed all lines approaching the station as occupied. This could mean only one thing – the train had derailed.

Marlow rang Electrical Control and asked for the traction current to be switched off and Young called the emergency services.

Engineering works at Nuneaton

Nuneaton station is situated on the West Coast main line between Rugby and Crewe, a section of line known as the Trent Valley route.

In January 1975 work started on the first stage of extensive alterations to the track layout. At the London end of the station there was a complex array of points and crossings linking the branches

▼As the derailment of the 23.30 Euston to Glasgow sleeper occurred at a station, the scene was one of severe destruction. The leading locomotive led all but the very last carriage of the train into derailment, with coaches slewing sideways destroying signals, point machines and lineside telephones. Electric locomotive No 86 242, which had failed soon after the start of the fateful journey, ended up mounting the platform – fortunately it did not displace the awning.

and main lines to the four platform lines and other tracks through the station. All this pointwork was expensive to maintain, and as it fell due for renewal it was decided to simplify the layout and to cut out many of the crossings.

At the time of the accident, the main lines at the south end of the station had a short section of plain track between new work in its final position and old track which had still to be replaced. As the two tracks had slightly different alignments a short but pronounced curve was put in as a temporary measure, with a 20mph speed restriction over it.

Advance warning signs

Speed restrictions on British Rail were, at that time, marked by advance warning signs. These consisted of yellow arrow-shaped boards with the speed in figures on top. At night the yellow boards displayed two horizontal lights and the figures were illuminated from behind.

The advance warning board at Nuneaton was placed about 1¼ miles out from the start of the speed restriction – an ample distance for trains travelling at the full 100mph line speed to slow down to 20mph before passing through the station.

After an advance warning sign, another indicator would be displayed at the start of the restriction. These were also illuminated at night.

Most speed restriction boards at the time of the accident were lit by paraffin lamps, but gas lit indicators fed from portable gas cylinders were becoming more widespread. The advance warning board at Nuneaton was gas lit, while the board at the start of the restriction was paraffin lit and was placed just before the temporary section of track.

Breakdown

On the night of 5 June, the 23.30 overnight sleeping car train for Glasgow left Euston on time. It was hauled by Class 86 electric locomotive No 86 242 and comprised 12 sleeping cars, two passenger brake vans and a buffet car.

At around midnight its electric locomotive developed a fault and the train came to a stop at

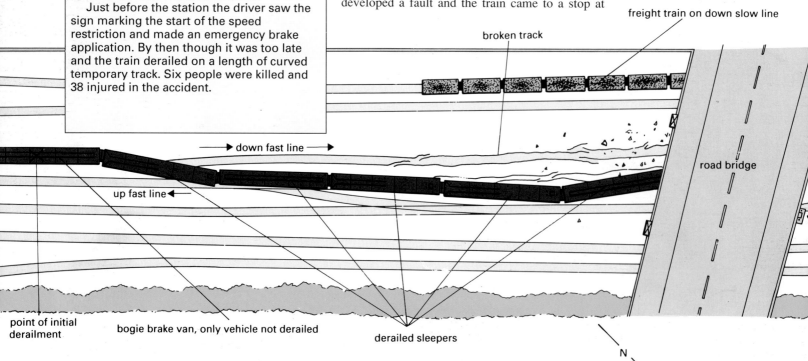

▲In the daylight of Friday morning the extent of the damage to the first six sleeper carriages could be seen from the road bridge looking towards the station. Rescue services spent many long hours searching the wreckage for survivors. All six fatal injuries were to passengers and staff travelling in these coaches.

Build up to disaster

On 5 June 1975, the 23.30 Glasgow night sleeper left Euston on time, but after just 28 minutes' running the engine failed at Kings Langley. Another locomotive was provided, but by then the train was well behind schedule.

Between Kings Langley and Nuneaton the train was driven at its maximum permitted speed, and as it approached Nuneaton station it was travelling at about 80mph.

Over a mile out from Nuneaton, the train passed a warning sign giving advance notice of a temporary 20mph speed restriction through the station, but all three lights on the sign were out and the driver assumed that the restriction had been lifted.

Just before the station the driver saw the sign marking the start of the speed restriction and made an emergency brake application. By then though it was too late and the train derailed on a length of curved temporary track. Six people were killed and 38 injured in the accident.

---

freight train on down slow line

broken track

down fast line →

road bridge

up fast line ←

point of initial derailment

bogie brake van, only vehicle not derailed

derailed sleepers

N

Kings Langley, with the locomotive a total failure. A relief Class 86 electric locomotive was sent from Willesden; the failed engine was left attached so that with both locomotives the train was a hefty 749 tons.

By the time the train got going again from its prolonged stop at Kings Langley it was 75 minutes late, so the driver, J McKay, set about regaining some of the lost time.

Lights go out

As the train approached Nuneaton, McKay was on the look-out for the warning board. The restriction was listed in the operating booklet called the Weekly Engineering Notice which gave details of engineering works and any related speed restrictions. He had also seen the board on a run during the previous night from Euston to Crewe.

The train passed a colour light signal showing green just over 1½ miles before Nuneaton station. McKay should have seen the warning board for the speed restriction about 200 yards ahead, but the next thing he saw was a warning board for the adjoining slow line ¼ mile further on.

The first thought which flashed through his mind was where was the warning board applying to his train? Even while he was thinking, the train was still speeding on at around 80mph – over 100 yards every three seconds. Nuneaton was fast approaching. The missing board raised doubts. Was the speed restriction still on? Another restriction further south between Bletchley and Rugby, listed in the Weekly Notice, had no warning boards in place and had seemingly been cancelled.

Trial of the driver

After the accident, driver McKay was charged on six counts of manslaughter. The case was brought as he had not observed the speed restriction.

Certainly the speed restriction was listed in the Weekly Notice and had not been cancelled – but so too was the one at Hanslope further south. The warning boards there were simply not in place, which was not within the rules.

As for the advance warning board for the Nuneaton restriction, the rule book said: 'After sunset two yellow lights (white lights on gas lit boards) must be placed as shown...and the speed indication must be illuminated.' They were not.

Others were also at fault. The track staff used incorrect methods so that the lights failed, and the preceding drivers did not report the gradual failure of the lights.

After a three-day trial McKay was found not guilty and discharged.

◄ **The two locomotives at the head of the train separated after derailment. The failed locomotive veered sideways and damaged about 150 feet of the platform.**

Class 86/2 electric locomotive No 86 242 (not under power) with front end on top of platform in contact with awning.

sleeping cars on their sides at right angles to track

overhead gantry displaced

restaurant car

150 feet of down fast line platform coping damaged

Nuneaton station

455 yards of fast lines and 175 yards of up slow line destroyed

sleeping car on side across up slow line

sleeping car upright but severely damaged

partly crushed sleeping car on side

Bogie brake van jammed against the south end of the down fast platform, upright but damaged beyond repair.

Class 86/0 electric locomotive No 86 006 came to rest between the up and down fast lines about halfway through the station.

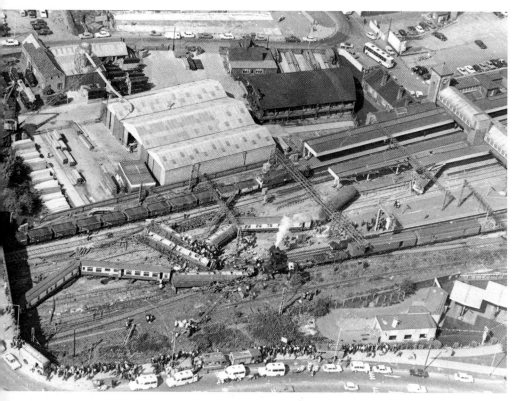

▲Apart from the destruction of the train, the derailment caused extensive damage to the stretch of track just before Nuneaton station. Three overhead line structures were demolished – one of which struck a passing freight train – and overhead wires were brought down. The supporting piers of a road bridge were also hit by the train as it careered off the tracks, but fortunately the damage was not sufficient to endanger its stability and it remained intact.

coaches jack-knifed right across the layout just before the platforms. Four passengers and two sleeping car attendants were killed and 38 passengers were injured in the accident.

What went wrong?

No fewer than 15 trains had passed the warning board between 10.39pm on 5 June and 1.54am (the time of the accident) on 6 June. The lights had gradually begun to fail until, by the time the Glasgow sleeper passed, all three had gone out. Six drivers saw that the light behind the figure 20 was out, yet not one had stopped to report the failure as they were required to do by the rules.

But why had the warning board lights gone out? It emerged that the permanent way staff were using an incorrect method of coupling the gas cylinders used to illuminate the sign.

The cylinders were designed to be used in pairs. Supply should have been taken from one cylinder, and when the gas ran low an automatic changeover valve should have switched to take the supply from the second, full cylinder.

But the staff at Nuneaton were in the practice of coupling the gas cylinders singly, manually changing over the supply when the gas in one was low and then replacing the empty cylinder. On the night of the accident, the gas cylinder in use at the speed restriction warning board became empty and the lights went out one by one.

At the inquiry, the inspecting officer felt that it was unlikely that an experienced driver should have decided that, because he could not see a warning sign, the speed restriction had been cancelled. He suggested that McKay had been intent on making up lost time and had forgotten the speed restriction.

The inquiry placed the major share of the blame on driver McKay, some of the responsibility on the crews of the preceding trains for not reporting the failing lights and a lesser share on the permanent way staff for incorrectly connecting the gas equipment at the warning board

Fatal decision

McKay decided that the Nuneaton restriction must also have been lifted, but by then the lights of the station were coming into view. Amidst the background of the station he suddenly saw the dimly lit 20 board marking the start of the restriction for the temporary curves into the station. He made an emergency brake application, but it was too late and the train ran on to the speed restricted curve at nearly 80mph.

The leading locomotive derailed and separated from the train, continuing well into the station and running between the tracks of the up and down fast lines, before finally coming to rest. The second, dead locomotive finished up on the down fast line platform, while the train piled up as

Action taken

The accident highlighted a degree of unreliability in the lighting of warning indicator boards. This led to an improved design for gas mantles and a new reporting system for monitoring the performance of all temporary speed restriction warning boards and indicators. The lights in the yellow warning boards were made to flash as an added distinction.

The practice of European railways was examined by the Railway Inspectorate and, as a result, the inspecting officer recommended that an improved design of board should be produced – possibly with a reflective surface – with better illumination. Today, advance warning boards are highly visible, with white figures displayed on a blue background.

The inspecting officer also concluded that an automatic warning system (AWS) permanent magnet should be placed at the

approach to an advance warning board. This would mean that the driver of an approaching train would receive an AWS caution indication exactly as if he were approaching a signal at caution. There are difficulties with this system, however, such as the possibility for confusion between an audible warning for a speed restriction close to a positive indication for a green colour light signal.

As part of signalling developments, speed restrictions for engineering work can now be keyed into the automatic train protection system (ATP) by beacons on the track. As ATP is adopted, it will provide fail safe speed indications on the driver's control desk and automatic brake applications if the driver fails to reduce speed to the required limits.

This 1990s development will mean that never again will a driver be able to forget a speed restriction.

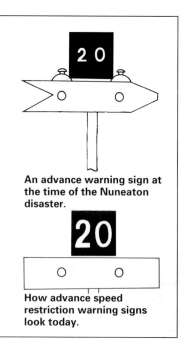

An advance warning sign at the time of the Nuneaton disaster.

How advance speed restriction warning signs look today.

Moorgate 1975

**A February morning in 1975 – rush hour on London's
Underground was progressing as normal, moving thousands
of commuters. But at 08.46, Londoners were stunned when a tube
train failed to stop at Moorgate station and hit the dead-end
wall of the tunnel at speed, killing forty-three people.**

The Finsbury Park to Moorgate branch, former-ly part of the London Underground system, has an unusual history. Unlike most parts of the system, it has changed its role on more than one occasion. It was originally built as an independent company – the Great Northern & City Railway (GN&C) – largely at the instigation of the Great Northern Railway (GNR), whose suburban ser-vices from King's Cross and Broad Street were becoming very overcrowded around the turn of the century.

The aim was to run through trains from the GNR line to Moorgate, which would be steam-hauled from the north to Finsbury Park, then an electric locomotive would take over for the final short run to Moorgate. The line was planned to run overground from Finsbury Park to the first station at Drayton Park, then descend in deep-level tube tunnels through three more stations – Highbury, Essex Road and Old Street – and finally to the ter-minus at Moorgate. At that point, passengers could change on to the Metropolitan and what became the City branch of the Northern line.

Since the intention was to run through trains from the GNR, the tube tunnels were 16ft (5m) in diameter – to allow for normal, main line stock. However, while the company was battling to get established and raise finance, the GNR lost inter-est, and although the tunnels were built for trains of main line size, the connection to the GNR was not made when planned. Therefore, the GN&C had to make its northern terminus underground, beneath Finsbury Park GNR station.

Tube trains brought on line
The main line sized tunnels played a major part in the accident of 1975. The line was electrified from its opening in 1904, with main line sized saloon trains. But the line was less successful than hoped, and in 1913 it was taken over by the Metropolitan Railway, even though it was physically isolated from it.

There were plans to extend the line, or to join it to the main Metropolitan line, which also served Moorgate just below ground level, but nothing was done. In 1939, London Transport transferred oper-ation of the branch to the Northern Line, although it was still physically separate. The old GN&C trains were scrapped and normal, small, tube-sized trains took over. It then became known as the Northern City line.

By the 1970s, plans had been revived to link the Northern City branch to the former GNR main line at Finsbury Park, as part of the GNR electrifi-cation. Through GNR-line British Rail (BR) trains would run in the large tunnels to Moorgate, form-ing a direct part of BR's Great Northern suburban services.

By the beginning of 1975, the Northern City line had been cut at its northern end. Trains termi-nated in the open air at Drayton Park. This was to allow work to be carried out between Drayton Park and Finsbury Park in building the link line between the Moorgate branch and the Great

▼Firemen at work in the confined space between the crumpled coaches and the wall of the blind tunnel. It took the fire brigade nearly three hours to hack their way through to the first coach. Working conditions were appalling, and exacerbated by the heat and fumes of the fire brigade's generators.

Northern main line, ready for the introduction of through BR electric trains in August 1976.

A normal rush hour

On the morning of Friday 28 February 1975, trains were shuttling normally on the 2³/₄ mile (4¹/₂km) double-line branch. A train had left Moorgate for Drayton Park at 08.44, and the signalman had reset the points and signals for the next southbound train to arrive at platform 9.

Moorgate Northern City platforms comprised an island, with the two sides in separate tunnels, numbered 9 and 10 as part of the platform numbering of the whole station, including the sub-surface Metropolitan and BR tracks. At the approach to these platforms was a scissors crossover, with a 15mph (24km/h) speed restriction through it.

A few passengers had wandered on to platform 9 after the 08.44 had left, to await the next train. Train No 272 left Drayton Park at 08.39, and made normal stops at the intermediate stations. After Old Street it accelerated to 35-40mph (55-65km/h). But then, instead of slowing to 15mph (24km/h) to go over the scissors crossover, the train continued at about 35mph (55km/h) into the platform.

The passengers waiting on the platform looked up as the train approached much faster than normal. Suddenly they realized it was going much too fast to stop; some even thought it was under power. The signalman in the cabin at the Drayton Park end of platform 10 heard the train come

through the crossover 'like an express'. He ran out and through to platform 9, and saw the back of the train passing him at about 35-40mph (55-65km/h). Suddenly there was a resounding crash as the train went past the end of the platform, through the sand drag, and into the short tunnel beyond, where it hit the end wall of the tunnel.

The short, blind tunnel was only 66ft (20m) long, yet only the back end of the third coach could still be seen. The three leading coaches had been compressed into the space of two by the violence of the collision. Waiting passengers had just witnessed the worst-ever accident on the London Underground. It also became one of the most horrific and long drawn-out for the trapped survivors and their rescuers.

The signalman telephoned the London Transport control office immediately to report the accident and call for assistance, and the guard

▲Passengers were trapped not only by the crushed fabric of the train, but also by other passengers, some of them injured (and some dead), lying on top of them. In certain cases, the injured were inaccessible by stretcher, and had to be handed out along a human chain of rescuers.

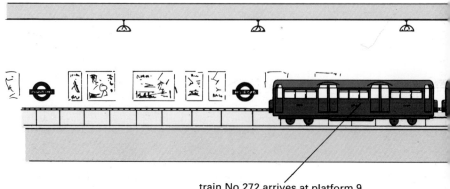

train No 272 arrives at platform 9 doing 35-40mph (55-65km/h) managed to get the doors open on the back three coaches – still in the platform – and what was left of the third coach from the front.

Just outside Moorgate station, a police motor cyclist was told by a passenger coming out of the station that there had been a crash down below. He left his motor cycle and made his way down the escalators to be met by a crowd of distraught passengers, dazed, and many of them black from head to foot. They had been covered in soot, which had been displaced in a massive cloud from the dead-end tunnel by the violence of the collision. He went back to the surface and called by radio to his control that there had been a major accident. The police control at Scotland Yard immediately started the major accident procedure.

Rescue difficulties

Following years of planning and joint exercises, the rescue services had basic plans for dealing with various emergencies, but were largely unprepared for the horrific nature of this disaster. Ambulances were soon on the spot, followed shortly by the fire brigade. As senior officers and their men went down to the platform, they were met with a battlefield scene. Railway staff and the first of the rescue services had started to help those passengers who were not badly hurt, or were just suffering from shock. The black cloud of sooty dust was settling everywhere, and much was still in the air.

At first, the rescue teams had to contend with passengers using other parts of the station at surface level. But gradually, the police closed off the station and nearby roads to give fire and ambulance crews space to bring in equipment.

As the passengers were still being detrained relatively easily from the back end of the third coach and the rear three coaches of the six-coach train, rescuers were trying to make their way into the blind tunnel to get at the front of the third coach and the leading two coaches. Only then was the full extent of the accident realized.

Because of the large diameter tunnels, the small-sized tube train had not been constrained by the tunnel as it hit the end wall, so the leading coach had jack-knifed up on striking the hydraulic buffers at the end of the platform, hitting the end wall near its top. The underframe had buckled in three places, leaving the front of the coach at a V-angle to the middle, another angular bend in the centre, and a further bend towards the rear. The back of the leading coach was impacted into the roof of the tunnel, with the front end of the second coach underneath it. All 52ft (16m) of the leading motor coach was compressed into no more than 20ft (6m). The front of the third coach had been driven over the top of the back end of the second coach. Rescuing the survivors was going to be a prolonged and difficult exercise.

▲Post mortem examination detected no disease that might explain why the driver of train No 272, Leslie Newson, failed to apply his brakes as he approached Moorgate station. In fact, Mr Newson was described by colleagues as a cautious driver, who entered stations slowly, and had never been known to overrun a platform.

No evidence

The train approached the station without slowing for the crossover, and continued under power through the platform until it ran through the sand drag, hit the buffers, and was thrown over them and into the tunnel end wall at between 35 and 40mph (55 and 65km/h).

The driver had acted normally on previous journeys that morning. There was no evidence of suicide and, although traces of alcohol were found in his body five days after the accident, there was no evidence to suggest that he had ever been a heavy drinker, or that he was drunk when he went on duty that day.

A suggestion was made at the inquest, but not proven, that the driver might have had a momentary brain spasm, which made him freeze.

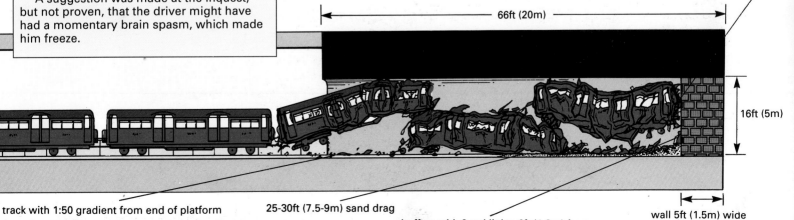

52ft (16m) leading coach compressed into about 20ft (6m)

66ft (20m)

16ft (5m)

track with 1:50 gradient from end of platform down to sand drag

25-30ft (7.5-9m) sand drag

buffers with 3 red lights 6ft (1.8m) from brick wall shunted into brick wall

wall 5ft (1.5m) wide

▲Where possible, firemen used hydraulic equipment to lift wreckage from the bodies, taking great care to avoid further injury, whether to the living or to the dead.

Working conditions were over 100°F (38°C), and it was not until late in the afternoon that the fire brigade were able to rig up an emergency airline to the end of the tunnel.

Cutting equipment
Rescue teams realized quickly that the possibility of fire and the danger of fumes made it too risky to use oxy-acetylene cutting equipment. There would also be an increased chance of further injuring trapped passengers.

However, they could use air cutting equipment, and an immediate priority for the firemen was to call in air cylinders from all parts of London.

Medical teams were soon at work in the wreckage, giving pain-killing injections to trapped passengers. Working conditions were appalling – with no trains operating to pull air into the tunnels, the temperature was rising. But the main problem was that of access through the twisted metal to the passengers, many of whom were trapped up to their heads by parts of the coaches, or by other passengers piled against them, some of whom had not survived. Rescuers had to crawl under bogies upended and jammed, but which might have fallen on top of them.

As the day passed, the teams gradually extracted passengers whose lives could still be saved, as well as many bodies. Dire working conditions demanded frequent periods of rest and recuperation. The rescue involved considerable control and organization of the different services on the spot, and the hospital needs for the injured; also the care of the bodies and counselling of the relatives and friends called to identify them. Voluntary services played an important role, too, with the Salvation Army and Red Cross helping and providing comfort to relatives of the casualties, and to the rescuers, most of whom had never before been involved in such an horrific accident. And the rescue teams, working in shifts, had to be provided with food, drink, and – eventually – washing facilities. The last of the passengers still alive was trapped for over 13 hours.

That was the end of only the first stage. Most of the wreckage of the front three coaches still had to be removed, and many bodies were yet to be recovered. It took another four days of careful cutting, jacking, supporting and winching of the wreckage before the last of the bodies, including that of the driver, were finally recovered late on Tuesday 4 March. In all, 42 passengers and the driver died, and 74 were injured in this, the worst train accident ever on the LT system.

What went wrong?
Nobody really knows why this disaster occurred. Neither the inquest nor the railway inspectorate inquiry came to a firm conclusion. The most astonishing thing was that several witnesses, waiting on Moorgate platform as train No 272 came in, saw the driver at the controls, staring straight ahead, as if frozen or paralysed, making no attempt to change the controls in a panic-brake application.

Evidence from the position of the electrical contactors proved the train had been under power until reaching the sand drag. The chief inspecting officer, Lt Col I K A McNaughton, stated that the possibility of it being a deliberate action could not be disproved. The driver appeared to be in good health, and there was no medical reason for his inaction, other than a suggestion of a passing brain spasm, which could not be proved. The train brakes were in good order, and there was no signalling fault. Moorgate became yet another mystery accident in the annals of railway history, the only comparable accident being that at Tooting Broadway in 1971, in which a driver was killed.

Lt Col McNaughton was determined that it would not happen again, giving recommendations to prevent trains approaching a dead-end underground station too fast.

Recommendations
Although the exact cause of the driver's actions are unknown, the inspecting officer's recommendations were intended to prevent anything like it happening again. He stressed that preventative measures must allow for the possibility of deliberate dangerous action on the part of a motorman.

While full automatic train protection, including an absolute control over the driver's actions, would be desirable, or an automatic driving system as on London Transport's (LT) Victoria line, it would be expensive to provide this on lines with older types of signalling. But LT lines are equipped with trip-cock train stops, and timing devices can be added to track circuit sections.

The recommendation was for speed-control track circuits to be used to ensure trains slowed down as they approached a terminus station, and could not accelerate under power towards the dead end. If they did, the timing circuit would not clear the train-stop trip arm, and the train would be tripped, and brakes applied automatically. In addition, the last signal before a dead-end track was to show a single yellow aspect for caution rather than the green aspect that had been standard until then – and this was to apply to BR lines as well.

As for Moorgate Northern City line, it was taken over in 1976 by BR Class 313 electric trains running through from the Great Northern line. They too have trip-cocks, similar to those on LT, for use on the underground section, so that speed controls linked to the trip apparatus prevent trains from entering a dead-end line too fast.

West Ealing 1973

A heavily loaded commuter train from Paddington, travelling at about 70mph (113km/h), was suddenly derailed when a battery box cover hanging down unseen in the late afternoon darkness hit point rodding and ripped points open under the train. Ten people died in this pre-Christmas tragedy.

The main line from London Paddington to the West has always been well aligned for speed right from the terminus, with 70mph (113km/h) allowed within a mile or so of the start. The route has four tracks westwards all the way to Didcot, over 50 miles (80km) from Paddington, paired by use with the down and up main lines, today called the fast lines on the south side, and the down and up relief lines on the north side. At intervals, crossovers link the main and relief lines. At Longfield Avenue Junction, between Ealing Broadway and West Ealing, a down main to down relief crossover gave trains running on the down main line a facility to cross to the down relief line, and – if needed – to take a right-hand divergence at West Ealing on to the Greenford branch.

The crossover at Longfield Avenue and the signalling in the area in the 1970s was controlled from Old Oak Common signalbox, a few miles towards Paddington. The signalling in the area had been modernized in the 1960s, with track circuit block and routes set by the Old Oak Common signalmen turning switches and pressing buttons on the track diagram in the signalbox. The signals were of an older style, known as searchlights. The three main aspects of red, yellow and green were displayed through one lens, with the different colours shown by a moving disc of coloured filters. The filters were positioned by electromagnetic controls in front of the main light. The second yellow light, to give the double yellow aspect, was placed above the main searchlight lamp.

Long suburban trains

Most of the suburban trains in and out of Paddington were (and still are) formed of diesel multiple units. However, several of the outer suburban peak hour commuter trains, particularly those running beyond Reading on the Newbury line and through Didcot to Oxford, were formed of locomotive-hauled trains of main line corridor stock, often in lengthy formations. One such was the 17.18 from Paddington to Oxford.

On Wednesday 19 December 1973, the 17.18 had 11 coaches, all of BR Mark I side corridor stock, four of which included first class compartments. Just before Christmas the train was well filled with commuters, and had many shoppers as

▶ **A general view of the derailment at West Ealing shows the Western class diesel-hydraulic locomotive No 1007 on its side at the bottom of the photograph. The down fast to slow crossover can be seen to the right of the further crane.**

67

well, although they were discouraged from travelling on the peak trains. The train had seats for 622 passengers, but a train count showed that 650 were on board, so some must have been standing in the corridors.

The locomotive was Western class diesel-hydraulic C-C No 1007 *Western Talisman*. In the original 1955 modernization plan, the Western Region of British Rail (BR) had gone its own way and adopted German pattern diesel engine power plants and hydraulic transmissions for its fleet of locomotives, rather than the diesel-electric arrangement used by other regions, and preferred by BR's top management. The result was a unique range of locomotive classes on the Western Region, much lighter than the heavy diesel-electrics elsewhere, but needing specialist facilities for maintenance. The most powerful class was the Western, of 2700hp and carried on two six-wheel bogies. All carried names prefixed by *Western*.

▼ The breakdown cranes got to work lifting the wrecked coaches on the morning of 20 December 1973. The rear coaches had been removed during the night, but major work could not start until all the casualties had been removed. Note the extra width between the up and down fast lines on the right, a consequence of the original 7ft ¼in broad gauge.

Unlocked box

The battery box doors of the Western class diesels were of hefty construction, weighing 80lb (36kg). They were hinged at the bottom and when horizontal were held by two folding metal stays.

When open, the doors were outside the maximum permitted width. Once the stays had been ripped apart by the impact with the platform coping at Ealing Broadway, there was nothing to stop the door from dropping to the vertical position, with its normal top edge lying below rail level. It should have been held in the upright position by two locks and a pear-shaped drop catch. Instead, it had been sent out unlocked and the catch had failed to drop to hold it. There was no proper final check procedure.

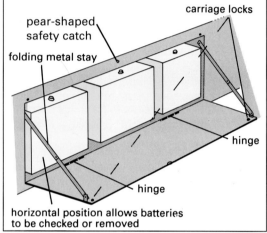

pear-shaped safety catch

folding metal stay

carriage locks

hinge

hinge

horizontal position allows batteries to be checked or removed

By the 1970s, the BR Board had shown its hand and was demanding an end to the hydraulic locomotives, which required costly maintenance. By then, too, the locomotives were beginning to show their age; they were not all that old by general standards, but 10-15 years was old for diesels.

No 1007 was already proving troublesome. It was based at Laira depot in Plymouth, and had been there from 8-12 December for what were called 'A' and 'B' examinations, which took place every so many hours in service. On 12 December it worked the 05.45 Plymouth – Paddington ser-

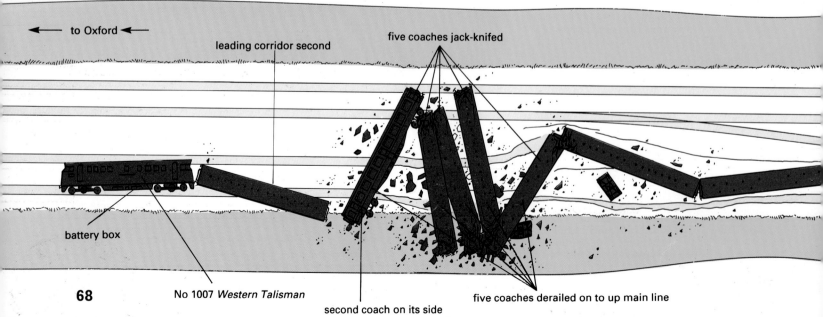

← to Oxford ←

leading corridor second

five coaches jack-knifed

battery box

No 1007 *Western Talisman*

second coach on its side

five coaches derailed on to up main line

vice and the 17.45 Paddington – Westbury. On arrival in Westbury it needed repairs because of loss of coolant fluid, transmission oil leaks and a reversing problem. On the following day the locomotive was able to run unaided back to Plymouth, where one of its two diesel engines was changed.

On 14 December No 1007 worked the 19.00 Plymouth – Bristol, but was again in trouble with an automatic warning system (AWS) fault. That was repaired, and on the following day it worked passenger trains to Exeter and on to Plymouth, but during the day developed another AWS fault. On 17 December it took the 05.45 Plymouth – Paddington train, but by Reading was in trouble once more, and had to have an assisting locomotive to get the train to Paddington. It then worked to Old Oak Common depot on one diesel engine and there it had repairs carried out on the engine that had not been changed at the Laira depot four days earlier.

While at Old Oak Common, the batteries used for starting the diesel engine and for powering the auxiliary equipment and controls were put on charge. The battery box on the south side was opened to allow the electrician to clip on the charging leads to the terminals.

The bottom-hinged battery box doors normally stood upright, locked by carriage-type locks. These locks were operated by a simple steel leaf, which had to be turned through a right angle by a square-ended key to engage in a slot in the battery box frame. As an added precaution, a pear-shaped safety catch that pivoted from the body could also hold the door in the closed position.

The battery boxes were located just below the main bodyside of the locomotive within the skirt of the body panels that extended downwards. When the battery doors were opened, they acted as a table, which allowed the battery cells to be pulled forward for examination or changing.

After the repairs were completed at Old Oak Common, No 1007 was sent back into service at 14.00, and was booked to haul the empty coaches to

▲ **No 1007 *Western Talisman* is seen here on its side. The space where the open battery box door had been can be seen on the lower side panels between the bogies just above the policeman.**

Check list to disaster

It was the lack of a final check on Western class diesel-hydraulic locomotive No 1007, after it had undergone repairs and battery charging at Old Oak Common depot, that led to it being sent back into traffic with the battery box door closed, but not locked, and with an additional safety catch not in position.

The bottom hinged door stayed upright for a time, but soon after leaving Paddington, hauling the 17.18 train to Oxford, the door dropped open and hit several objects at Acton and Ealing before the stays were ripped off.

The door dropped to below rail level and smashed into point rodding, which caused facing points to move under the locomotive, and derailed the whole train.

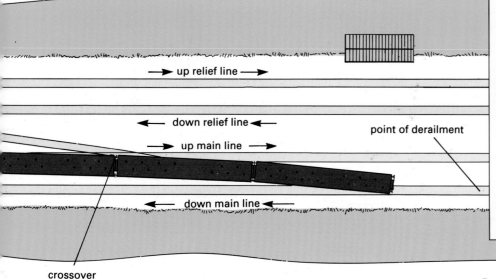

→ up relief line →

← down relief line ←

point of derailment

→ up main line →

← down main line ←

crossover

→ to Paddington →

▲ Five coaches from the middle section of the train jack-knifed in the derailment (this picture shows three of them). Nearest the camera, on the left, is the front of the fourth coach. The back of the fifth is in the centre, the front of the sixth is partly overturned on the right, and on the extreme right can be seen the seventh coach.

Built for speed

Brunel, the engineer of the line from Paddington to the West, built a route in the 1830s to Reading and Bristol with easy gradients for most of the way and few curves calling for speed limits. Even in steam days, the express long distance trains to the South West of England, Wales and the West Midlands were able to take advantage of the superbly laid out line to accelerate quickly. But so too could the outer suburban trains, many of which ran on the main lines at express speeds until they were diverted off the main lines on to the relief lines or branches to make their first calls at such places as Slough, Twyford for the Henley branch, or Reading.

Paddington to form the 16.48 train to Worcester. After the Worcester train had departed, No 1007 ran out to Paddington Yard carriage sidings and then back to platform 2 to couple on to the coaches forming the 17.18 for Oxford.

The 17.18 was 11 minutes late in starting, but once on its way the journey seemed normal, except that the driver felt a lurch on approaching Ealing Broadway station at 70mph (113km/h). He thought it was a bad rail joint and decided to report it at Reading. Less than half a mile ahead, as the locomotive reached the facing points of the crossover from the down main to the down relief at Longfield Avenue, its back end bounced into the air. No 1007 rolled over on to its right-hand side and scraped along the down and up main tracks for about 200yd (180m) before coming to a halt.

Massive derailment

The sudden stop from a speed of 70mph (113km/h) caused chaos. The leading corridor second had derailed to the left but was still attached to the locomotive by its buffers, and stayed upright. The next five coaches jack-knifed, concertina fashion, and were at right angles to the track, spread over all four tracks, with the second coach on its side. All six sustained serious damage to their bodies, with some locked together in a tight mass.

The remaining coaches were derailed on to the up main line. Luckily, no other train was approaching on any of the other three lines, or there would have been a major disaster. It was bad enough with 10 passengers dead and 94 injured, of whom 53 needed hospital treatment.

It was not hard to find clues as to the cause of the sudden derailment. Along the line from Paddington were damaged lineside fixtures and fittings. At Old Oak Common a 'limit of shunt'

sign, about 2ft 11in (89cm) from the left-hand rail and 12in (30cm) above rail level, had received a hefty blow; while at Acton, cable brackets on the platform wall had been damaged, and coping stones on the ramp approaching Ealing Broadway platform were dislodged.

At Longfield Avenue something had hit the point and facing point lock rodding between the point motor and the switch blade with such force that the rodding was bent and the point machine wrecked, forcing the point blades to move to the reverse position under the locomotive, so diverting the rear wheels towards the up main line.

Examination of the locomotive showed that the battery box door was the culprit. It was not locked, and the pear-shaped catch had not dropped to hold it closed. The door had remained closed on its own while the locomotive was travelling to Paddington with the empty coaches, and while it shunted on to its own coaches. But at some point, after leaving with the 17.18 train, the door had dropped to the horizontal position, and been held in position by stays, where it projected about 12in (30cm) outside the normal maximum loading gauge. The door struck the limit of shunt sign, and later, as it hit coping stones at Ealing Broadway, the stays were ripped away. This allowed the door to fall vertically to a position about 2ft (60cm) outside the left-hand rail and 6in (15cm) below it. The next objects in its path were the point rods of the facing points at Longfield Avenue, which it hit at 70mph (113km/h), ripping the point blades open.

Clearly, the battery box had not been locked after the repairs and battery charging at Old Oak Common. The accident showed a lack of any inspection system to ensure that body doors, battery box doors, hatches and the like were securely locked before locomotives were sent back into traffic. An unauthorized modification had also been made to the pear drop catches at Laira, allowing them to remain raised, although done with the intention of helping them to drop.

Recommendations

Lt Col I K A McNaughton, who chaired the inquiry into the accident, found there was no proper system for a final look round locomotives after repairs were carried out at Old Oak Common. Such a check should ensure that everything had been correctly 'boxed up' – the term used when everything was put back into place after repairs.

The check should cover any part of the locomotive that had been removed or opened to give access to equipment inside the locomotive, such as bodyside doors, panels or roof hatches. A responsible person should be designated to see that all these parts were properly in position and secured before locomotives were sent back into service. A new design of safety catch was also to be produced, and Lt Col McNaughton criticized Laira depot for having made a modification to the existing pear-shaped drop catch to the battery box doors without authority.

Eltham Well Hall 1972

**After a day at the seaside, tragedy struck an
excursion train returning from Ramsgate to north London
when its drunken driver took it through a 20mph (32km/h) curve
at over 60mph (97km/h). The derailed train overturned,
killing five passengers and the driver.**

The east Kent seaside resorts of Ramsgate and Margate are popular destinations for daytrippers from London, not just those from the south and east of the capital, which is served by regular trains to the coast, but also for those living in the north and west suburbs, from where special excursion trains were run in the 1970s.

Various cross-London rail links were used to transfer trains from the north London main lines to the Southern Region. Trains from the Midland lines out of St Pancras to Bedford generally used the route from Cricklewood to Acton and Kew, and then went up the South Western Windsor line to Clapham Junction, using the maze of junctions and spurs to get to Brixton and across to Lewisham. Once there, they were on one or other of the direct routes from London to the Kent coast.

Between London Bridge and Dartford there were three parallel routes through the south-east

suburbs: the most straightforward for cross-London excursions was the Bexleyheath line to Dartford. This was not laid out for high speed, and in the early 1970s the speed limit was 60mph (97km/h). The track had its ups and downs, with some gradients as steep as 1 in 68, but the most constraining features were 20mph (32km/h) speed restrictions at Dartford and at Eltham Well Hall, the latter having a sharp curve with a radius of 264yd (241m).

Most passenger trains on this route were local electric services, stopping at all stations. As the Eltham Well Hall stop was just east of the curve, its sharp radius was of little consequence to them. But the few non-stopping trains had to take it with great care.

On Sunday 11 June 1972 the London Midland Region of British Rail (BR) had arranged an excursion to the Margate seaside, starting from

▼ **Having been derailed at speed through the sharp curve at Eltham Well Hall, the rear end of Class 47 No D1630 was surprisingly little damaged, even though at first it remained coupled to brake second No M35302 (on the right) after they jack-knifed. The bogie on top of the locomotive came from the near end of the coach. Behind can be seen the fifth and sixth coaches of the excursion train from Ramsgate, which became uncoupled and ran on past the locomotive.**

Kentish Town, just outside St Pancras. The train's route took it north-westwards to Cricklewood as part of its almost circular trip round the northern, western and southern suburbs in order to reach the Southern Region and the line to Margate. The train had 10 coaches of BR Mark I main line corridor stock, all except one having compartments from a side corridor, the remaining one being an open second with saloon-style seating. The train was well filled, many passengers being railwaymen and their families. Motive power was provided by Brush Class 47 diesel locomotive No D1630, allocated to the London Midland Region. As far as Cricklewood the locomotive had a local crew, but from there on a Southern Region driver took over right through to Margate.

The outward journey was uneventful, with the driver making several brake applications for signal checks and the station stop at Margate. He then worked the train on empty to Ramsgate sidings. The brakes were clearly in good working order. After reaching Ramsgate at 11.00, the driver and a shunter arranged for the locomotive to be uncoupled and run round the train to the other end, where it would be recoupled ready for the return journey that evening. The driver then went off to take up other duties, as he was not rostered to drive the return trip.

Irregular booking on

The driver booked to work the return excursion, scheduled to leave Margate at 20.05, was supposed to sign on at Hither Green depot at 15.22 and travel as a passenger from Hither Green to Dartford, changing there into a train for Ramsgate. He was to be accompanied by a secondman. The driver lived near Rainham (Kent), the next station east of Gillingham, and was thus already half-way to Ramsgate. Instead of travelling to Hither Green to book on and then having to go all the way back again, he telephoned to the motive power supervisor at Hither Green to say that he would be on duty and was travelling direct from Rainham to

Ramsgate by train.

The secondman reported in person to Hither Green and he went to Ramsgate as a passenger in the regulation way. The driver, who had actually set off from Rainham at about 17.00 – nearly two hours after his official signing-on time – and his secondman met at about 18.30 on the locomotive for the return excursion, the train at this time still standing in Ramsgate sidings.

Soon after 19.30 the guard joined the train and carried out the brake test in conjunction with the driver, after which the empty train was ready to leave for Margate. It arrived there at 19.59, in

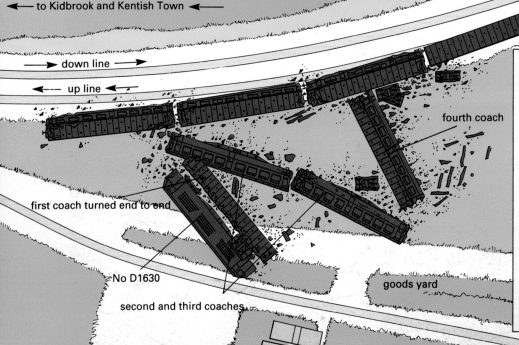

to Dartford and Margate →

tenth coach stayed on the rails

← to Kidbrook and Kentish Town ←

sharp curve with 20mph (32km/h) speed restriction

→ down line →

← up line ←

fourth coach

first coach turned end to end

No D1630

second and third coaches

goods yard

Drink was a factor

A seaside excursion returning from Margate to north London approached the sharp curve at Eltham Well Hall, which was limited to 20mph (32km/h), at over 60mph (97km/h). The heavy Class 47 diesel locomotive rolled as it entered the curve, derailed, and turned over on its side, dragging the train off the rails behind it and badly damaging the front coaches. Five passengers and the driver died.

At the post-mortem the driver was found to have three times more alcohol in his blood than was the limit for car drivers: he had clearly been drinking before taking up his duty, and probably continued while he was driving the train. The secondman was criticized for drinking while on duty, but as he did not know the route, he was not aware of the speed restriction.

◄ On the left of this shot is the back end of the leading coach, brake second No M35302. On the right can be seen the roof of the second coach, corridor second No 25614, lying on its left-hand side, while the crane is attached to the fifth coach, just beyond.

▼ Once the wreckage of the coaches which had stayed near the track had been removed, the cranes got to work on those that had been spreadeagled away from the line. Here, the crane is lifting the second coach. On the right is the back of the first coach and on the left can be seen the sharp curve of the track, which proved too much for the excursion train travelling at over 60mph (97km/h).

good time for the passengers to get on and for the train to leave at 20.05. However, when the guard gave the right away signal for the train to start nothing happened, as neither the driver nor the secondman were on the locomotive. (Witnesses later said that they had been seen leaving the station, but the secondman could not remember where they went.) They returned a few minutes later and the excursion train eventually left Margate at 20.13.

The guard becomes uneasy

The journey was normal, but the train was stopped briefly by red signals at Sittingbourne and again at Rainham. The guard thought the speed was a little high round the curves between Gillingham and Chatham, but the driver braked sharply and had the train under control as it went round the spur from Rochester to Strood for the line to Dartford.

Speed was about right through Dartford, but approaching Eltham Park the guard again became concerned, since they were travelling faster than appropriate at the point where the train should have been braking for the 20mph (32km/h) curve at Eltham Well Hall, now about half a mile (0.8km) ahead. The guard made a quick application of his vacuum brake handle, so as to attract the driver's attention without releasing enough of the vacuum in the system to apply the brakes, but it was too late. The train was already running

through Eltham Well Hall at about 65mph (105km/h), with the sharp curve just beyond the far end of the platform. (The secondman did not know the line, and was unaware of the restriction.)

The speed was too much for the heavy locomotive. As it swung to the right on the curve it leaned to the left, and the wheels lifted off the right-hand rail. The locomotive continued to roll to the left and overturned into the goods yard on its left side. The train started to follow the locomotive, but the leading coaches soon went their own way. The first coach turned end to end and finished up alongside the overturned locomotive, although still upright. The second and third coaches finished on their sides, forming a letter 'N' between the first coach and the fourth, which had jack-knifed, and was lying partly overturned and at right angles to the line. The remaining coaches had started to overtake the wreckage of the leading coaches, and stopped alongside them, all derailed except for the tenth.

Casualties were heavy: the driver and three passengers died almost instantly, while two more passengers died later. No fewer than 126 people, including the secondman, were injured, 40 of them seriously. The second and third coaches were so badly damaged that they were cut up on site, and only the last four coaches were lightly damaged.

How could an experienced driver, who knew the line, forget a well-known hazard? He had sev-

▲ The front end of locomotive No D1630 was badly damaged, and the driver died in it. The locomotive tipped over on to its left-hand side as it swung round at a right angle to the line. On the left is the back end of the first coach.

eral landmarks, and it was shortly before dusk, so there was enough daylight to see where he was.

The first clues came just three days later, when the inquest into the fatalities was opened by the coroner. A leading pathologist, who examined the driver's body and took samples for his post-mortem, found that the driver's blood had an alcohol content of 278mg per 100ml – more than three times the limit for motorists. Clearly the driver had taken alcohol during the day.

At the inquiry into the accident, conducted by Colonel J R H Robertson, witnesses began to fill in the details of the driver's whereabouts and actions during the day, before he took charge of the train. But in any derailment of this nature, checks and tests had to be made into all the factors. Was the track in good order? Were the train brakes working?

With the train spreadeagled across the coal yard, well beyond the point of derailment at the end of the platform, it must have been travelling fast, certainly well above the 20mph (32km/h) restriction. Checks on the track showed that it was in good order for trains travelling at the proper speed, and examination of the train's brake gear proved that it had been working satisfactorily. Besides, the brakes had been used several times during both the outward and return trips without any problem.

There was only one other factor: how had the train been handled by its driver? There was no doubt in Colonel Robertson's mind: the driver had not applied the brakes on the steep falling gradient through Eltham Well Hall. Furthermore, as the inquest heard from the pathologist, the driver had been drinking alcohol during the day, before taking up duty, and again after reporting to Ramsgate to take over the train. His two brothers told the inquiry that he had drunk 2½ pints (1.4 litres) of beer with them at lunchtime, and the secondman said that the driver had told him he had been

drinking sherry, too. The secondman also said that the driver's breath smelt strongly of drink when he joined the locomotive at Ramsgate. Even so, he had taken the secondman to the staff association club at Ramsgate, and both had three drinks before leaving with the empty train for Margate. There was also a suspicion that the driver had had yet more to drink on the locomotive; to reach the blood alcohol levels found at the post-mortem, the driver would have to have drunk 8½ pints (4.8 litres) of beer, or the equivalent in spirits.

The evidence suggested the driver was a heavy drinker, although unaffected by it. Nonetheless, Colonel Robertson concluded that the driver was responsible for the accident, with his ability to drive safely impaired by alcohol taken both before and during the journey. None of the supervisors or other staff who had seen the driver before the journey realized his condition, since he spoke and walked quite steadily.

Averting similar incidents
The accident inevitably raised the question of whether train drivers should be given breath tests, but Colonel Robertson felt that existing rules, forbidding staff to report for duty under the influence of alcohol, and banning drinking of alcohol on duty, were adequate. Also considered was whether drivers should be seen by a supervisor when reporting for duty, and whether booking on by telephone was satisfactory.

Finally there was the question of warnings for the speed restriction. A marker with the figure 20 was sited at the start of the restriction, but too late for a train that was not already slowing down. While advance warnings with automatic warning system (AWS) magnets had been devised for high speed lines after the Morpeth 1969 derailment, the Bexleyheath line is not a high speed route. Instead, Col Robertson recommended restrictive signal aspects with approach control on the signals leading to the curve.

Hixon 1968

An express thunders at 75mph towards an unmanned level crossing over which is slowly passing a 100 ton transformer on a low loader. The tragedy that followed showed serious flaws in safety procedure.

At 12.26pm on Saturday, January 6 1968 the driver of electric locomotive No E3009, hauling the 11.30am Manchester – Euston express, approached Hixon level crossing on the Stoke-on-Trent – Colwich line. He suddenly saw, about 400 yards ahead, a long low-loading transporter lorry almost stopped across the level crossing.

The transporter was carrying a large, heavy transformer from the English Electric Company's works at Stafford, a few miles away, to a depot at Hixon just beyond the level crossing.

Because of a slight hump in the road over the crossing and the overhead live wires of the electrified line, the transporter's crew were checking clearances as the transporter crept forward at no more than 2mph.

There was little that the train driver could do. He made an immediate brake application but it had no real effect. There was just not enough distance for the train to stop – on the falling gradient of about 1 in 600 it would have needed over 1500 yards from its speed of 75mph.

The train hit the transporter with its heavy transformer, and threw the whole assembly aside. Inevitably the locomotive was badly damaged and derailed, finishing up about 100 yards beyond the crossing with the leading coaches, partly destroyed, zigzagging across the track behind it.

Three men on the locomotive – the driver, his secondman and a spare driver travelling in the cab – and eight passengers were killed; over 40 passengers and a restaurant car attendant were injured. There were no injuries to the crew of the transporter or the police escorting the load.

The transporter lorry was designed specially for carrying large, heavy loads. It consisted of tractor units at the front and back for power and steering and a main centre section consisting of a steel girder framework with a low centre well carried on two four-axle bogies pivoting at each end. These were linked to the tractor units which guided the whole assembly around bends in the road.

The underside of the well section was only a few inches above the road surface. It was possible for it to touch the ground if the road was humped, with the wheels at the ends of the unit in a dip or on a slope.

Movement of very large loads such as this has

▶ After the collision with the transporter on the automatic half barrier (AHB) crossing, only two of the 12 coaches of the train were left on the rails, although six others remained more or less upright. The transformer was pushed aside and ended up alongside the train – the transporter carrying it was sliced in two.

always been subject to special rules by the Ministry of Transport and can take place only by special order as an abnormal load. The order specifies the route to be taken, largely to ensure that the road is suitable and that there are no weak underbridges or low overbridges. Usually such movements have a police escort. It was not the practice to list any exceptional hazards, such as level crossings, which were visible and capable of being understood by the driver of the vehicle.

Crossing controls

The level crossing at Hixon was of the type known as automatic half barriers (AHB). In the 1960s these were fairly new. Right from the dawn of the railways, level crossings were always regarded as a special hazard. Animals were considered the main problem – farmers needed to drive cattle and sheep over crossings from fields on one side of the line to those on the other. To stop animals straying, level crossings had gates which were closed across the railway when the road was opened and vice versa.

Many crossings were controlled from a signalbox alongside, with signals to control the trains.

▲The four leading coaches and the engine were badly damaged in the collision. Over 200 yards of track were torn from their fixings, and a signalbox, disused since the introduction of the barrier, was demolished. Eleven people died in a collision caused, according to the inquiry report, by ignorance, and by a failure at all levels to carry out the correct procedures.

Some boxes simply worked the gates; the gateman was advised when trains were coming by bell signals or indicators from the next signalbox along the line. Others were fully fledged signalboxes acting as block posts to operate the block system.

By the 1950s – with growing motor traffic, particularly in towns – level crossings were causing long road delays. After investigating crossing control systems used in other countries, the Ministry of Transport's railway inspecting officers and BR chose the AHB type of crossing. These have a lifting barrier dropping across the road on each side of the railway. The barriers cover only half the road – traffic is prevented from entering the crossing but has a clear way off because the exit side is open with no barrier.

Operation of the barriers is triggered by the trains themselves when they occupy a track circuit and depress a treadle which sets off a sequence of warning lights and bells for road users at the crossing. This is followed by the descent of the barriers.

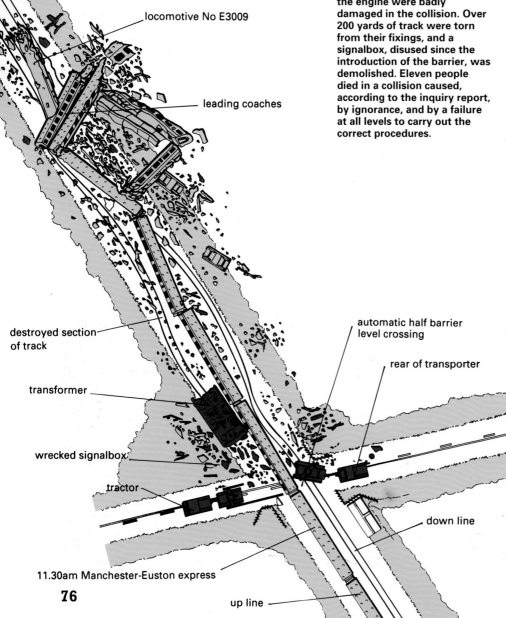

to London

locomotive No E3009

leading coaches

destroyed section of track

transformer

wrecked signalbox

tractor

11.30am Manchester-Euston express

automatic half barrier level crossing

rear of transporter

down line

up line

A few seconds later the train passes, after which the barriers rise to allow road traffic to continue.

Up to the time of the Hixon accident the sequence for barrier operations gave a minimum of 24 seconds from the start of the warning bells and flashing red lights to the passing of the fastest train, with eight seconds warning, eight seconds for the barriers to come down and eight more seconds until the train passed. A notice alongside the crossing advised road users to phone the signalman in an emergency or before crossing with exceptional or heavy loads or cattle. The first AHB had been installed in 1961 and by 1968 there were over 360 on BR.

The inquiry

A judicial inquiry was used at Hixon because all the authorities – including both road and rail sections of the Ministry of Transport, the inspectorate and British Railways – were involved, as well as the men driving and escorting the load.

The inquiry was wide ranging. It was clear from the evidence that the transporter crew had no real understanding of how AHB crossings worked. Certainly they did not realize the speed of operation with a minimum of only 24 seconds from the start of the flashing warning lights to the arrival of the train at speed. Nor did they realize that the barriers were not linked to railway signals and that there was no way of stopping a train if a road vehicle was stuck on the crossing. The transporter crew were under the impression that the police were in charge, and paid little heed to the working of the crossing.

There was doubt whether the transporter would pass under the railway's electrified overhead lines, which are never tightly strung but droop slightly. The transporter, travelling at no more than 2mph, slowed to a crawl as its crew checked for clearance under the electrified wires. The 148ft long transporter would have had to be moving at least at 6mph to pass over the crossing within the 24 seconds warning time.

The police constables accompanying the load had driven beyond the crossing – they did not appreciate the rapid operation of the barriers and the arrival of a train, nor were they aware of the existence of the telephone by the crossing to call the signalman at Colwich, several miles away, who supervised the crossing.

Indeed, the police had received no special training or advice on the procedures for large loads at AHBs. Nor had the Chief Constable of Staffordshire appreciated that this was a new hazard which his force ought to know about. The government departments which had prepared and sent out notices describing the new crossings had not clearly emphasized the changes.

In simple terms, the safety of the public using the new crossings was no longer guaranteed by the railway. Instead, the public had to look after its own safety.

▼The driver of locomotive No E3009, which was hauling the Manchester – Euston express, made an immediate brake application about 400 yards from the Hixon crossing. But after the barrier was activated, nothing could stop the crash. From a speed of 75mph almost four times the distance would have been needed to avert a collision.

What went wrong?

The inquiry concluded that the accident arose from many failures, from government departments down to men on the ground. The real cause was ignorance. Neither the police accompanying the load nor the crew of the transporter telephoned the signalman for permission to take the load over the crossing. They did not realize how short a time they had until the train arrived.

The road crew did not appreciate the meaning of the emergency notice. The sign was not easily read from a moving vehicle, and was not noticed by the policemen.

The directors of the haulage firm were at fault because, following a recent near miss at another AHB, BR had told the firm that drivers of large loads must telephone the signalbox before crossing. The firm's directors found BR's letter so arrogant that they took no action.

The possibility of a long slow vehicle taking minutes to pass over a crossing had not even been considered, let alone discussed, by the Ministry of Transport. The telephone procedure was hidden away in notes sent to chief constables as though it was unimportant.

Even though it had been realized in 1965 and 1966 that the emergency notice requiring drivers to telephone before crossing with large loads was not entirely clear, no revision was undertaken. Apart from the letter to the haulage firm, neither BR nor the ministry sent out advice to the main haulage firms warning of the hazards of AHB crossings and the steps to be taken for slow moving vehicles.

The Ministry, the railway inspectorate and BR had decided that the responsibility for safety at level crossings was to be transferred to the public on the road. But they did not tell the public what they were supposed to do.

▲An injured passenger is lifted gently from the wreckage. The transporter crew, who helped with the rescue operation, spoke later of their horror at seeing the express bearing down on them: 'The barrier arms were up and there was no warning or anything – no bells or flashing lights... Then the train was approaching. I couldn't jump – it was too late. I stayed at the wheel,' recounted the rear driver. The 148 feet long transporter, inching over the crossing while crew checked clearances, failed to cross within the 24 second warning time.

The main recommendations

The time of the operating sequence should be extended to a minimum of 32 seconds before the arrival of the fastest train – eight seconds for the warning, eight seconds for the barrier to lower and 16 seconds to the arrival of the fastest train. A steady amber light should be installed to show for five seconds before the red lights start to flash. This five seconds was to be in addition to the 32 seconds of the operating cycle. The steady amber light also allowed the flashing red lights to become a mandatory stop indication which made it an offence to pass the red lights.

Movement orders for abnormal loads must include details of AHBs on the route and an instruction to the driver to telephone for permission to cross. There should be mandatory signs approaching AHB crossings requiring drivers of large or slow vehicles to telephone the signalbox.

Wherever possible dual carriageways should be provided over AHB crossings, otherwise double white lines should be used to discourage zigzagging around lowered barriers. Yellow box markings could be introduced on crossings. Penalties should be more severe for drivers who fail to use safety procedures.

The road sign indicating a level crossing should be improved, as the new 'barrier' sign did not convey the meaning of a railway crossing.

The resumption of installation of AHBs (suspended after Hixon) was recommended.

In 1978 the AHB timing sequence was reduced to three seconds steady amber road signal and 24 seconds from the start of the flashing red lights to the passage of the fastest train. This was adopted for crossings of up to 15m in length between barriers.

For longer crossings one extra second was added to the timing sequence for every additional three metres. This meant a 55ft (16.8m) long vehicle travelling at only 3½mph would clear the crossing if it began to cross as the timing sequence was triggered, before the arrival of the fastest train.

Hither Green 1967

**Poor track maintenance and a dubious line
speed limit led to one of the worst post-war rail disasters
in Britain at Hither Green, near London, when a crowded
multiple-unit train jumped the rails at high speed.**

A Sunday evening train, crowded with passengers returning from the south coast to London, suddenly left the track at 70mph in the south-east London suburbs after the third coach derailed. Four coaches flipped on to their sides and 49 passengers were killed with many more injured – all because a short, triangular fragment of rail had broken off under the train. From the chaos, investigators had to find out how the rail had fractured, and why.

A seaside excursion

Sunday 5 November 1967 was not one of the best days to spend at the seaside, but despite being cold and damp, the Southern Region's south coast trains were well filled. The 19.43 Hastings to Charing Cross was one of those trains. It consisted of two six-coach diesel-electric multiple units (DEMUs) forming a twelve-coach train. These were of the unique Southern Region type with heavy diesel-electric power cars at either end of each six-coach set, unlike the lightweight diesel trains with underfloor bus-type engines used elsewhere.

About half of each power car was taken up with the driver's cab, guard's compartment and engine room with a diesel generator unit, while the rest of the coach was an open passenger saloon. The three second class trailer coaches in each set were also of the open saloon pattern, while the single first class coach had a side corridor with separate compartments.

The Hastings line, which branched off the Charing Cross – Dover main line at Tonbridge, has a number of narrow tunnels so that special coaches no more than 8ft wide were needed. The Hastings DEMUs were of this pattern.

An overcrowded train

The 19.43 was well loaded, especially the front unit, as some stations on the Hastings line had short platforms where only the leading coaches could load passengers. People were unable to walk through the train to look for seats further back since, although the coaches within each unit had inter-coach gangways, there was none between the motor coaches of the two units.

The train picked up more passengers at Tonbridge and Sevenoaks so that the aisles of the

▶ The corridor first class coach is hoisted away for inspection. Four coaches behind the leading power car flipped over and slid along the tracks crushing people underneath as the side walls disintegrated.

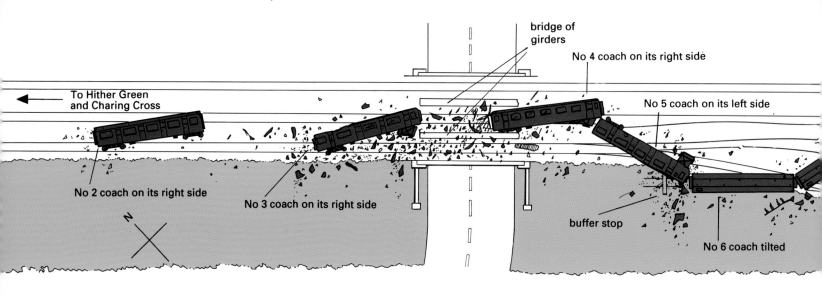

bridge of girders

No 4 coach on its right side

To Hither Green and Charing Cross

No 5 coach on its left side

No 2 coach on its right side

No 3 coach on its right side

N

buffer stop

No 6 coach tilted

▲In the diagram above, the leading coach, which was the only one still on the rails, had come to a halt about 220yd (201m) further on.

▼The triangular piece of rail which came away from the joint was restored to its proper position at the inquiry to show how the various pieces fitted together. The train was travelling from right to left, from the running-off end of the first closure rail to the running-on end of the second.

open second class coaches and the side corridor of the first class coach of the leading unit were crammed with standing travellers.

The driver slowed for the 60mph speed limit through Chislehurst and then applied power to accelerate to 70-75mph, the train's maximum speed, although the line limit between Chislehurst and Hither Green was 90mph. With signals showing green as far as he could see, he shut off power and coasted through Grove Park, with just a few miles to go before reaching Charing Cross.

Suddenly, as he passed the Continental freight depot on the left and prepared to brake for the 60mph limit beyond Hither Green, he felt the train drag. Several severe snatches followed, something banged and the brakes came on sharply.

He looked out and in the darkness lit by nearby lights saw that his motor coach was on its own. The rest of his train lay some 220yd behind, spreadeagled across the down and up fast lines and an adjoining siding. The second and third coaches were both detached and both came to rest on their right sides. The remainder of the train was still

coupled together, but coach No 4 had slid along on its right side while No 5 had done so on its left. The last coach of the front unit and the rear six-coach DEMU were all totally derailed and had jack-knifed across the tracks, but at least the coaches remained upright.

The derailment was seen by the Hither Green signalman three-quarters of a mile away and by a staff member at the Continental freight depot. It was a horrific scene which met the rescue services, all of which arrived with remarkable speed. The police got there within five minutes, ambulances a minute later and the fire brigade just two minutes after that. With the coaches of the front unit sliding to a stop on their sides, all were severely damaged with smashed windows and two losing parts of their roofs; it was inevitable that casualties would be high.

Nothing could be done for the 49 passengers already dead and it took four hours to get the last of the 78 injured passengers out of the wreckage. Of these, 27 were severely injured. It was remarkable that even more were not killed and injured considering how crowded the train was and how the second through to the fifth coaches had overturned at such speed.

A simple fault
Examination of the line soon showed the cause of the derailment. A triangular piece of rail, about 5½in long at the top, had broken away at a joint.

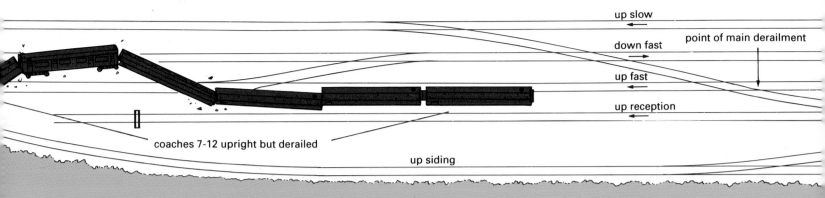

up slow

down fast   point of main derailment

up fast

up reception

coaches 7-12 upright but derailed

up siding

One of the metal fishplates on the inside edge had also fractured at this joint of the right-hand rail.

It seemed to the investigators that the fragment had broken away under the train, possibly as the heavy leading motor coach passed over the joint. The leading wheels of the front bogie of the third coach then became derailed at the break, although the remaining coaches jumped the gap despite battering the broken rail end. The derailed wheels slid on for 463yd until they struck a single slip diamond crossing. Here all the coaches except for the front one became totally derailed.

The track on the up fast line approaching the scene of derailment at that time consisted of different types of rail and fastenings. First there was a trailing crossover from the up slow line laid in bullhead rail on wooden sleepers, which was nearly worn out and was due for replacement within a few weeks. Then came two short lengths of track called closures, before a length of continuously welded track. This led on to another closure length before the next set of points and a crossing.

The two closure lengths after the trailing points were of different patterns of flat-bottom rail. The first was laid on concrete sleepers, except for two wooden ones at the beginning and end, while the second lay entirely on concrete sleepers. The running-on end of the second length had the piece of broken-off rail and a broken fishplate. The break in the rail had started with a crack from the first bolt hole, running diagonally into the rail head, and the whole piece had broken down to the foot near the rail end.

The inquiry

Damning evidence was soon heard at the inquiry, chaired by the Chief Inspecting Officer of Railways, Colonel D McMullen. This suggested a catalogue of woe as far as track maintenance standards were concerned on the Southern Region's South Eastern Division tracks.

At that time the track was divided into sections for maintenance purposes with a permanent way inspector for each section and gangs of about a dozen men for maintenance and small repair jobs. There was another team of two which went round the tracks in the district checking rails for cracks with ultrasonic test equipment. The limitations of the equipment, however, meant that not all types

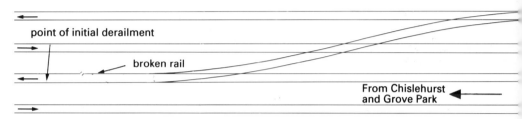

point of initial derailment

broken rail

From Chislehurst
and Grove Park

of crack could be discovered.

It soon became clear that the track near Hither Green was not in the best condition and that some was due for renewal at the time of the derailment. Wooden sleepers were past their best; fastenings could not be kept tight and some concrete sleepers were loose, broken or missing.

The gang had found it difficult to maintain the level of the track. At joints the sleepers were pressed down into dirty stone ballast contaminated with slurry which had formed from a mixture of dirt, dust and rain water. This meant that the rail ends were working up and down as the wheels of trains passed over, putting immense strain on the rail. Moreover, a concrete sleeper at the end of the first closure length had cracked some time before the accident and been replaced by a shallower wooden one.

▲The point of initial derailment on the closure length immediately after the trailing points, in the lower diagram, was 463yd (423m) before the diamond crossing, where almost the entire train jumped the rails.

▼Rescue services were fortunate in having excellent access to the site of the disaster. Police, ambulance and fire brigade personnel were all on the scene within eight minutes of the derailment.

Eventually the constant hammering of the rail had its effect. A crack developed from the end bolt hole. It should have been detected by the ganger with the ultrasonic test equipment but he hadn't been over that section since June, five months before, when it hadn't shown up. However, on the 23 October, two weeks before the accident, the ultrasonic equipment had identified no fewer than five cracks further south on the up fast line between Chislehurst and Grove Park. Clearly the track was not in the condition it should have been for frequent fast trains.

Another factor was the line speed limit, which had been raised from 75mph to 90mph between Chislehurst and Hither Green in July 1967 to allow certain types of electric train to run faster. Nobody had told the local men or even asked their opinion as to whether the track was fit for higher speeds. The chief permanent way inspector for the district told the inquiry that he didn't think the track was suited for higher speeds. Unfortunately, at the regional headquarters he had failed to pass on his observations to the senior civil engineering officers who authorized the speed increase.

What went wrong?

Colonel McMullen concluded that the accident had been caused by the piece of rail breaking away, thereby derailing the leading wheels of the third coach. When they hit the crossing a quarter of a mile ahead the rest of the train was thrown off the track. He was lenient in apportioning blame to the staff on the ground, saying that they couldn't have foreseen the crack in the rail head. It probably hadn't been present when the ultrasonic test was made five months before and might not have been detected even then.

As for the support of the rail end, clearly the joint had been working up and down. The fractured rail had been newly laid only 10 months before and the joint was no worse than others. It didn't seem to call for any special measures other than packing and tamping. However, there wasn't enough clean ballast under the sleepers – this should have been improved when the length was relaid the previous February. The staff also should have looked a little closer at the joint between the closure lengths when the concrete sleeper cracked and was replaced.

Colonel McMullen placed the responsibility for the unsatisfactory state of track maintenance generally on the local permanent way staff, the chief permanent way inspector, the district inspector and the chief civil engineer. He also blamed top staff for agreeing to the increase in line speed to 90mph when the track was not even fit for speeds above 60mph – the speed limit imposed immediately after the accident.

Colonel McMullen made several recommendations, remarks and conclusions to prevent a possible recurrence.

▼Monday morning and the salvage operation is underway. The rear six-coach DEMU lies jack-knifed across the tracks while some of the coaches of the front set have already been removed. The site is less than a mile from the scene of the Lewisham disaster in 1957, where 90 people died.

Recommendations

● The use of closure lengths of jointed track between continuously welded lengths and points and crossings to be abandoned.
● Steps to be taken to improve rail joint supports.
● More frequent ultrasonic testing with improved testing equipment.
● Improved maintenance standards.
● Priority replacement of jointed track by continuously welded rail on main lines and heavily used commuter lines.
● A rethink on the design of motive power to see whether heavy traction motors could be carried on parts of the bogie which are sprung to the wheels, rather than as dead weight directly on the wheel sets.
● Redesign of rail with thicker web between the head and foot.

Thirsk 1967

As diesel and electric power replaced steam in the 1960s, the speed of goods trains increased, and so too did the number of derailments. The worry was that a second train could be involved, as happened at Thirsk, when an express hit a derailed wagon, killing seven passengers.

During the 1960s, as steam was phased out on British Rail (BR) and more diesel and electric locomotives came into service, goods trains began to run faster. There were various reasons: one being that more wagons had automatic vacuum brakes so could stop more rapidly than when they had just a steam brake on the locomotive and a hand brake on the guard's van. Another reason was that loads were lighter in the 1960s, because trains were made up of fewer wagons. Also, diesel locomotives could accelerate more rapidly than steam locomotives, and were designed to travel faster than the average steam locomotive intended for goods haulage. Finally, since the new freight trains travelled faster, they could be interwoven between express passenger trains on the same track, instead of needing separate lines.

Derailments increase

As the speed of goods trains rose, so did the number of derailments. The standard British goods wagon was small compared with those of main-

land Europe or North America. Only about 16ft (5m) long, with a wheelbase of 10ft (3m), there was not enough length for good stability, and if springs and suspension were not carefully maintained, or if couplings were slack, or the load was not evenly positioned, wagons could make alarming movements at speed. They might swing from side to side, or develop a twisting movement backwards and forwards, particularly if there were track defects. Such defects might be only minor variations of level between the two rails, or a dipped joint between adjoining rails, but they could cause wheels to drop into the dip and quickly rise out again, with possible weight transfer so that the springs were not pressing down on the axle boxes for a few seconds.

By the mid-1960s, operators were trying to get better use from the wagons by quick turn-rounds when loading and unloading, and faster journey times, so a wagon might make a return journey in three or four days instead of the three weeks or more which had been common in steam days. The

▼On 31 July 1967, a cement train derailed south of Thirsk. Although most of the rear wagons fell down the adjoining embankment, one of them slewed round to obstruct the path of the fast-approaching 12.00 King's Cross – Edinburgh express, hauled by locomotive No DP2, on the down fast line. It could not stop in time and the left-hand side of the locomotive struck the cement wagon, crushing the cab. The driver and his secondman survived, but many of the passengers were not so lucky.

wagons were running much higher mileages than ever before, but not receiving the specialized maintenance that used to be given to the small pool of wagons carrying perishable goods normally used on the fast freight trains of steam days.

Speeds rose from the 30mph (50km/h) or so of the average goods train in steam days, to 45-50mph (70-80km/h) with diesel or electric haulage. But the penalty was an alarming rise in goods train derailments, where one set of wheels left the track because of a combination of forces, and the wagons behind piled up against the wagon initially derailed, causing much destruction. Where just a goods train was involved, there was usually no more problem than wreckage, damaged goods and wrecked track, although that was bad enough. But if a train was coming in the opposite direction on a double-track route, or if the wreckage spilt over other tracks carrying fast passenger trains on multi-track routes, then the danger of a major disaster became acute unless the goods train's crew could contact the controlling signal-box quickly, or put down detonators and flags far enough away (usually 1-1¼ miles/1.6-2km) from the hazardous wreckage before another train approached.

So great was this danger, both potentially and actually, that the railway inspectorate held a special investigation into all the contributory factors. It was realized that the old-type short British wagons were unsuited to high speeds, and lower speed limits were imposed to keep them below 40mph (64km/h). New wagon designs appeared, with longer wheelbases and new suspension systems. Among these were cement wagons, called Cemflo. They had four wheels with an axle spacing of 15ft (4.5m), and weighed nearly 36 tons when loaded. They had originally been designed in the early 1960s to travel at 60mph (97km/h), but following derailments the maximum had come down to 50mph (80km/h), and then 45mph (70km/h) in 1966. One of their regular workings was between Cliffe, in North Kent, and Uddingston, just outside Glasgow. Complete trains of these wagons ran for Associated Portland Cement. The company owned the wagons as a company train, but their design and maintenance had to conform to BR standards.

A derailment blocks the fast line

On the afternoon of 31 July 1967, the 02.40 Cliffe – Uddingston cement train, with 26 wagons and a brake at each end, was travelling north on the down slow line of the main East Coast route. It was just over two miles (three kilometres) south of Thirsk, travelling at about 45mph (70km/h), when the rear wheels of the 12th wagon derailed to the left. The train continued for about 170yd (155m) before the coupling between the 11th and 12th wagons broke. This pulled apart the vacuum brake pipe, letting air into the system and automatically applying the brakes on both parts of the train. But while the front of the train continued to a safe stop about ¼ mile (0.4km) ahead, most of the rear wagons derailed and fell down the embankment into a field below. The rear six wagons remained alongside the track, and the front of the 23rd slewed round to lie about two feet (0.6m) on to the adjoining down fast line.

The cement-train guard was travelling in the rear guard's van, looking out through the side ducket, when he saw wagons ahead of him break out to the left and roll down the embankment. He also realized that a wagon had gone to the right and was obstructing the down fast line. As soon as his van came to a stop he got down with his red flag and detonators and ran back to protect the down fast line. He had gone only about 100yd

▼As side impact with the heavy cement wagon ripped open the compartments of the derailed leading coaches of the King's Cross – Edinburgh express, still travelling at about 50mph (80km/h), seven passengers died and 45 were seriously injured.

← To York

field

rear six wagons remained alongside track

embankment

23rd wagon derailed on to down fast line

▲When the wreckage of the express carriages was inspected, questions arose as to the need for improved safety standards when running diesel freight trains much faster than their steam-hauled ancestors, both when interweaving them between express passenger trains on the same track, and when running on separate slow lines.

Key to trains

 02.40 Cliffe - Uddingston cement train

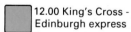 12.00 King's Cross - Edinburgh express

when he saw a diesel-hauled express approaching at speed, the 12.00 King's Cross – Edinburgh train. He waved his flag, but it was too late; although the brakes were hard on, the express train – still travelling at about 50mph (80km/h) – hit the wagon.

The left-hand side of the locomotive cab was crushed, and derailed to the right on to the up fast line, taking the first seven coaches of the 13-coach train with it. The leading three coaches were severely damaged, with the side panelling of the front one ripped off, and its compartments on the left of the coach demolished. The corridor of the next two coaches was on the left side, and although the left-hand side body panelling was badly damaged, the compartments on the right of the coach were not so badly affected. The damage to the front coaches caused heavy casualties, with seven passengers killed, and 45 severely injured.

The driver of the express and his secondman had lucky escapes in view of the damage to the locomotive. They had been travelling at about

The goods train derailment problem

The derailment and collision at Thirsk was just one of a rising number of goods train derailments in the mid-1960s. These were caused by the higher speeds of goods trains hauled by diesel and electric locomotives, and by more intensive use of wagons without a corresponding rise in maintenance standards of older, short wagons, or improvements in the track standards of lines used by goods trains. The wagons involved at Thirsk were fairly new, and longer than the old types, but the effect of wear in the suspension had not been appreciated.

At Roade, on the main line out of Euston, there were two goods train derailments resulting in collisions with passenger trains – one in 1967 and another in 1969. The peak of goods train derailments was reached in 1969, with a total of 383. Subsequently, better maintenance of wagons and track, elimination of many older wagons, and the introduction of new types designed for higher speeds resulted in the total number of derailments dropping to 223 in 1971 and to 56 in 1991-92. However, many of these are still due to technical faults.

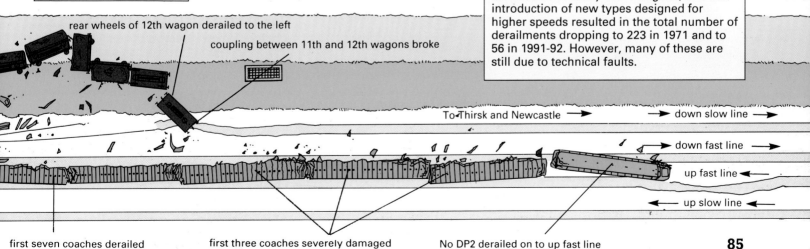

rear wheels of 12th wagon derailed to the left

coupling between 11th and 12th wagons broke

To Thirsk and Newcastle →   → down slow line →

→ down fast line →

→ up fast line ←

← up slow line ←

first seven coaches derailed   first three coaches severely damaged   No DP2 derailed on to up fast line

▲The toll of dead and injured might have been much higher had it not been that the main impact from the stationary cement train was taken by the corridor side of the express coaches. Further suffering was reduced thanks to the pilot of a Royal Air Force aircraft from nearby Topcliffe spotting the crash and radioing for help.

Uneven rails
Approaching the point of derailment there were slight variations in cross levels: the right-hand rail was ¹/₂in (13mm) high at 43yd (40m) from the derailment, and the left-hand rail was ¹/₄in (6.4mm) high; then the right-hand rail was ⁵/₈in (16mm) high, and the left-hand rail ³/₈in (10mm) high. These tiny irregularities were probably enough to set up the fatal rolling.

75-80mph (120-130km/h) when the driver saw what he thought was haze or dust. As a reflex action he shut off power and started to make a brake application, then realized there was a train ahead on the slow line that appeared to have derailed. He made an emergency brake application at once, applied sand to the rail to help braking, and shut down the diesel engine to reduce the risk of fire. He could do no more to avoid the collision.

The express locomotive was No DP2, a unique engine not owned by BR, but by its builders, the English Electric Company. It was undergoing extensive running trials as one of the prototypes for a new class (to become Class 50). Its unusual number was derived from its role as **D**iesel **P**rototype No 2, the first English Electric prototype diesel being the original Deltic diesel. Unfortunately, DP2 was too badly damaged in this accident to warrant repair; by this time much of its running experience and equipment had already been assessed.

The track is scrutinized
Col Dennis McMullen was appointed inspecting officer for the accident. His first problem was finding out why the wheels on the rear axle of the 12th wagon had derailed. So, measurements were taken along the track approaching the point of derailment. These showed slight variations (no more than ¹/₄in/6.4mm) in cross levels, which would have set up a slight rolling. These are small variations given the line speed and the speed of the cement train, but combined with worn suspension in the 12th wagon, they might have been more than the wagon suspension could cope with.

No real cause was found to explain the derailment, and several wagons from the train were taken to Doncaster works for measuring and testing, on a roller rig and out on the line. The tests included running with the couplings slightly slack

– so the buffers were not quite in contact – and running tight coupled. The worst results were achieved with slack couplings, when the wagon moved from side to side, becoming increasingly unstable. The wagons were fitted with suspension links between the springs and the underframe, with the links intended to damp out oscillation. However, wear and tear – possibly because of the abrasive effect of the cement dust – meant that the wagons were more likely to swing from side to side because the suspension did not provide firm control. (The wear on the suspension links on the cement wagons gave them an average life of only 5000 miles/8050km; the same links on other wagons would last for 80,000 miles/128,700km.) On the first wagon to derail there was another factor: the wheels on the derailed axle had a ¹/₃₂in (0.8mm) difference in diameter – within the specified limits, but in combination with other wear on the wagon, and the slight track defects, had caused additional wear on one flange, and could have helped to initiate the derailment.

Immediately after the derailment, the maximum speed of the cement wagons was reduced to 35mph (60km/h), but Colonel McMullen recommended that the whole design of the suspension, the maintenance of wheel diameters and the buffer/coupling arrangements should be looked at, and track maintenance standards tightened.

The Thirsk accident was one of several freight train derailments involving other trains in the 1960s and early '70s. Initially, freight trains with older-style wagons had to cut back their speeds to the levels of the steam era, but as new, larger and heavier wagon designs came into service, alongside new suspension systems, the freight train derailment problem of the new diesel and electric era declined. Moreover, as freight carryings by rail declined, the total numbers of wagons in service went down dramatically and, with tight control of maintenance, standards are higher. However, freight train derailments still happen, and from 1986 to 1990 an average of nearly 93 freight trains were derailed each year.

Recommendations
There was no clear cut cause of the Thirsk derailment; several individual small faults on the track and on the wagon initiated the derailment. As an immediate preventive a 35mph (60km/h) speed limit was imposed on the cement wagons, but that brought operating restrictions. As longer-term solutions, a new design of friction link to support the springs was developed; a smaller difference was allowed on the diameter of wheels on the same axle (¹/₁₀₀in/0.25mm instead of ¹/₃₂in/0.8mm); and couplings between wagons were tightened so as to bring buffer heads together. If necessary, spring buffers were to replace hydraulic buffers. Finally, track maintenance standards had to be improved and more stringently monitored so that minor track irregularities could not combine with wagon defects to cause derailments.

Stechford 1967

It was just a hand signal by a shunter to a guard, but it was mistaken by the locomotive crew as a signal to start a shunting move – right into the path of a fast-approaching electric train. Nine people died in the collision.

Stechford is a junction station on the main route between Birmingham and London Euston. It is situated about 3½ miles out of Birmingham. A secondary route avoiding the city, the Grand Junction line, diverges at the station to the north. (The name is used because a little further north these become the tracks of the original Grand Junction Railway from Birmingham to Manchester, which opened in 1838 and arrived in the city via Aston.)

At the Coventry end of the station are down sidings on the south side, with more sidings on the up side beside the station itself. No 1 up siding has two links to the up Grand Junction line to allow run round movements. (Note that in this area, down lines run towards Birmingham, while up lines go towards Coventry and London.)

On 28 February 1967, an engineer's ballast train, which had been working on the down line, arrived at Stechford from Coventry at about 2.50pm. To clear the main line it was backed temporarily into the down sidings. After a through

train had passed, the ballast train began shunting to the up side ready to return to Coventry. It drew out of the down siding on to the down main, ran through the station and on to the down Grand Junction line.

When the back of the train was clear of the crossover between the up and down Grand Junction lines, it stopped and set back through the crossover to stand on the up Grand Junction line alongside the platform. Normally it would have been put into No 1 up siding to allow the locomotive to run round. On this occasion, however, the train was too long.

If the train had been split into two, the locomotive could have run round with the train in the sidings. But the shunter in charge wanted to save time and do it in one go. The only way this was possible was for the wagons to stand on the up Grand Junction line and for the locomotive to go back to the down Grand Junction line. It could then reverse through the station on the down main line (the way it had come, but now in the wrong

▼The leading coach of the Manchester to Coventry EMU express lies on its side on the night after the collision. The driver saw the diesel locomotive arriving on the diamond crossing seconds before impact but had no chance of stopping. He was killed instantly.

The unauthorized movement

The ballast train arrived at Stechford from Coventry and backed into the down sidings before manoeuvring to return to Coventry. It was too long, however, to do it in the normal way.

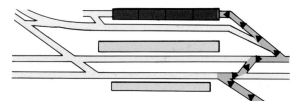

Normally, it would have crossed over to No 1 siding where the loco could run round.

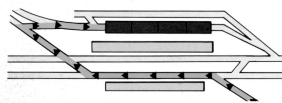

However, it went through the station and backed on to the up Grand Junction line.

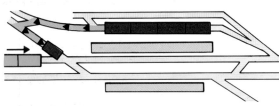

The loco then returned to the down line ready to move back through the station but moved too early and into the EMU's path.

A disastrous hand signal

With No D5002 standing on the down Grand Junction line, the shunter at the crossover signalled to a guard on the ballast wagons to come back to the end of the train. The secondman on the locomotive took it as a signal to move forward and instructed his driver to restart. Seconds later, seeing their route through the station was occupied, the brakes were applied but not in time to prevent the up main line being fouled. The oncoming EMU had no chance of stopping in time, struck No D5002 a glancing blow and slewed across the tracks before ending up on the far side.

direction), over a crossover to the up main line at the Coventry end and reverse back on to the up Grand Junction line. It wasn't an authorized move, nor was it signalled, but the shunter was planning to arrange it with the power signalbox at Birmingham New Street.

The crossovers and siding connections were controlled locally. The down sidings were controlled by the Stechford shunting frame, while the Grand Junction crossover was worked by a small ground lever frame near the points. Both had to be released electrically from New Street.

With the train on the down Grand Junction line the shunter had obtained the release to shunt it on to the up Grand Junction line. He still had control of the crossover after the locomotive had been uncoupled from the ballast wagons and run forward to the down Grand Junction line. He immediately reset the crossover points so that the line was set from the down Grand Junction line, across the up main and on to the down main.

At this moment, the shunter saw the guard of the ballast wagons walking towards the Coventry end of the train. He wanted him to remain at what

▼Two nurses from East Birmingham Hospital climb along the wreckage of one of the overturned leading coaches in an attempt to reach a trapped passenger. The roof was ripped open as the EMU slewed out of control through a tangled mass of overhead gantries, catenary and electrical equipment. Medical teams arrived within six minutes of the accident.

Key to trains

■ No D5002		▢ Coventry – Birmingham EMU
▨ Manchester – Coventry EMU		

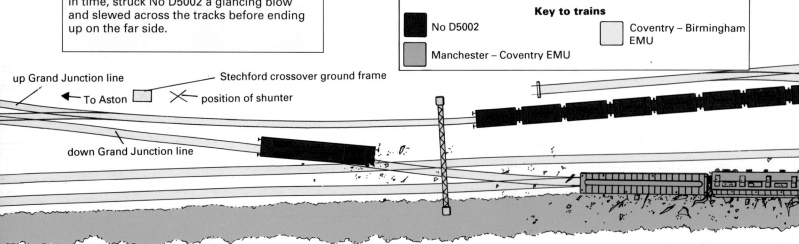

up Grand Junction line
— Stechford crossover ground frame
← To Aston   ✕ position of shunter

down Grand Junction line

← From Birmingham New St

▶ Emergency service personnel hold up blankets to screen bodies being lifted from the wreckage. Doctors and nurses had to give blood transfusions to trapped passengers as it took several hours before all the victims could be extricated.

would become the rear end, however, ready for departure. He shouted and waved to the guard to return to the western end of the train. The guard had no idea what the shunter was planning to do.

Meanwhile, the secondman on the locomotive, a Bo-Bo Type 2 (later BR Class 24) No D5002, was looking out of the left-hand side of the cab from the far (Birmingham) end of the engine. He saw the shunter wave his hand and took it as a signal to move towards the station along the down Grand Junction line.

He told his driver, who was at the same end of the locomotive, and restarted. Almost immediately the secondman saw a local electric train arriving on the down main line at the station, the one they were heading for. He realized there was something wrong and shouted. The driver managed to stop the locomotive just as it reached the diamond crossing with the up main line, but it inched a little too far forward and fouled the crossing.

Just then, a four-car electric multiple unit, heading from Manchester to Coventry, was approaching at speed on the up main line. There was no time for evasive action. It hit No D5002 a glancing blow and was thrown upwards. The train flipped, careered across the tracks and crunched to a halt across the down main line about 200yd (183m) further on. The leading two coaches were ripped open and were lying on their sides, the third coach was tilted with the fourth upright but totally derailed.

The electric train driver didn't stand a chance. His last signal had been showing green and, without warning, the diesel locomotive had appeared from the left, right in front of him. He was killed instantly, together with eight passengers. Sixteen more, six of them railwaymen learning the line, were injured. Neither of the men on the diesel locomotive was hurt.

What went wrong?

The whole area of the Western Division lines around Birmingham, including Stechford and part of the Grand Junction route, was controlled by the power signalling centre at New Street, which had been commissioned as recently as July 1966. The signalmen working the shunting frames did not have freedom of action unless they obtained a release from New Street.

If a through train was to be signalled, the levers at the frames had to be at normal. The New Street signalman would cancel any releases, thus locking the shunting and ground frame levers, with the points set for the through routes. Only then could the signals be cleared for the through train on the main lines.

When the ballast train went into and out of the down sidings, New Street had to release that part of Stechford shunting frame to allow the Stechford signalman to change the points from the down sidings to the main line. At the same time, New Street set the points towards the down Grand Junction line (these points could not be switched at Stechford). After the train had stopped beyond the crossover, and signals behind it had gone to

Ground frame control
Modern power signalling schemes with large centralized signalboxes look after vast lengths of line. Edinburgh signalling centre, for example, controls the East Coast main line from Berwick to Dundee.

Little-used points are often controlled locally by ground level frames or larger shunting frames. The latter, such as the Stechford shunting frame at the Coventry end of the station, are sometimes old signalboxes with mechanical levers adapted for their more limited use.

This method is used to save on the provision of relays, cabling and other equipment to little used points. Equipment to work the release is all that is needed at the power centre.

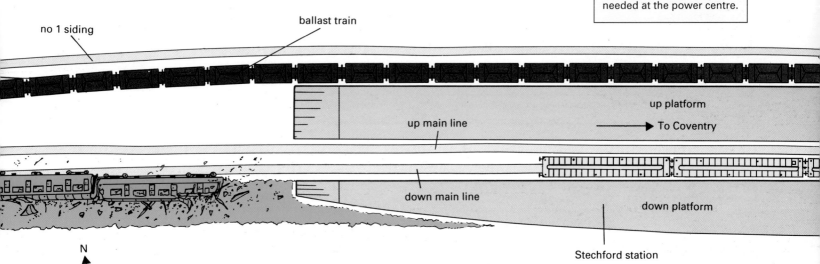

no 1 siding

ballast train

up platform

up main line ——▶ To Coventry

down main line

down platform

Stechford station

N

▲A rear view of the overturned leading EMU coach shows how completely the roof was ripped off as it ploughed past the overhead gantries.

danger, a release was given by New Street to the shunter at Stechford crossover ground frame. He could now change the crossover points, allowing the train to set back to the up Grand Junction line and then for the locomotive to return to the down Grand Junction line.

Because the Grand Junction crossover did not affect the main lines, however, the release given to the Stechford crossover ground frame did not stop the signalman at New Street from clearing the signals for through moves on the main lines, and did not have to be cancelled. That was the position when the diesel locomotive was standing on the down Grand Junction line. Certainly the New Street signalman did not know that the locomotive was going to move as it did. He cleared the signals for the electric trains on the main lines.

Strict rules had been drawn up to say what moves were allowed under local control. The wrong direction move planned by the shunter for No D5002 to run back through the station on the down line was specifically banned except in an emergency, and then only with the approval of the main signalman. There was not an emergency on the day of the accident, nor had the shunter obtained the approval of the New Street signalman.

The inquiry

The inspecting officer, Colonel D McMullen, was quite certain that the accident happened when the locomotive was making an unauthorized move. For that move he placed most of the blame on the shunter at the crossover frame. He hadn't told the driver of No D5002 what he was planning, he hadn't asked for New Street's permission before the move started, and it wasn't allowed in normal working in any case.

The signalman working Stechford shunting frame also had to take some responsibility since he must have known what was being planned and knew that it was against the rules. Although he couldn't order the shunter not to carry it out, he could have used his greater experience to press him into doing it another way.

As for the crew of No D5002, the secondman had accepted the wave of the shunter without querying it. His driver had accepted the secondman's assurance that it was alright to move, even though the route they were taking had no proper signals. He also should have questioned the shunter. He was further at fault for not ensuring that the secondman went to what would be the leading cab to get a better view and apply the brake if necessary. Had the secondman been there he would have seen the down train entering the station just a few seconds earlier, and the locomotive might have stopped short of the crossing.

Colonel McMullen commented that the run round move should have been made in the sidings, as was normal, by splitting the train. This would have meant leaving half in the down sidings, shunting across to the up sidings, running round, and placing this part in a dead-end siding. The locomotive could then have returned to the down sidings to pick up the rest of the train and repeated the operation. It would probably have taken almost an hour. The shunter was trying to save time, but it was a short cut to disaster.

Settle 1960

**A single nut and bolt, which held part
of the slide bar assembly of a Britannia Pacific,
No 70052 *Firth of Tay*, worked loose while the engine was
working hard, leading to the derailment of a train
on the opposite track. Five were killed.**

The night of 20-21 January 1960 in the high Pennines of north west Yorkshire was cold, wild and stormy. Snow whipped up by gale force winds made the conditions on the Midland main line between Carlisle and Leeds particularly unpleasant, but the snow was not so heavy that trains had to be stopped. The 9.05pm train from Glasgow St Enoch to London St Pancras had not been affected by the weather, although it had left Dumfries two minutes late and was still just those couple of minutes late leaving Carlisle for the climb to Ais Gill summit, 48 miles ahead. At the head of the light eight coach formation, which included three sleeping cars, was Britannia Pacific No 70052 *Firth of Tay*.

The Leeds-based driver and fireman worked the train from the start at Glasgow and had taken over No 70052 at St Enoch – another crew had brought the engine from Corkerhill depot. The driver did not check the engine then, as the Corkerhill fitter had made an examination before it was sent out. At Dumfries, the driver walked round the Pacific, felt the bearings and examined the corks in the oil lubricating holes, seeing nothing wrong. After Carlisle, where the engine took water and the fireman pulled the coal in the tender forward, the train set off towards Leeds.

No 70052 handled the train with ease up the 15 mile climb at 1 in 100 between Appleby and Ais Gill summit, which it breasted at about 35mph, having worked fairly hard uphill. The two lost minutes had been regained and the engine crew were preparing for the level stretch across the Pennine plateau for the 15 miles to Blea Moor, followed by the 15 mile drop down the other side, mainly at 1 in 100, to Settle Junction.

As the driver eased the regulator and notched up the valve gear for the gentle fall after Ais Gill summit, he heard a repeated knocking which he thought was coming from one of the big ends – the bearing by which the connecting rod rotates on the crank pin on the centre driving wheels. He could not tell from which side the knock was coming, so he shut the regulator.

The noise became worse, so he opened the regulator slightly to keep steam on to the cylinders to try to cushion the knock, but reduced speed by applying the brake. He decided that he would stop the train at Garsdale, to find the source of the noise.

▼Side panelling from the first three Glasgow to London express coaches was ripped away by the running plate and smokebox of the Leeds to Carlisle goods train engine, a Crab 2-6-0, as it derailed on the track that had been churned up by the flailing connecting rod assembly of the express.

▲Snow continues to swirl around railway workers as the Crab is lifted back on to the track. Conditions on this high Pennine route were not bad enough for trains to be prevented from running, but they hampered the driver of the express as he attempted to make an accurate assessment of the state of his engine.

Key to trains

■ 9.05pm Glasgow to London express train

▨ 10.40pm Leeds to Carlisle goods train

When the train stopped near Garsdale signalbox, the driver got down and, by the light of a small torch, first looked at the left side, feeling all the bearings, then walked round to the right. He looked at the cylinder covers, felt the crosshead, checked the bearings and the corks in the holes, but saw nothing wrong. He looked closely at the valve gear but all appeared to be well. It was dark, snow was blowing round the engine in the freezing wind, settling a few inches deep, and the driver had only a small pocket torch – not the best of conditions in which to carry out an examination. The driver decided to carry on, but at reduced speed, and stop again at Hellifield, 25 miles on just beyond Settle, where there was a small motive power depot.

He restarted No 70052, and as they passed the signalbox the signalman called to the crew that the engine was knocking badly, but the train continued at what the driver thought was about 20mph. As the train reached the falling gradient, it was difficult for the driver to keep steam on yet hold the train in check with the brakes. The knocking got no worse except when the regulator was eased or shut.

As the train passed Settle distant signal, the fireman on the right of the engine called across to the driver that he could see sparks flying from the right of the engine and that ballast was being thrown up against the cab. The driver made a full brake application. Almost immediately a down goods train passed in the opposite direction, and at the same time *Firth of Tay* started to shudder. The train came to a halt soon after.

The crew of the goods train, which had been travelling at about 20mph, working hard on the rising gradient, had seen the express coming and the fireman saw sparks from the approaching engine. As the two engines passed each other, the engine of the goods train, an LMS Class 5 2-6-0, lurched and rolled to the right and the engine, tender and leading eight wagons were derailed.

Full horror

As the trains stopped and the crews got out, they saw the full horror of what had happened. Although the express train was still on the rails, the right hand sides of the front three coaches had been partly torn away and ripped apart. Worst was the third coach with its passenger compartments on the right – the side panelling was destroyed and the interior of five compartments badly damaged. The five passengers who were killed and most of the eight injured were in this coach.

The goods train guard had been thrown across his guard's van by the force of the collision and had received head injuries, but he was able to walk three quarters of a mile to Settle signalbox for first aid. The goods train fireman had run back to Settle

Loose slide bar nuts

A loose nut on the slide bars of No 70052 over the previous few days had not been tightened properly. The motion was potentially dangerous before the engine left Glasgow.

The nut above the lower inside front end of the slide bars worked loose and fell off with the bolt three miles north of Kirkby Stephen. Over the next ten miles the remaining three bolts on the slide bars fell out or sheared off.

The two lower slide bars fell off, leaving the crosshead without support – the engine ran for 20 miles in this state and the piston rod eventually broke away from the piston. The connecting rod/crosshead/piston rod swung down, dug into the ballast and forced the opposite track out of line. A goods train derailed on the deformed track and the engine fell to the right, hitting the side of the express train.

← To Settle ←

right hand side of first three coaches ripped away

N

Slide bar construction

The slide bar on a Britannia Pacific was of a three piece design. The lower two pieces were fixed to the top part with four bolts, one at each end of the two lower parts. Bronze packing pieces maintained a gap between the top and bottom sections, and the two separate lower pieces allowed the T-shaped crosshead to move between them.

The four bolts were inserted upwards from the bottom, with the nut on top. A steel feather was inserted just inside the bolt head, engaging with a slot in the bolt hole to stop the bolt turning when being tightened, and a split pin above the nut stopped the nut unwinding. Being right under the steam chest, access to the bolts was awkward.

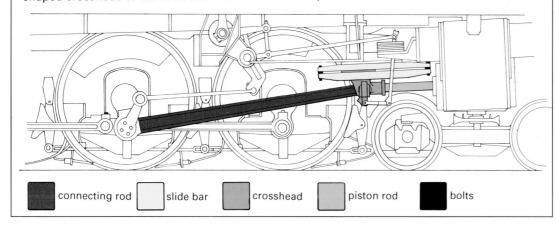

■ connecting rod	□ slide bar	▨ crosshead	▨ piston rod	■ bolts

▼When the blizzard eventually died down, the extent of the destruction caused by the passage of the Crab was fully revealed. One of the damaged coaches was, fortunately, a guard's van, but the people in the right-hand passenger compartments of the next coach accounted for most of the five dead and eight injured in the crash.

signalbox to raise the alarm and the signalman called the control office and Hellifield to alert the rescue services.

Now the detective work started. What had caused the knocking and how was the goods train derailed into the side of the express?

What went wrong?

The permanent way and locomotive department engineers soon found the immediate cause of the collision still attached to No 70052. The locomotive's right-hand piston rod, crosshead and connecting rod assembly had broken away. The piston rod had fractured immediately behind the piston, which meant that the rod was free at the front end. It was still attached to the crosshead, which was also free because the crosshead's bottom slide bars were missing, and there was nothing to support the crosshead.

The gudgeon pin holding the little end bearing of the connecting rod to the crosshead was still in place, and the big end bearing of the connecting rod was still held on to the crank pin in the centre driving wheel. The whole of the piston rod/crosshead/connecting rod assembly was free at the front end, the union link having fractured, and at first it had flailed round as the wheels revolved, then dug deeply into the ballast between the up

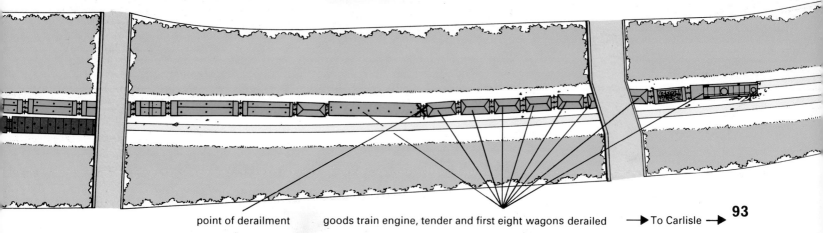

point of derailment   goods train engine, tender and first eight wagons derailed   → To Carlisle →

▲Two steam-powered cranes came alongside in order to reposition the derailed goods train on the track. A winch was also clamped to the rails so that the movement of the goods train engine could be controlled.

Rapid relief
The accident happened at 1.48am, yet despite the country area, the darkness and the bad weather, the first ambulance arrived at 2.05am, just 17 minutes later. The injured passengers were taken to hospital in less than 40 minutes, and the remaining passengers stayed in the less damaged coaches until they were ferried by ambulance to Settle station, at about 4am, for a hastily arranged relief train, which left at 5.19am.

and down tracks.

It finally assumed a trailing position, with the connecting rod bent and twisted in such a position that it was pushing the crosshead into the ballast, or on to the nearer rail of the down track as it went along, wrecking the track in front of the goods train. That accounted for the derailment of the goods train whose engine fell to the right, smashing into the leading express coaches, causing all the casualties, then scraping the sides of the last five coaches.

It was astonishing that when the connecting rod/crosshead assembly of No 70052 swung down and dug into the ballast, it did not pitch the locomotive off the track. The track was on an embankment at that point, so the ground beneath the track was softer than natural ground, and the weight of the engine was enough to drive the connecting rod and piston rod 6ft down into the ballast as it somersaulted and twisted to a back facing position, inclined out towards the other track which it could almost reach. So how had the crosshead and piston rod come adrift?

Missing slide bars

It was immediately obvious that the bottom slide bars on the right side of No 70052 were missing, leaving the crosshead without support. A search of the line found various parts of the slide bars over the final ten miles of the climb.

About three miles north of Kirkby Stephen, ten miles back along the line from Garsdale, a nut and bolt were found. A mile closer, another nut was picked up; after two miles the inner bottom slide bar, and then, seven miles after the first find, the outer slide bar. By this time, nothing had been supporting the crosshead as it moved to and fro with the piston. There is considerable upward and downward force on the crosshead which the slide bars normally restrain. Just as the second slide bar

fell off, the driver became aware of the knocking. When the train stopped at Garsdale, in the dim light of his torch and the swirling snow, the driver clearly did not see that the bottom slide bars were missing, even though he had felt the crosshead with his hand.

As the engine went on, speed was much higher than the 20mph which the driver thought he was running at. The inquiry inspecting officer, Brigadier C A Langley, said that, according to the signalbox registers, he had averaged 42mph from Garsdale to the point of the accident.

Reports ignored

The failure of the right-hand motion assembly arose because the bolt at the front end of the lower inside slide bar had been loose. The stresses on the slide bars were demonstrated by the sheared and bent split pins once the loose nut had vibrated free. The loose nuts had not been properly tightened when reported, both on the previous night at Leeds and two nights before that at Polmadie. Brigadier Langley found that loose slide bar nuts had been reported ten times since a major overhaul at Crewe works, four months before the accident.

The nuts were difficult to get at because they were right under the steam chest, above the cylinder. But the nuts and bolts found on the line afterwards were badly worn anyway, and should have been changed, rather than simply tightened. In addition, the steel feathers were missing and the slots in which they fitted were filled with dirt. Maintenance of these nuts and bolts was not being done properly at many depots, said Brigadier Langley, but the basic cause was poor design.

This had already been recognized and a new arrangement adopted with a longer bolt inserted from the top, with the nut at the bottom and a deep split cotter, instead of a split pin, stopping the nut from turning. At first the modification was carried out only when engines required overhaul, but after the Settle accident a specific programme was undertaken to fit the new bolts to all engines with these slide bars.

Recommendations
Brigadier C A Langley found that poor maintenance of the bolts had led to several failures. He recommended that maintenance staff should be reminded of the essential need for proper attention to be given to securing fastenings during maintenance work.

The nuts at the front of the slide bars were hard to reach. It was recommended that a new method of fitting the bolts should be used so that the nuts would be more easily accessible – this, along with ease of maintenance, should be given special attention in new locomotive designs.

Brigadier Langley took the terrible prevailing weather conditions into account when he did not criticize the driver of No 70052 for not noticing the missing slide bars when he stopped at Garsdale to investigate the source of the noise.

Dagenham East 1958

**Travelling slowly through thick fog, a heavy
steam-hauled commuter train ran into the back of another on a
line equipped with a pioneer automatic warning system (AWS).
How did it happen, and why were ten passengers killed?**

The London, Tilbury & Southend (LTS) line has always been one of the most intensively worked commuter lines in Britain. Even in late Victorian years the seaside resort of Southend was a popular residential area for the middle class City office workers and the town was served by two railways to London – the Great Eastern via Shenfield to Liverpool Street and the LTS through Upminster to Fenchurch Street.

Much of the LTS route lies along the Thames marshes and low lying ground to the north of the river estuary. Between Pitsea and Chalkwell the line actually runs along the estuary shore line. As a result, it has always had a problem with fog and, until the Clean Air Act of the 1950s began to take effect, this was compounded by smoke billowing from thousands of house chimneys. However, at the time of the crash the line had a good safety record due to installation of the automatic warning system (AWS) at distant signals, which had been completed in 1948.

On the afternoon of Thursday 30 January 1958, smog reduced visibility in places to less than 20 yards. By nightfall peak services were running late and drivers were having difficulty in seeing signals at all, let alone what colour was displayed through the spectacles of the semaphore arms lit only by an oil lamp. Even the bright beam of light from the odd colour light could hardly be seen until trains were close to.

The 6.20pm train with 11 non-corridor coaches, hauled by an LMS 2-6-4 tank engine, was eight minutes behind schedule when it left Fenchurch Street. It lost more time as most of the distant signals were at caution and the driver had to crawl through the murk and darkness looking for the home and starting signals.

The train stopped as booked at Barking and

▼Firemen search for survivors amongst the wreckage of the timber-bodied coaches which shattered into matchsticks when the collision occurred. At the subsequent inquiry, it was recommended that they be replaced by stronger all-steel stock. The bunker of the 6.35pm's engine can just be seen on the left.

▲The 6.35 embedded in the back of the 6.20, showing the way the roof of the rear coach slid over the cab of the bunker-first running BR 2-6-4T. Clearing wreckage on a foggy night was itself a hazardous business.

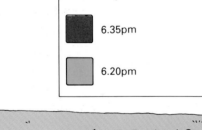

Key to trains

■ 6.35pm

■ 6.20pm

was checked at Upney, although the home and starting signals cleared as it reached them. But Becontree distant was clear and the driver accelerated to about 20mph, although not for long because the intermediate block distant ahead was at caution. Although the next signal – the intermediate block home signal – was clear, the long horn warning of the AWS told him that Dagenham East distant, below the intermediate home signal, was at caution. He ran very slowly forward looking for Dagenham East home signal, when suddenly he felt a bump to the rear of the train; the brakes came on automatically and the train stopped.

The fireman went back to see what had happened and to his horror he saw that the following 6.35pm train from Fenchurch Street had run into the back of the 6.20 train. The BR standard 2-6-4 tank, running bunker first, had demolished most of the last coach, a wooden-bodied brake third, and

pushed it part way into the coach ahead, telescoping one into the other.

Lineside residents heard the crash and quickly called police and ambulance services. When the rescuers arrived they found a scene of carnage. Both trains were crowded, with over 500 passengers in each. But most of the casualties were in the back coaches of the 6.20pm train. Ten passengers lay dead and 93 people were injured, including the

Clear signals to disaster
The 6.35pm train from Fenchurch Street ran past Upney starting signal at danger in thick fog. Becontree signalbox had just closed, while the 6.20pm train from Fenchurch Street was approaching Becontree, and all signals there were left in the clear position. But with the 6.35 now in the section without authority its driver saw Becontree's green signals and caught up and collided with the 6.20pm train just before it arrived at Dagenham East.

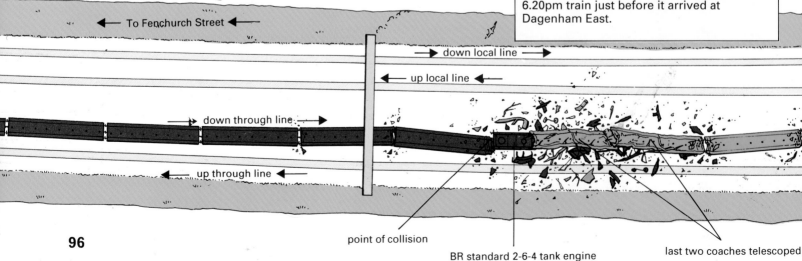

← To Fenchurch Street ←

→ down local line →

← up local line ←

→ down through line →

← up through line ←

point of collision

BR standard 2-6-4 tank engine

last two coaches telescoped

6.20's guard; 72 needed hospital treatment.

Foolproof signals

LTS line drivers naturally placed great reliance on the AWS distant signals, and there were plenty of them because the signals and signalboxes were closely spaced. In the three miles between the Upney approaches and Dagenham East there were four block sections with four distant signals and five stop signals, all upper quadrant semaphores.

After Barking, the next signalboxes were Upney, with distant, home and starting signals, and Becontree. This box not only had a distant and home signal, but also controlled an intermediate block section ahead of it with its own distant signal underneath Becontree's home signal, and an intermediate block home signal just over ³/₄ mile beyond; Dagenham East's distant signal was underneath it.

As usual, the intermediate block section had a track circuit from Becontree home signal to the intermediate block home signal. All the signalboxes had modern block controls, although not full Welwyn control, but it meant that if the track circuit approaching the home signal was occupied, the block indicator for the rear section was maintained at 'train on line'. The signal controlling entry to a block section could not be cleared (and then only for one pull) unless the forward section block indicator was at 'line clear', and the signal levers were interlocked in such a way that they had to be pulled in order. 'Line clear' could not be given to the rear unless the distant and home signals were at caution and danger respectively.

The 6.35's driver told Brigadier C A Langley, who chaired the inquiry, that he had passed Upney

▼Seen on the rear bogie of a Stanier 2-6-4T is the pickup receiver for the Hudd automatic warning system. This device detected whether distant signals were at clear or danger, and until this accident had a good safety record.

The AWS
The AWS fitted to the LTS line was the Hudd system, which used a magnetic transfer between track-mounted magnets to a receiver on the locomotive. There were two track magnets about 200 yards before the signal to which they applied – first a permanent magnet then, 15 to 20 yards later, an electromagnet. These magnets could either apply or cancel the braking system.

If a distant signal was at caution as the locomotive passed over the magnets, a continuous horn sounded on the locomotive and, if the driver did not operate a cancelling handle, the brakes would be applied automatically. When he acknowledged the warning a visual indicator disc, normally all black, changed to black and yellow as a reminder that he had passed a distant signal at caution. If the system was at clear the second (electro) magnet was energized, cancelling the horn and preventing the brake application, leaving the indicator at all black. Thus the driver had a short horn to indicate that the line ahead was clear and a long horn for caution.

To Upminster

N

▲Part of the twisted wreckage of one of the destroyed coaches. The cylinder is part of the oxy-acetylene cutting equipment that was used to speed recovery of the carriages.

distant signal at caution and was stopped at the home signal for two minutes. Then it was cleared and he crawled forward to the starting signal which was clear. Becontree distant was clear, so he accelerated to about 15mph. He saw all of Becontree's signals at clear and Dagenham East distant at clear. All of a sudden a red light loomed out of the fog and the collision occurred.

Different stories
The Upney signalman told a different story. He said he stopped the 6.35pm train at his home signal and then cleared that signal to allow the train forward to wait at his starting signal. He left the signalbox for a couple of minutes to go to the toilet and when he returned found that the track circuit to the starting signal was unoccupied. He telephoned a warning to the Dagenham East signalman who tried to get a lineman to alert the 6.20's driver, but it was too late.

But there was an added complication: since the Becontree signalman had been working for more than 12 hours, he had just closed the signalbox with the 6.20pm train in the section. This meant that the block instruments were switched through from Upney to Dagenham East and all of Becontree's signals, including the intermediate block signals were pulled to clear, thus losing two block sections. Because of the block locking, closing a signalbox and switching through the instruments could only be done in a clearly defined way. With the 6.20 between Upney and Becontree,

Becontree could switch out only if the sections on to Dagenham were clear, with line clear on the instruments to allow him to pull the intermediate block signals. Then he immediately gave 'train entering section' to Dagenham so that the signalman there would put the block indicator at 'train on line' when he switched out.

If the indicator for the section to Dagenham was at 'line clear' when he turned the closing switch, a false line clear would be sent back to Upney while the 6.20 train was still in the section. This would allow the Upney signalman to clear his starting signal for the 6.35 train, while the 6.20 had not reached Becontree. Not only that but with all Becontree signals at clear after switching out, the 6.20's driver would have seen green signals – which he did. Had the 6.20 train run past Upney starting signal at danger or had the Upney signalman seen a false 'line clear' and been able to clear his starting signal? That was the puzzle which Brigadier Langley had to sort out in his enquiry.

Other factors such as an altered time in the Upney train register book on the arrival time of the 6.35 and missing entries in the Becontree register, together with conflicting evidence on telephone calls, added to the confusion. All the signalmen involved were certain that the closure of Becontree had been correctly carried out and that at no time was a false 'line clear' given to Upney. Indeed they did not know it was possible. After a long consideration of the detail Brigadier Langley concluded that the 6.35 train had gone by Upney starting signal at danger and that its driver missed it in the thick fog. The clear signals which followed led him to believe the line was clear. As for AWS, it was only fitted to distant signals and could not prevent a driver running by a stop signal at danger. Brigadier Langley's recommendations to London Transport aimed to eliminate the repetition of such a dangerous sequence of events.

Coppenhall Junction 1962

Severe weather on Boxing Day 1962 caused frozen points at Crewe and trains to bunch up on the main line from the north. A driver tried to obtain instructions at a red signal, but the telephones were dead. He drove his train on, failing to see a train standing ahead; 18 people died in the collision.

The Christmas period has always brought heavy traffic to the railways, even though today British Rail does not normally operate trains on Christmas Day or Boxing Day. But in 1962 trains were running on 26 December, and all were well loaded. Boxing Day that year was on a Wednesday, and many passengers were returning home during the evening ready to restart work on the following day, since the trend of taking several days' holiday at Christmas had not yet developed.

During the late afternoon, as darkness fell, several trains were heading south on the West Coast main line towards the great junction at Crewe. One of them, the 4.45pm from Liverpool Lime Street to Birmingham, had joined the West Coast line at Weaver Junction. It was electrically hauled as far as Crewe, following the commissioning of the second stage of the West Coast electrification at the beginning of that year. But the main line from Scotland would have to wait another decade for the overhead catenary, and in 1962 Anglo-Scottish trains were mostly diesel-hauled. Steam locomo-

tives were still used on some services, but on that afternoon, the Mid-day Scot, the 1.30pm Glasgow – Euston express, was hauled by a heavy 1-Co-Co-1 diesel locomotive, then known as a Type 4 (but later as Class 40).

The weather was cold that Christmas, heralding one of the coldest winter periods for some years, with heavy snow in many parts of the country up until the early weeks of 1963. The severe cold during the afternoon of Boxing Day caused points in the Crewe area to freeze, and by the time it was dark, around 4pm, trains were heavily delayed, with staff struggling to get salt and oil to the point switches in order to free them.

Bad weather backlog

On the West Coast main line from the north, trains were beginning to bunch up in such a way that they were being stopped at signals approaching Crewe. Following trains were then being checked and stopped at signals further back, and with periods of slow running from signal to signal, yet

▼ **When the Mid-day Scot ran into the back of the Liverpool – Birmingham train, the two rear coaches of the latter were telescoped by the force of the collision. The back of the seventh coach – an open second – was totally destroyed, and this is where nearly all the casualties occurred. The eighth coach was a corridor brake second, with the brake and luggage end leading. The buckeye coupling between the seventh and eighth coaches fractured, and failed to keep the two coaches apart.**

more trains behind were being delayed and stopped. This domino effect meant that by the time the 4.45pm from Liverpool approached Winsford station, seven miles from Crewe, it had to reduce speed ready to stop at signal number CJ114, about $^3/_4$ mile ahead.

As part of the electrification of this route, the signalling had been modernized with four-aspect colour-light signals, track circuiting, and equipped with the automatic warning system. But to keep costs within limits there was no centralized signalling control centre, and signals and points were controlled from the existing old-style signalboxes, which had been retained, with their lever frames adapted to work the new signals.

Automatic signalling system

Through Winsford station there were just two tracks, an up and a down line carrying all traffic. But south from Winsford to Crewe there were four tracks, from east to west known as the up slow, up fast, down fast and down slow lines. Winsford station signalbox controlled the points where the two tracks became four and on the up line there was a colour-light signal WS28/9, which controlled the split from one up line into two. The next signals, $^3/_4$ mile ahead, were carried on an overhead gantry CJ (for Coppenhall Junction) 114 for the up fast, and 116 for the up slow line. Another $^3/_4$ mile on was another pair: CJ110 for the fast line and 112 for the slow line. Normally these signals worked automatically, and all had lineside telephones to their controlling signalbox, which in this case was Coppenhall Junction. The down line signals, which were from 230 to 500yd away from the up

line signals, also had telephones, but these were to Winsford station signalbox.

The 4.45pm from Liverpool was braking as it passed Winsford signal W28 and 29 at 5.26pm, ready to stop at signal CJ114. The driver telephoned to the signalman, as required by the famous Rule 55, and was told to wait until the signal cleared. After a while the signal cleared to single yellow, and the 4.45pm train went forward to stop at signal CJ110. But here the lineside telephone was not working, because a switch on the telephone at CJ114 had not returned to normal after the earlier call, and all the up telephones on this section were on a common circuit. The secondman on the electric locomotive then called the Winsford signalman from the down line telephone 230yd away and, after he had checked with Coppenhall Junction, was told to wait for the signal to clear.

Meanwhile, the 1.30pm from Glasgow (the

▲ The last coach of the Liverpool – Birmingham train was driven partly through the seventh. Surprisingly, the back of the eighth coach, with the passenger compartments, stood up well to the collision, because the buffers of the Mid-day Scot diesel locomotive (seen extreme right) hit the buffers of the coach.

Taking risks

When very cold weather caused points to freeze at Crewe, trains from the north were delayed and started bunching, stopped at signals further back.

The driver of a Liverpool – Birmingham train telephoned the signalman at Coppenhall Junction for instructions and he was told to wait for the signal to clear. When it did, he drove his train to the next signal. But a switch in the telephone did not reset properly, so that when the secondman and driver of the following Mid-day Scot tried to telephone the signalman they could not get through.

Instead of trying another telephone 500yd away, the Mid-day Scot's driver took his train forward past the red signal without finding out if the line was clear. He drove too fast and hit a standing train ahead, killing 18 passengers and injuring 34.

Key

[grey] 4.45pm Liverpool – Birmingham express

[black] 1.30pm Glasgow – Euston express

← To Coppenhall Junction and Crewe ←   all injuries and deaths occurred in these two coaches

ed 'Stop!', and about a coach-length away was the back of the standing 4.45pm train.

It was too late: the heavy diesel ploughed into the back coach and pushed the whole of the front train forward, the two trains eventually stopping about 25ft apart. But the damage had been done. There were about 300 passengers on the 4.45pm train. Eighteen lay dead or died later, and 34 others, including the guard, were seriously hurt, all in the back two coaches of the 4.45. But why had the Mid-day Scot driver not seen the back of the train ahead, nor its oil tail lamp showing a red light?

Colonel D McMullen, the inspecting officer, had no doubt that excessive speed was a factor. The Mid-day Scot had passed Winsford station at 5.51pm. Yet, just 10 minutes later, it hit the back of the 4.45pm train. It had taken two minutes to stop at signal 114 and the driver and secondman would have been trying to telephone for at least five minutes. In the three remaining minutes, the train had restarted, accelerated, and reached the back of the standing train ³/₄ mile ahead. That meant an average speed of 15mph and an impact speed of about 20-25mph.

Colonel McMullen held the Mid-day Scot driver responsible for the accident: for not using one of the down line telephones; for not ensuring the line was clear to the next signal (which he could not ascertain in the dark); and for running too fast. Although the 4.45 train's oil tail lamp did not shine brightly against the strong electric light of the signal beyond, the signal itself was obscured by the silhouette of the standing train when a following train got within about 100yd of it.

Mid-day Scot), which passed Winsford station at 5.51pm, had come to a stop at signal 114. The secondman could get no reply on the telephone, nor from the adjoining telephone for signal 116. Instructions said that any other nearby signalpost telephone should be tried, but the down line telephones were nearly 500yd away. The Mid-day Scot driver decided to carry on slowly to the next signal. He was allowed to do this, according to the rules, under clearly defined circumstances, but had to ensure that the line was clear to the next signal, and travel slowly, ready to stop short of any obstruction. And he had to stop at the next signal, regardless of the aspect shown, to report his actions.

The Mid-day Scot went forward. The driver said later that as he could see signal CJ110 ahead at red, he went no faster than 5-6mph. About halfway to the signal, it changed to single yellow, but the driver did not accelerate, as he intended to stop at the signal. Suddenly, his secondman shout-

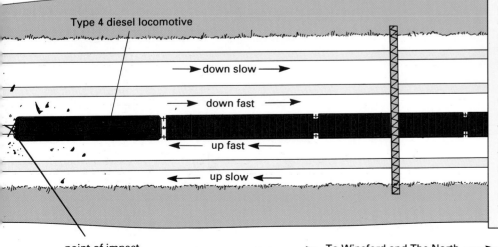

Type 4 diesel locomotive

→ down slow →

→ down fast →

← up fast ←

← up slow ←

point of impact

→ To Winsford and The North →

Lewisham 1957

**When the driver of a steam train passed warning
signals and ploughed into the back of a stationary electric train,
the accident was serious enough – but when the collision took out the
supports of an overhead flyover, bringing 350 tons of steel bridge
crashing down, disaster turned to tragedy.**

The combination of a dark winter evening, thick fog, signals missed, trains running out of proper order and the collapse of a heavy girder bridge led to the worst ever accident on the Southern Region of British Railways.

The two trains involved in the initial collision at Lewisham, in the south-east of London, were overcrowded, with nearly 1500 passengers in the 10 coaches of the electric train and 700 passengers in the main line steam train which ran into it. Casualties were inevitably high: 89 passengers and a train guard were killed and over 100 passengers were seriously injured.

The line was equipped with colour light signals controlled partly by track circuits which, although installed about 30 years earlier, were just as effective as the newer installations of the 1950s. So how did the collision happen?

Fog causes disruption

Wednesday 4 December 1957 was one of those days when fog had been hanging around the Thames basin in London. By dusk it had thickened up in places so that visibility was little more than 10 to 15 yards. Elsewhere, visibility was better at about 50 yards. The eastern section of the

▼Rescuers work in the wreckage of the 4.56pm Cannon Street to Ramsgate train with the collapsed bridge girders above them. The second coach was totally crushed; this is the third coach (No 4378), the front part of which was destroyed.

▶The scene from the wrecked bridge, looking south , on Friday 6 December after the engine of the Ramsgate train had been removed. A further disaster was averted on 4 December when the driver of a train approaching on the left-hand track over the bridge saw the leaning girders and stopped his train. It ran on to the bridge and was leaning but did not derail. All passengers were safely evacuated.

Signalling system

The signals at St Johns were controlled from the signalbox near the station, although a lever could not be pulled to clear a signal if a train was on the section of line beyond that signal. Many of the signals not controlling junctions were automatic and not worked by levers. The next signalbox ahead was Parks Bridge Junction which controlled the local and through trains and also a connection to the Mid Kent branch to Hayes.

Trains were not offered and accepted as in manual block working but were simply described on the train describer. These clockwork instruments consisted of a clock face with a pointer towards up to 12 descriptions around the face and levers operated by the signalman to identify trains to the next signalbox down the line. There were two describers for each track, one to say what type of train was coming and one to say where it was going.

Driver's view of signals

Normally signals were on the left of the line, but those between New Cross and St Johns were on the right. This was partly for space reasons and partly because when the signals were installed in the 1920s many of the steam engines on the line at that time had right-hand drive.

Later Southern steam engines had the driver's controls on the left, so that the right-hand signals had to be picked out before becoming obscured by the locomotive boiler.

The extent to which the boiler restricted the driver's view depended on the type of locomotive. The Battle of Britain class Pacific involved in the collision at St Johns had a particularly wide, flat-sided casing, restricting the forward vision of the driver to a narrow spectacle glass.

In fog, if the driver could not see the signals on the right, he would either cross the cab to look out of the right-hand side or ask his fireman to look out for the signals for him.

It was doubtful whether the driver of the Ramsgate train realized he could not see the signals through the fog. He did not cross the cab, and only asked the fireman to look out when he saw the lights of St Johns station.

Southern Region, with its dense network of routes out of the main London termini, was badly affected and trains from Cannon Street and Charing Cross were running late and out of order.

The routes from these two termini combined in a complex track layout as they approached London Bridge, but by New Cross there were just four tracks – down and up local and down and up through – all equipped with colour light signals. At St Johns, the next station, a branch diverged from the local lines towards Lewisham Junction, while the local and through lines curved sharply to the right under a massive girder overbridge carrying the railway from Nunhead to Lewisham.

At about 6pm several trains were running on the down through line between London Bridge, New Cross, St Johns and beyond. The 5.05pm Cannon Street to Hastings train, steam hauled by a Schools class 4-4-0, had left Cannon Street 38 minutes late; it passed through St Johns at 6pm.

The train had lost more time during its journey as the driver, cautious after passing successive yellow signals, searched for signals in the fog. Even though colour light signals with their powerful electric lights can penetrate fog, in places the fog was so dense that night that the beams of light could barely be seen more than 20 yards away. The fireman of the 5.05 train said afterwards that some could not be seen even at that distance.

The driver of the 4-4-0 was seated on the left-hand side of the engine. Even though the boiler of the Schools class locomotive was not as large as those of other engines – notably the Battle of Britain class which was involved in the accident – his view of signals on the right-hand side of the track was partially obscured. As the train continued running slowly on towards Hither Green he asked his fireman on the right-hand side of the engine to look out for the signals through the fog.

Three minutes behind the steam train was the 5.16pm Cannon Street to Orpington electric train. With the driver right at the front and no massive boiler to obscure his vision, the driver had a better view of the signals both on the right and left. Even so, some signals were still difficult to pick out in the fog until they were very close. The train was travelling slowly, running past successive yellow signals as it was following the Hastings train ahead.

A few minutes behind was the 5.25pm Charing Cross to Hastings train, formed of a diesel-electric unit, with the driver right at the front like the electric train ahead. It had passed green signals until North Kent East Junction on the London side of New Cross, but then slowed as its driver saw yellow signals through New Cross and St Johns until it was stopped by a red signal at Parks Bridge. This was the setting for the drama which followed.

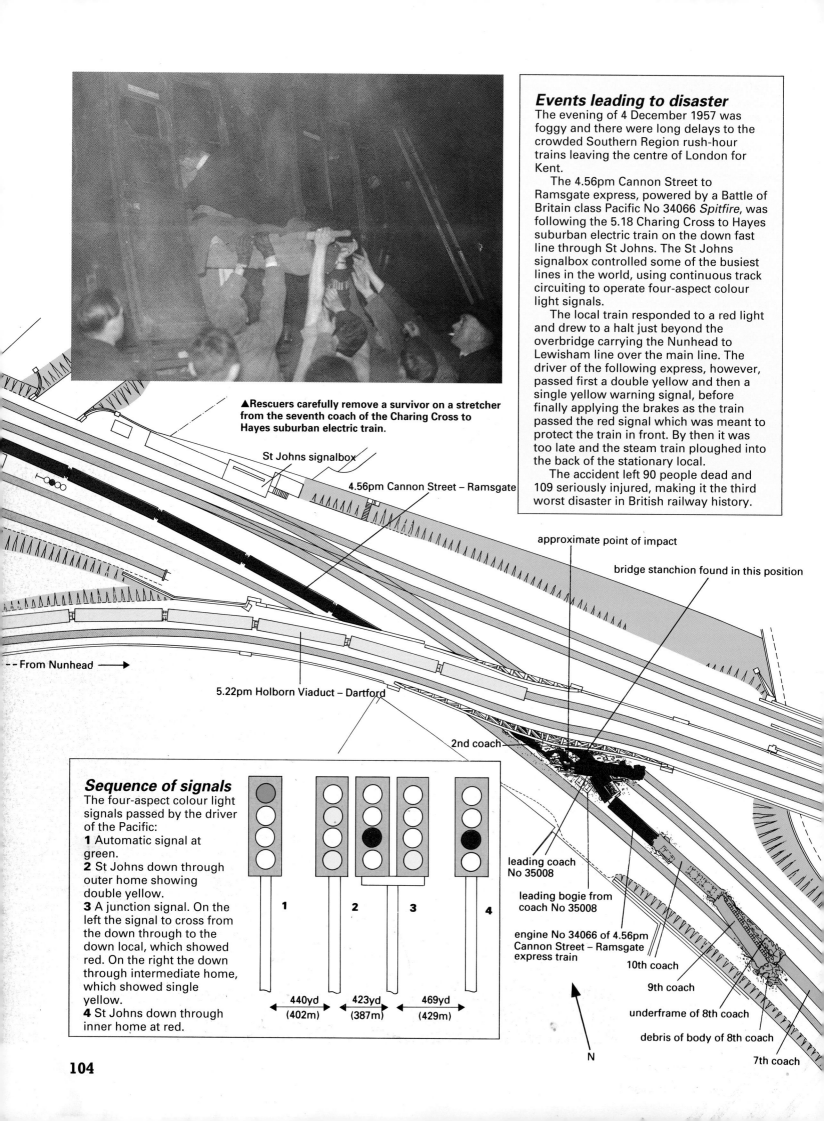

Events leading to disaster

The evening of 4 December 1957 was foggy and there were long delays to the crowded Southern Region rush-hour trains leaving the centre of London for Kent.

The 4.56pm Cannon Street to Ramsgate express, powered by a Battle of Britain class Pacific No 34066 *Spitfire*, was following the 5.18 Charing Cross to Hayes suburban electric train on the down fast line through St Johns. The St Johns signalbox controlled some of the busiest lines in the world, using continuous track circuiting to operate four-aspect colour light signals.

The local train responded to a red light and drew to a halt just beyond the overbridge carrying the Nunhead to Lewisham line over the main line. The driver of the following express, however, passed first a double yellow and then a single yellow warning signal, before finally applying the brakes as the train passed the red signal which was meant to protect the train in front. By then it was too late and the steam train ploughed into the back of the stationary local.

The accident left 90 people dead and 109 seriously injured, making it the third worst disaster in British railway history.

▲Rescuers carefully remove a survivor on a stretcher from the seventh coach of the Charing Cross to Hayes suburban electric train.

St Johns signalbox

4.56pm Cannon Street – Ramsgate

approximate point of impact

bridge stanchion found in this position

-- From Nunhead ➔

5.22pm Holborn Viaduct – Dartford

2nd coach

leading coach No 35008

leading bogie from coach No 35008

engine No 34066 of 4.56pm Cannon Street – Ramsgate express train

10th coach

9th coach

underframe of 8th coach

debris of body of 8th coach

7th coach

N

Sequence of signals

The four-aspect colour light signals passed by the driver of the Pacific:

1 Automatic signal at green.

2 St Johns down through outer home showing double yellow.

3 A junction signal. On the left the signal to cross from the down through to the down local, which showed red. On the right the down through intermediate home, which showed single yellow.

4 St Johns down through inner home at red.

1   **2**   **3**   **4**

440yd (402m)   423yd (387m)   469yd (429m)

Signalman's confusion

The signalman at Parks Bridge could not see the train in the fog. He did not know which train it was or where it was going. He thought from the train describer that it was an electric train for the Mid Kent line which branched off to the right at Parks Bridge.

The signalman could not clear the signals to the Mid Kent line because he already had a train coming on the up through line from Bromley North, and also another heading down the Mid Kent line from Lewisham station.

The diesel train driver telephoned the signalman from the signalpost to identify the train, but the signalman did not know from which signal the driver was speaking and thought the driver had given the number of the signal behind.

In the meantime the 5.18pm Charing Cross to Hayes, which had left Charing Cross 30 minutes late – three minutes behind the diesel – approached St Johns. This was the electric train that the signalman at Parks Bridge had mistaken the diesel for. Its driver had seen the yellow signals at St Johns and drew to a halt at the signal showing red behind the diesel train. The back of

the 5.18pm train was on the curve just beyond the Nunhead to Lewisham overbridge.

The 4.56pm steam train from Cannon Street to Ramsgate, hauled by Battle of Britain class 4-6-2 No 34066 *Spitfire*, had been badly delayed on the empty run from the sidings to Rotherhithe Road. It did not leave Cannon Street until 6.08pm but then had green signals as far as New Cross.

The next three signals, all on the right of the line, were at double yellow, single yellow and red, the last being at the country end of St Johns platform.

Driver W J Trew was on the left of the cab and his fireman, C D Hoare, had seen the green signal at New Cross and called across to tell Trew what aspect it was showing. Then Hoare carried on firing ready for the start of the climb to the North Downs, assuming that Trew would see the next two signals. Although these stood on the right of the track, they were on a left-hand curve and, in clear weather, would be seen easily by the driver in spite of the restrictions caused by the huge boiler. Neither driver nor fireman were expecting the fog to be so thick at this point. Whether Trew actually saw the next two signals telling him to

Key to trains

- 4.56pm Cannon Street – Ramsgate
- 5.18pm Charing Cross – Hayes
- 5.22pm Holborn Viaduct – Dartford

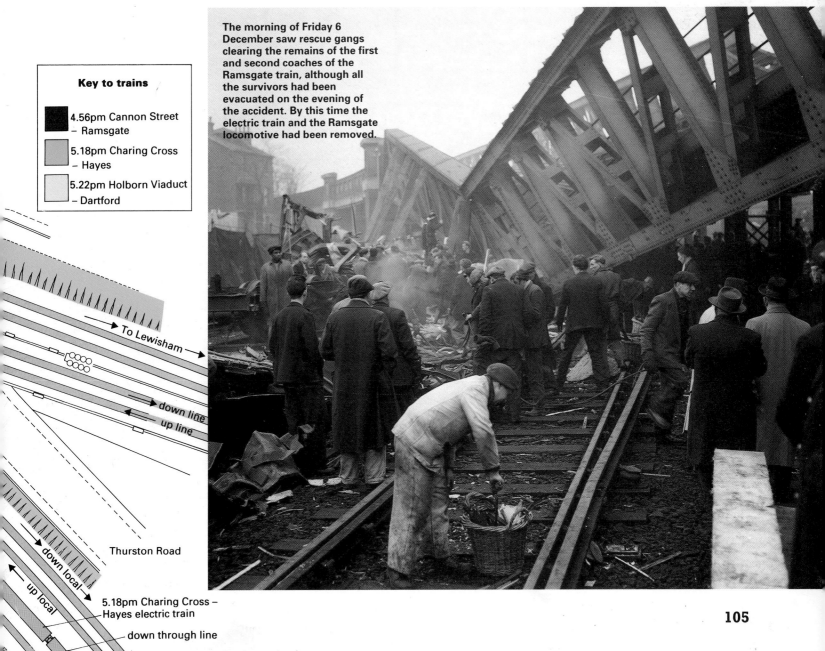

The morning of Friday 6 December saw rescue gangs clearing the remains of the first and second coaches of the Ramsgate train, although all the survivors had been evacuated on the evening of the accident. By this time the electric train and the Ramsgate locomotive had been removed.

To Lewisham

down line
up line

Thurston Road

5.18pm Charing Cross – Hayes electric train

down local
up local

down through line

slow down was never established.

The next thing Trew saw was the station lights as the train ran into St Johns. Just as Trew called to Hoare to look out for the signal at the end of the platform, Hoare saw the glow of the signal light through the thick fog. It was red.

Hoare called the indication to Trew. The driver pulled down the brake handle to apply the brake, but it was too late. Just 138 yards beyond the red signal was the back of the 5.18pm Charing Cross to Hayes electric train, standing on the rising gradient with its brakes hard on.

The Ramsgate train was travelling at around 30mph, and the brake blocks had hardly begun to grip the wheels when the big Pacific locomotive ploughed into the rear driver's cab of the electric train. The force of the collision thrust the rear two coaches of the electric train forward and as these were both of a stronger BR standard pattern than those ahead of it, the ninth coach over-rode and completely destroyed the weaker body of the eighth coach.

The sudden stop by the engine caused the leading coach of the Ramsgate train to burst out to the left of the curve. This forced the tender up and out immediately beneath the flyover, where it hit and displaced one of the stanchions supporting the bridge girders above.

Within seconds of the initial collision 350 tons of steel bridge collapsed on to the leading coaches of the Ramsgate train. What remained of the first coach after the collision was crushed by the bridge. The whole of the second coach was flattened and the leading part of the third was

wrecked. Of those killed it was thought that 37 were in the electric train, mostly in the eighth coach, and 49 were in the front three coaches of the steam train. Remarkably, the engine itself was not derailed and damage to it was not extensive.

A couple of minutes after the accident, the 5.22pm Holborn Viaduct to Dartford train approached the collapsed bridge. Fortunately it was moving slowly up to a red signal, and when the motorman saw the girders at an angle he was able to stop the train just in time.

▲Battle of Britain class 4-6-2 No 34066 *Spitfire* which headed the Ramsgate train was repaired and returned to service. It continued to be based at Stewarts Lane depot and used on main line services to the Kent coast until electrification in 1961. After that it was used on surviving steam services on the main line out of Waterloo to the south west until it was withdrawn for scrap.

What went wrong?

The inspecting officer who chaired the inquiry into the collision placed the blame for it solely on the driver of the Ramsgate train. He concluded that the driver did not see the two signals at caution and the St Johns signal at red and did not apply the brake until his fireman called out that the signal was red.

The fireman's actions were not criticized since he probably did not realize how thick the fog was in the cutting between New Cross and St Johns.

The signalman at Parks Bridge mistakenly stopped the Hastings diesel train thinking it was bound for the Mid Kent line, but he was in no way responsible for the collision.

Action taken

Like many inquiries at this period into accidents caused by drivers passing signals at danger, the inspecting officer recommended the adoption of the warning type of automatic train control, today called the automatic warning system (AWS).

Although the SR management had their reservations about AWS, it was eventually installed. However, the system has since been blamed for several accidents where repetitive cancellation by drivers acknowledging caution signals has led to accidental cancellation at red signals. Now BR is testing a new system – automatic train protection (ATP) – which will prevent a train from running into danger.

Barnes Junction 1955

**Mistakes made by two signalmen working
under pressure defeated the locking on a line equipped with
Sykes lock and block instruments, and led to a collision between
an electric train and a goods train, and to a major
fire in which 13 people died.**

The Windsor line (thus known even though its trains went to destinations other than Windsor) out of London's Waterloo station never had the glamour of the adjoining main line, which runs parallel as far as Clapham Junction. In Southern Railway (SR) days, and right up to the end of steam out of Waterloo in 1967, the main line had its long-distance express trains. These ran to Bournemouth, Weymouth, to Exeter in the far South West, and originally to Ilfracombe and into Cornwall as far as Padstow.

In contrast, the Windsor line – apart from sharing the route from Waterloo as far as Clapham Junction – had little to do with the main line services. It carried mainly suburban and outer suburban trains, serving Thames Valley destinations such as Windsor, Weybridge via Staines, and Reading. It also provided inner London services round the Hounslow and Kingston loops to form the well-known roundabout services starting and ending their journeys at Waterloo.

In addition, the Windsor line had links with main lines north and east from London via its connection at Kew to the North & South Western Junction line. This gave access to Willesden, Cricklewood, and by other junctions and spurs right round to east London. These links brought a large number of goods trains from north of London to destinations on the SR.

From Waterloo as far as Barnes Junction, three miles (five kilometres) west of Clapham Junction, the Windsor line had four tracks almost all the way, with just a short length of three tracks running out of Waterloo. Between Clapham Junction and Barnes Junction the four tracks were called the down local, the down through, the up through and the up local. At Barnes Junction the route split into two, via Richmond and via Kew, each of them double track.

Sykes lock and block

The signalling along this section was controlled from signalboxes at Clapham Junction 'A', Clapham Junction 'E', Point Pleasant Junction, Putney, Barnes East and Barnes Junction. As far as Point Pleasant Junction the signals were colour lights, but between there and Barnes Junction they were upper quadrant semaphores. On this stretch of track the block sections were controlled by Sykes lock and block, which provided the signalmen with added safeguards to ensure that only one train could be in a block section at a time.

Sykes lock and block worked either by means of treadles on the track that could be depressed by

a train's wheel flanges, or by track circuits controlling locks connected to the block instruments and signal levers. The effect was that signals could not be cleared unless the previous train had operated the treadle or track circuit beyond the next signal. Furthermore, the block instruments could not be placed in the clear position for a train to enter a section unless the previous train had been proved to have left the section at the signalbox ahead. It was the same system that was in use at the time of the 1947 disaster at South Croydon.

The Sykes instruments used on what were

▼Wreckage from the Barnes Junction collision between an electric train and a goods train was loaded on to wagons after the accident. On the goods train, a container next to the guard's van was destroyed in the initial impact.

London & South Western Railway routes west of Clapham Junction provided only two indications to show the state of the block section. This was by means of a small semaphore indicator: horizontal meant that either no train had been accepted by the box ahead, or that there was already a train in that section; and lowered indicated that the line was clear for the next train to be sent into the section. The Sykes instruments at Croydon on the Brighton line and also on the South Eastern lines were slightly different: a lowered semaphore meant that no train had been signalled, or that the line was clear for a train. The indicator was raised to the horizontal position only when a train was actually in the section.

A hard night's work

At around 11.00pm on Friday, 2 December 1955, train services were still fairly intense on the Windsor line, with passengers on their way back home from London restaurants, theatres and concerts. Between 10.42pm and 11.12pm Waterloo sent out no fewer than eight electric trains on the Windsor line alone. Six of these were signalled to run on the down through track: five via Richmond, and one via Kew. The remaining two ran on the local line and then to Richmond.

The last train to get through was the 11.03pm Waterloo – Kingston, which called at Barnes

▲Firemen struggled to damp down the blaze when the leading coach of the 11.12pm from Waterloo was destroyed after colliding with the goods train. The fire probably started when external metalwork made contact with the live conductor rail.

Junction at 11.27pm. During this same half hour, four up trains passed through Barnes Junction, two from Kew and two from Richmond. And to add to the workload of the signalmen, there was the 10.55pm cross-London goods train scheduled, steam hauled by a Stanier LMS Class 8 2-8-0 from Battersea to Brent, near Willesden.

The signalman at Barnes Junction must have been very busy: racing up and down the frame, changing the route for trains from the local to Richmond, through to Richmond, local to Kew or through to Kew, or vice versa, re-setting the points and locking levers, and pulling and restoring signal levers as the trains went past.

To further complicate the situation, not all the signalboxes were open at that late hour. Barnes East, situated about 1/4 mile (400m) on the Waterloo side of Barnes Junction, had been correctly switched out and closed for the night at about 9.45pm. Just after 11.00pm, the signalman at Putney wanted to switch out and go home, even though it was still 45 minutes before the booked

Improper use of the release key

A signalman at Barnes Junction, working under pressure after an earlier power failure, forgot that he had a goods train approaching on the down local line.

The signalman at Point Pleasant had not received train out of section for the goods train, yet still offered the 11.12pm Windsor train to Barnes Junction. The Barnes Junction signalman used the release key wrongly, to unlock the instruments that had been protecting the goods train, and accepted the 11.12pm train, which then ran into the goods train.

The type of block indicator used on the line was criticized, since it did not distinguish between a train in the section, and no train signalled – this could have misled the Point Pleasant signalman.

The goods train guard killed in the accident had not changed the right-hand side light from red to white to show his train was on the local track. Seeing three red lights on the goods train, the 11.12's driver may have thought it was on the through line. He did not live to tell what he had seen.

Key to trains

10.55pm Battersea – Brent goods train

11.12pm Waterloo – Windsor and Chertsey passenger train

To Kew Chiswick and Richmond ◄

time to close the box for the night.

Switching out

In order to close a signalbox, all the signals it controlled on the main lines had to be pulled to the clear position, and the block instrument circuits switched through between the signalboxes on each side. There was a set procedure for this to be done safely. With Sykes lock and block the signalmen at the boxes on each side had to use the plunger on their instruments to give a line clear on the semaphore indicators. This enabled each line at the box to be switched out, and released the lock on the starting signals there. The signalman at the closing box could then pull his signals to clear. After he had turned the switch to link the block instruments between the boxes on each side, bypassing his own box, the signalmen at both ends of the now lengthened block section had to test the bells and indicators to make sure they were working. Then they had to use the release key on the Sykes instruments to cancel the line clear that had been given to the closing signalbox to restore the block indicators to normal; otherwise a false line clear would be transmitted to the box at the other end of the lengthened block section.

It was against the rules to close a signalbox with a train in either the forward or the rear section, so the Putney signalman refused to accept the Battersea – Brent goods train from Point Pleasant. This enabled him to switch out at 11.08pm. A minute or so later, Point Pleasant Junction offered the goods train (which had already passed Clapham Junction) directly to Barnes Junction on the down local line. It was accepted. The goods train ran the two miles (three kilometres) to Barnes Junction home signal (¼ mile/400m or so from the signalbox) in about seven minutes. After a few minutes the home signal was cleared, and the goods train moved forward towards the platform starting signal, which was at danger.

What happened next?

Quite what action the signalman at Barnes Junction took after that was never fully resolved. Three electric trains had been signalled on the down through line, and they overtook the goods train at different places. The signalman at Barnes Junction said that he offered the goods train forward to Grove Park signalbox, the first on the Kew line. He intended to signal it right across the junction, over the up and down Richmond line connections with the down through and up through/local tracks (beyond the limit of the diagram below), after the 11.03pm Waterloo – Kingston train had cleared the junction, having stopped at the down through platform.

The signalman at Point Pleasant Junction now had the 11.12pm Waterloo – Windsor/Chertsey train approaching from Clapham Junction on the down local line. He had not received the train out of section bell signal from Barnes Junction for the

▲A breakdown crane stands on the down local line at Barnes Junction after the underframe of the burnt-out driving trailer coach in the foreground had been lifted off the line, and taken into the goods yard to be cut up.

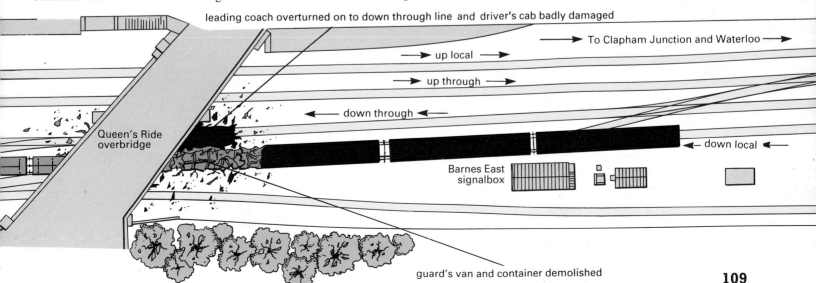

leading coach overturned on to down through line and driver's cab badly damaged

To Clapham Junction and Waterloo →

up local →

up through →

down through ←

down local ←

Queen's Ride overbridge

Barnes East signalbox

guard's van and container demolished

▲ This photograph shows the site of the collision between the 11.12pm Waterloo – Windsor/Chertsey passenger train and the Battersea – Brent goods train.

Barnes East signalbox, which was closed at the time, is in the centre of the picture. Just beyond the signalbox is the home signal controlled by both Barnes East and Barnes Junction. Next to the signalbox is the rear unit of the electric train.

The electric train

The four-coach electric train forming the 11.12pm service to Windsor and Chertsey was made up of two two-coach units, classified as 2-NOL. They were rebuilt in the 1930s from old LSWR steam coaches on to new underframes. They had timber bodies with individual non-corridor compartments, but the driver's cab and guard's van – which were added on to the old bodies – had timber frames with steel panels. The fire probably started from an arc as the steel panels bridged the conductor rail to earth before the current could be cut off (the old-style circuit breakers then in use were slow to react to short circuits).

goods train but – against the rules – still offered the 11.12pm train, which was accepted by Barnes Junction (despite the goods train still standing at his platform starting signal). The block instrument semaphore indicator in Point Pleasant junction dropped to the line clear position, his starting signal was unlocked, and he cleared the signals for the four-coach electric train, which ran on into the section ahead, towards Barnes Junction.

Were the red lights visible?

The electric train driver probably saw the Barnes Junction home signal at clear, still with its arm raised and showing a green light in the darkness for the goods train just beyond it. Whether he saw the red tail lamp and two red side lamps on the guard's van of the goods train nobody will ever know. He certainly made a semblance of a brake application, but nevertheless, at 11.28pm the electric train hit the back of the goods train at about 35mph (55km/h) and demolished both the guard's van and a container on a wagon next to it. The driver's cab of the electric train was badly damaged and probably the passenger compartment next to it.

The leading coach overturned on to the down through line, right under an overbridge. Within a minute or so, the external metalwork of this coach must have made contact with the live conductor rail, and an electric arc was created, setting the timber body of the coach ablaze. The inferno gutted the whole coach. About 30 to 40 passengers were in this coach: 11 were killed, as were the electric train driver and the goods train guard. About 20 passengers received severe injuries.

But how did the 11.12pm train get into the section when it was still occupied by the goods train, and protected by Sykes lock and block instruments

– specifically designed to prevent signalmen's mistakes occurring?

The signalman's doubtful testimony

The Barnes Junction signalman told the inquiry inspecting officer, Lt Col G R S Wilson, that he had not accepted the Windsor electric train from Point Pleasant, and there must have been a fault in the Point Pleasant equipment. He said he was concentrating on getting the goods train crossed over to the Kew line. But witnesses – including the electric train drivers on the through line who had overtaken the goods train – had seen the signals at Point Pleasant correctly set at danger behind the goods train. For them to have been cleared again for the Windsor train would have needed a release from Barnes Junction.

Much of the Barnes Junction signalman's evidence disagreed with the evidence of others, or with the recorded times in other signalboxes. During the late evening, Barnes Junction signalmen were not required to keep a detailed train register, but the time of offering the goods train forward to Grove Park signalbox on the Kew line recorded in the register at Grove Park was 11.28pm – not a few minutes earlier, as claimed by the Barnes Junction signalman.

Misuse of the release key

Despite the protestations of the Barnes Junction signalman that he knew nothing of the Windsor train, Lt Col Wilson concluded that he must have taken some action for the Windsor train to have been given clear signals at Point Pleasant. There could have been a sudden and unexplained failure of the locking at Point Pleasant, which allowed the signalman there to clear his signals for the Windsor train, but no evidence of this was found after the accident. Alternatively, the signalman at Barnes Junction, on being offered the Windsor train irregularly by Point Pleasant, had either forgotten the goods train, or thought he had not cleared the instrument after Putney had switched out, and then wrongly used the release key to unlock the section. This would have given line clear to Point Pleasant while the goods train was at his home signal. Lt Col Wilson was certain that the release key had been used, and blamed the Barnes Junction signalman for the accident.

Recommendations

As a short-term measure, the inspecting officer recommended the installation of track circuits approaching Barnes Junction home signals. These were not normally provided with Sykes lock and block, but would give greater safety. He also discussed making the LSWR-type block indicator match those on the other sections of the Southern Railway, with the semaphore arm raised to mean only that a train is in the section. In the longer term, Lt Col Wilson recommended the introduction of total signalling modernization, with track circuits and colour-light signals.

Didcot 1955

**Anticipation of an afternoon out in London turned to
terror when a Sunday excursion from South Wales derailed.
It was diverted on to a goods loop to avoid engineering work
but the driver missed the signals and took the crossover
far too fast. Eleven passengers were killed.**

In the steam era, railways traditionally carried out engineering work on Sundays when fewer passenger and goods trains ran than on weekdays. On double lines, one line was often blocked for work to be done on it during what was called a possession. The remaining line was kept open as a single line, with trains running on it in both directions under the control of a pilotman, who either accompanied each train or personally ordered it through. But where the route had more than two tracks it was often easier to close one pair and divert trains on to the other.

For major works a double line would sometimes be closed completely, and trains diverted by an alternative route. This often meant a lengthy detour. Sunday 20 November 1955 was just such a day on the Paddington – Cardiff main line. The principal work was in the Severn Tunnel, which was closed to ordinary trains for its regular Sunday maintenance. This meant all trains had to be diverted through Gloucester. But even on the Cardiff – Gloucester line the main lines were blocked for track relaying, with a crane lifting in complete track panels near Lliswerry. Here there were goods loops, over which passenger trains were run under special regulations.

Further east, between Swindon and Didcot, there was more engineering work. There were bridge repairs near Wantage Road, with a 15mph speed restriction for passing trains. Approaching Didcot, old ballast was being recovered from the up main. As at Lliswerry there was an up goods loop alongside the up main from Steventon, and all trains were to be diverted on to this loop at Milton signalbox, about two miles west of Didcot.

Normally the goods loops were worked on what was called permissive block, which meant that more than one train could be in the block section at one time, each train being checked as it entered the section slowly, and its driver being

▼Britannia Pacific No 70026, *Polar Star,* lies embedded in the soft ground after rolling down the embankment following the derailment. These engines had left hand driving controls, but the signals on the WR were sited to be seen best from right hand drive GWR engines.

told how many trains were ahead of him.

This applied only to goods trains, however. If the loop was to be used by passenger trains in an emergency, or while the main line was blocked by engineering work, then normal absolute block regulations applied, with not more than one train being allowed in the block section at one time. The rules also said that a passenger train must never enter a goods loop unless the signals were clear for it and the driver was instructed to do so by the signalman, or by a handsignalman provided to carry out that instruction.

Sundays often saw the running of special excursions which used stock that would otherwise stand idle, and which gave passengers a chance to go to places not normally served by through trains. Usually these outings were from towns or cities to seaside or country destinations, but on Sunday 25 November 1955 an excursion had been arranged from Treherbert to Paddington, to give people in the Rhondda Valley the chance of an afternoon in London. The 10-coach train ran down the Valley line to Cardiff, where it reversed. Britannia Pacific locomotive No 70026, *Polar Star,* was then coupled on to the back, and became the front of the train onward to Paddington.

The British Railways (BR) Britannia class engines were then fairly new to the Western Region (WR) and in many ways were unfamiliar to WR drivers and firemen. The main difference from the old Great Western Railway (GWR) engines was that the driver's controls were on the left instead of the right. Britannias also had very large, long boilers, and a smoke deflector on each

▼A general view of the wreckage after the derailment. The bracket signal to the right of the vehicles on the track in the background was the one missed by the driver, who should have been looking out on the left hand side of the engine.

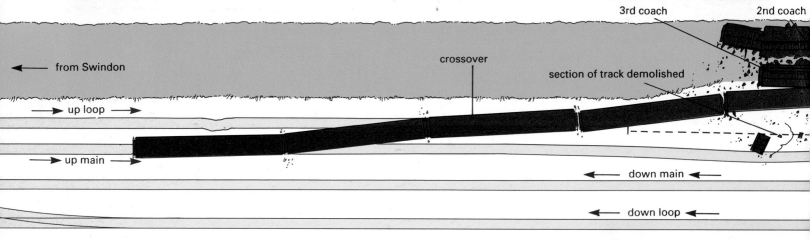

▲Gangs with breakdown tenders work by the light of lamps behind the overturned locomotive. This underside view shows the spring assembly behind the driving wheels, while to the right is the leading bogie.

the 15mph restriction for the bridge work near Wantage Road. The driver then opened the regulator for the train to accelerate, and had reached 40mph by Steventon.

About a quarter of a mile beyond Steventon was the AWS ramp for Milton up main distant signal, itself a further quarter of a mile on, but on the right of the engine between the down and up main lines. It was at caution because the Milton home signal was at danger. The bracket home signal, also carrying the main to goods loop signal, was also to the right, and the line itself was on a gentle right hand curve. As the train approached the home signal the signalman in Milton signalbox already had the points set from the main to the goods loop, and cleared the left hand signal for the train to proceed on to the goods line.

No time to react

The crossover points were sharply curved, with a 10mph speed limit through them. But the excursion train hadn't slowed down, and was still accelerating. The driver saw the point blades ahead of him set towards the goods loop, but his emergency brake application came too late.

The big Pacific swung to the left as it entered the facing end of the crossover, then almost immediately swung back to the right as it trailed through the points on the goods loop at about five times the speed limit. It was too much for the engine and the track. The left hand rails of the goods loop burst away and the engine derailed to the left, ploughing into the soft ground alongside the track on top of the embankment.

Still moving forward, the engine rolled to the left down the bank and overturned into the field. The leading coach overtook the engine and simply overturned on the earth; it wasn't badly damaged. But the following four coaches were wrecked as they toppled on top of each other, the body of the fourth coach separating altogether from its underframe. The rear five coaches were little damaged and stayed in line and upright. But the damage to the second, third, fourth and fifth coaches was such that 11 passengers were killed and 157 were

side of the smokebox – a feature unknown on GWR engines. Add the fact that GWR signals were sited to be seen best from the right hand side of the engine, and it is clear that driving the Britannias on the WR called for extra care.

The 8.30am Treherbert – Paddington train was due to leave Cardiff at 9.53am but actually left at 10.00am, having already lost a few minutes. The Cardiff based driver had driven Britannia Pacifics to London on a couple of occasions, and though he didn't drive on the Paddington route every day he knew the line. The engine was fitted with the GWR type of automatic train control, today called the automatic warning system (AWS).

At Lliswerry the AWS caution siren sounded on the engine because the distant signal was at caution, as the train was to be switched through the goods loop – which it negotiated at the correct low speed. After stops at Gloucester and Swindon the train was still 10 minutes late as it slowed for

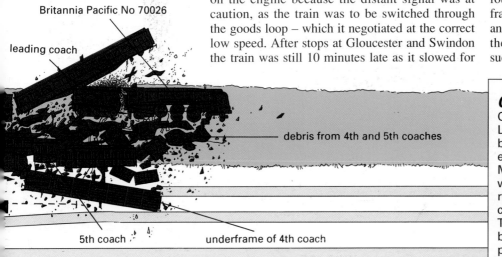

Britannia Pacific No 70026

leading coach

debris from 4th and 5th coaches

5th coach

underframe of 4th coach

> ### *Crossover calamity*
> One Sunday in 1955 a South Wales to London passenger excursion train, headed by a Britannia Pacific, was diverted by engineering works on to a goods loop at Milton, near Didcot. The crossover points were sharply curved, with a 10mph speed restriction, but the train entered the crossover at around five times this speed. The engine derailed and rolled down the bank, taking five coaches with it. Eleven passengers were killed and 157 injured. The driver was blamed for the accident.

→ to Didcot →

▲The fifth coach of the train, a former GWR side corridor third, with a steel panelled body on timber framing, lies on its side. Beyond is the sixth, a former LMS coach converted to a cafeteria car. This part of the train over-ran the engine and front four coaches which lay behind the trees.

injured, 62 of them so badly that they had to be hospitalized. What had gone wrong, and why hadn't the AWS warning alerted the driver to the Milton distant signal at caution?

This was the puzzle facing the inspecting officer, Brigadier C A Langley. The line was equipped with AWS ramps at distant signals, so that when the shoe of the engine AWS equipment was lifted by the ramp, a caution indication sounded in the cab if no electric current passed from the ramp into the engine equipment. And with the Milton distant signal at caution the ramp was not electrified. The engine had AWS equipment, and the driver and fireman, who both survived the accident, told the inquiry that the AWS had been working correctly earlier on the journey, but that it must have failed at Milton.

So why was the caution horn not heard by the crew? More to the point, why did the driver not see the distant signal at caution, the main to goods loop home signal at clear, and the main line home signal at danger?

The driver's view

The driver said that as the train approached Milton distant signal he saw the fireman having trouble putting on the exhaust steam injector to get water into the boiler. He didn't see the distant signal, didn't hear the AWS siren, and didn't acknowledge the warning. He was still concerned about the injector as the train approached the home signal, and didn't see that signal either. He added that it wasn't easy to see the Milton signals from the left hand side of a Britannia cab. He had got grit in his eye before when he leaned out, and normally his fireman would look out, but on the excursion train his fireman was having trouble with the injector.

The fireman had acknowledged the AWS warning earlier on the journey, but denied doing so at Milton. The guard knew of the diversion and was waiting for the train to slow down, but the train

derailed before he could do anything. He had been reluctant to apply the brake earlier.

After the accident the engine AWS apparatus was tested and found to be in working order, although dirt and congealed oil had prevented the caution horn from sounding properly. But if not acknowledged, the brakes should have applied automatically.

Brigadier Langley concluded that the AWS was working correctly, and that the driver must have operated the acknowledgement handle without realizing he had done so. Either that or the handle was operated by the fireman, as earlier on the journey, even though firemen weren't permitted to touch the AWS. Had the large ejector remained on to release the brake after the train slowed down for the Wantage Road speed restriction it would have counteracted the AWS brake application, but the siren should have been heard.

The inspecting officer blamed the driver for the accident, for not properly looking out for signals, and so failing to see the Milton distant signal at caution, even though he had received a copy of the weekly notice listing all engineering work, speed restrictions and diversions. He also criticized the district signalling inspector, for not having a handsignalman at the home signal to instruct drivers to proceed on to the goods loop in accordance with the rules; and the guard, for not applying the emergency brake when he realized the train wasn't slowing down.

Brigadier Langley was also critical of the lookout from the Britannia Pacifics, with the driver on the left trying to see signals sited for right hand drive GWR engines. The Milton signals were partly obscured from the left side by the smoke deflector and handrails alongside the large boiler. But he put the brunt of the blame for the accident on the driver, for failing in his prime duty of looking out for signals.

Sutton Coldfield 1955

**Diverted on to a secondary route while track
was being renewed, an express train approached a 30mph
restriction on a sharp curve at Sutton Coldfield doing nearly
twice the permitted speed. The engine overturned and
17 people died in the wreckage.**

Sutton Coldfield lies north of Birmingham on the Lichfield line, which is used today for local commuter services. The line continues north-eastwards as far as Wichnor Junction, where it joins the former Midland Railway main line from Derby which reaches Birmingham via Tamworth and Castle Bromwich. As a through passenger route it was often used when the main line was obstructed for repairs or renewals. The line was never intended for fast running and included steep gradients with long lengths of 1 in 100 and curves with speed limits between 20 and 50mph.

After leaving Lichfield City station for Birmingham, trains were – and still are – faced with almost seven miles of climbing at 1 in 100, apart from a short dip near Shenstone, before reaching a summit near Four Oaks. Then came two miles of falling gradients, also at 1 in 100, but with a sharp right-hand curve of 660yd radius which demanded a speed restriction of 40mph. At the end was a tunnel 171yd long, leading into Sutton Coldfield station.

Here the gradient changed again to a climb, but, on emerging from the tunnel, the curve became left-handed through the station, much sharper at 330yd radius and with a speed limit of 30mph. It was of little consequence to stopping trains but one to be taken with great care by those running through non-stop.

Line blocked

On the afternoon of Sunday 23 January 1955, the main line through Tamworth was blocked by track renewals so trains between Derby and Birmingham were being diverted via Lichfield and Sutton Coldfield.

The 12.15pm express from York to Bristol, a ten coach corridor train, was hauled by LMS Class 5 4-6-0 No 45274 and had arrived at Derby 30 minutes late at 3.09pm. Time was saved on sta-

▼The overturned 4-6-0 heading the diverted York to Bristol express came to rest straddling the down platform and down running line. Such was the force of the impact that the wreckage to its right is actually two coaches, an ex LMS corridor third and corridor brake third.

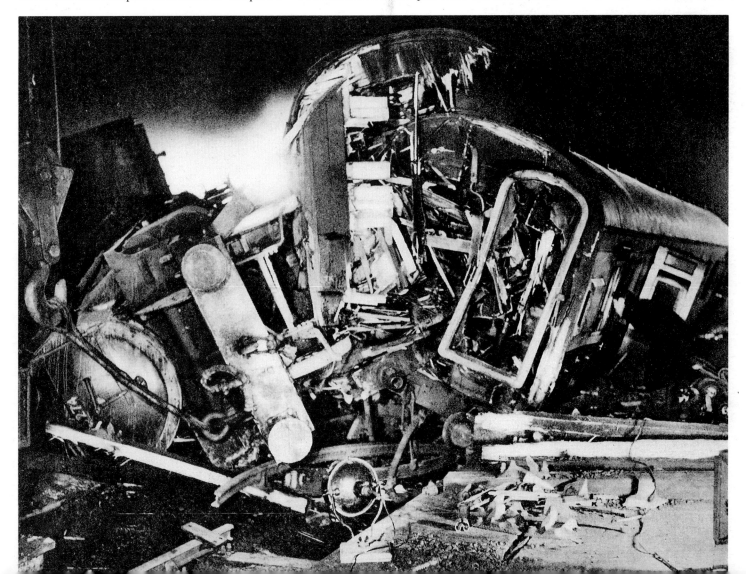

As the express approached the tunnel before Sutton Coldfield, the guard became concerned, knowing that at the other end was the sharp left-hand curve with its 30mph restriction. At the time he estimated they were travelling at between 55 and 60mph. He momentarily applied the vacuum brake, not long enough to reduce speed, but more in the hope of attracting the driver's attention.

The train swept into the tunnel at nearly 60mph. As it emerged into the station, the locomotive lurched violently round the curve, derailed, and overturned. The first five coaches spreadeagled into a pile behind and alongside – the first three were badly damaged while the fourth and fifth were totally wrecked. The first coach was turned round completely as the rest of the train pushed it past the engine. Of the remaining five coaches, four were derailed and slightly damaged although the coach bodies remained intact.

The train was crowded, with 300 passengers. Twelve died immediately and two more later. The conductor driver and the fireman were also killed as was another driver travelling on the train who

▲The damage to No 45274 bears dumb witness to the fact that the train was travelling far too fast as it shot out from Sutton Coldfield Tunnel. The right hand locomotive footstep was found 60yd further back towards Lichfield, suggesting that the locomotive slid on its side for that distance.

tion work and it was away again at 3.13pm, just 13 minutes late and with a Gloucester crew having taken over.

The driver was a main line man who normally worked the Tamworth route, but didn't know the line through Sutton Coldfield. He therefore asked for a conductor driver – one who knew the diversionary road – to accompany him. This extra driver joined the engine at Burton-on-Trent and took over the controls with the regular man standing behind him. At Lichfield, however, the regular driver left the engine to travel in the leading coach as far as Birmingham. The conductor driver was left to drive the engine on his own, accompanied only by the fireman.

On departing Lichfield he at once attacked the climb towards Four Oaks. Having crested the summit, however, the regulator was still open on the falling gradient and the speed of the train continued to rise above the 40mph restriction on the right-handed curve.

Exceeding the limit

The local line from Lichfield to Birmingham was often used on Sundays as a diversionary route for trains running from Derby to Birmingham.

The Gloucester-based driver who had taken over a late running ten-coach York to Bristol express at Derby did not know the local route through Sutton Coldfield; so he asked for a conductor driver with route knowledge to travel on the footplate with him.

The booked driver left the engine in the charge of the conductor driver and went to sit in the train.

As the train sped downhill towards Sutton Coldfield the worried guard applied the brake briefly to warn the conductor driver of the sharp curve through the station, but the train took it far too fast and overturned in the station.

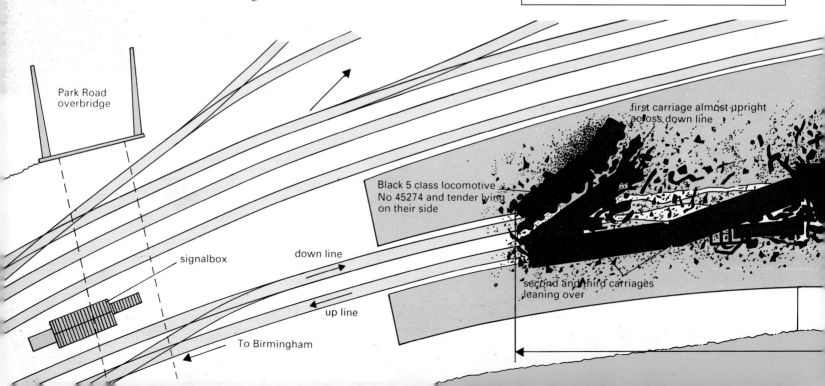

Park Road overbridge

signalbox

down line

up line

To Birmingham

Black 5 class locomotive No 45274 and tender lying on their side

first carriage almost upright across down line

second and third carriages leaning over

died later. However, the regular driver, travelling in the badly damaged leading coach, escaped with his life, although he was injured and severely shocked.

The inquiry

How could a conductor driver, with so many landmarks to go by, ignore a severe and well-known speed restriction? After all, he was only there because of his local knowledge of the line, so the exit from Sutton Coldfield Tunnel into a sharp curve with a permanent 30mph speed limit must have been familiar to him. Although it was midwinter it was still daylight when the accident occurred at 4.13pm, so he couldn't have lost his bearings. The inquiry, which was chaired by the chief inspecting officer of railways, Lieutenant Colonel G R S Wilson, set out to answer these and other questions.

The whole basis for a driver taking a train along a particular section of line is his knowledge of the route – road knowledge, as it is called. Before a driver can drive unaccompanied, he must know the line intimately; every curve, gradient, speed limit and, of course, every signal. He must know where the stations are, and the signalboxes, indeed everything to make the journey safe.

Until recent years, new drivers learned the road by travelling with another driver on the locomotive. When he felt he knew the line he signed the route card to say that he was able to drive trains along that section. There was no examination of his knowledge. The driver simply assured his foreman that he knew the line and signed for it. After that he could be rostered to drive on that line. Today route training is much more formal.

On that Sunday the driver of the York to Bristol express didn't know the line through Sutton Coldfield, so he asked for a driver who did know the line to conduct him. The rules for such an event were quite clear. If the conductor driver was familiar with the type of locomotive then he would take over the controls and drive. If not, then the booked driver would drive and the conductor driver would stand behind him and tell him where the

signals were and when to slow down or speed up.

When the conductor driver joined No 45274 at Burton, he took over the controls while the booked driver stood behind him. But No 45274 was riding very roughly and the booked driver had difficulty standing because of a pain in his leg caused by an injury two years earlier. When the train reached Lichfield he went back to ride in the first coach leaving the conductor driver in sole charge. This was against the rules since the booked driver should have remained on the footplate.

The conductor driver had confirmed his knowledge of the route through Sutton Coldfield only six days before when he re-signed the route card for the line. He was based at Burton-on-Trent and regularly drove local passenger and freight trains over the route. He hadn't driven many expresses on it, however, the last occasion having been the previous July. Nor did he drive Class 5 4-6-0s very often, but the controls were similar to those on the 2-6-4 tank engines normally used for stopping passenger trains.

▼**Railwaymen worked grimly throughout the following day clearing the wreckage. The inspecting officer found that there was a kink in the track but put the accident down mainly to the excessive speed of the train.**

Speed signs
Sutton Coldfield brought the widespread introduction throughout BR of the LNER style cut-out figures for speed restriction marking. However, with modernization and the higher speeds of the 1960s and '70s, even these were found to be inadequate.

After the 1974 Morpeth accident, illuminated signs at braking distance with AWS (automatic warning system) magnets were adopted in some locations. But after further high speed derailments, again at Morpeth (southbound – not covered after the 1974 accident by these improvements), and at Paddington, the guidelines for their provision were widened.

Today, most restrictions are marked either by floodlit signs and AWS, or by signs alone, both at braking distance and at the start of the restriction.

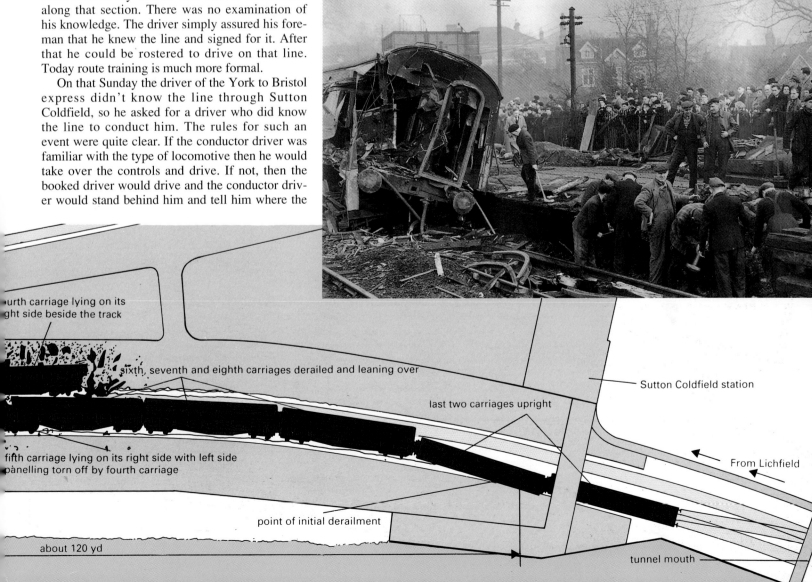

urth carriage lying on its ght side beside the track

sixth, seventh and eighth carriages derailed and leaning over

last two carriages upright

Sutton Coldfield station

fifth carriage lying on its right side with left side panelling torn off by fourth carriage

From Lichfield

point of initial derailment

about 120 yd

tunnel mouth

▲The guard of the ill fated express had put the brakes on briefly to warn the driver that the train was going too fast but did not want to offend him by putting them on fully. But the driver did not take the hint, with fatal results.

A near miss

Immediately after the derailment, the ticket collector and a fireman travelling to another duty pulled themselves from the wreckage. Both realized that another express, the 1.20pm Bristol – York, was due to pass the other way at any moment.

Being a Sunday the station was closed, as was the signalbox. All signals for the two running lines had been left in the clear position. The two men raced to the box and fortunately found the door unlocked. They quickly put the signal levers back to danger and the fireman, despite shock and injuries (he had been travelling with the other driver who died later) grabbed a handful of detonators and ran down the line in the Birmingham direction. He managed to put them on the rails at the approach to the home signal.

Fortunately, the driver of the express had seen the distant signal at caution and was coming to a stop anyway. It had been a near thing and the two men had certainly prevented a collision between the second train and the wreck of the first.

The conductor driver was known to work trains a little harder than other men and was always keen to regain lost time. The York – Bristol express was 15 minutes late leaving Lichfield and had already picked up some of the lost time.

Test trips after the accident suggested that No 45274 was being worked hard and may well have touched 60mph on the falling gradient from Four Oaks towards Sutton Coldfield as it entered the tunnel. There was no brake application although speed may have been reduced slightly as the gradient changed to a climb on emerging from the tunnel into the station.

Lieutenant Colonel Wilson concluded that the train was travelling at between 55 and 60mph as it swung into the sharp curve. The first sign of derailment was on the first length of rail beyond a trailing crossover immediately after the end of the tunnel.

After the accident, a detailed examination of No 45274 showed nothing that would have distracted or disabled the driver and fireman. There had been no blow-back of hot gases through the firebox door, the water gauge glasses were intact and no pipes were broken which would have caused jets of steam and boiling water to escape. The brakes on the locomotive and train were found to be in good working order.

Detailed measurements on the track, though, showed that the nominal 330yd radius left-hand curve as the line emerged from the tunnel was not even. It tightened to 180yd radius over a distance of 26ft from the end of the tunnel (where it was 440yd), before opening out to 330yd over the next 30ft or so, thus forming an 'elbow'.

An extraordinary lapse

Lieutenant Colonel Wilson concluded that the conductor driver had not simply misjudged the speed approaching Sutton Coldfield, but had made no attempt to slow down for the severe speed restriction. 'It is difficult to explain this extraordinary lapse on the part of a driver with such a long record of trustworthy service and who had an intimate knowledge of all the characteristics of the route', he commented. One possible explanation was that he was intent on regaining time and he simply forgot the speed restriction, which required no special action for a stopping train.

The Gloucester driver was criticized for leaving the engine and riding in the first coach. He claimed that the rough riding caused him leg pains but the inspecting officer didn't accept his excuse and said he should have stayed on the engine.

The report was mildly critical of the guard. Having become concerned at the speed, and having briefly operated his brake, he should have had the courage to apply it fully, even though he was anxious not to take control out of the driver's hands. As for the derailment itself, Lieutenant Colonel Wilson felt that it would have occurred even without the elbow on the curve.

The speed restriction was not marked on the lineside in any way. Restrictions were listed in the operating booklets for the area and drivers were expected to know them off by heart as part of learning the road. Only the LNER had a policy of marking speed restrictions using cut-out signs which showed the speed in figures near the start of the restriction. The GWR also marked a few special restrictions with signs, but, generally, the LMS left its permanent restrictions unmarked.

Lieutenant Colonel Wilson said that the system of relying on route knowledge had worked well, with few accidents attributed to excessive speed. Before Sutton Coldfield, the previous one was 24 years before at Carlisle. But with higher speeds being introduced due to dieselization and more intensive use of locomotives, with drivers needed to work over more routes, he felt that memory alone was probably not enough. He recommended a review of marking speed limits and that the LNER system should be considered, with possibly even more elaborate equipment such as speed recorders on trains.

Recommendations

Lieutenant Colonel Wilson made the following recommendations:
● The provision of lineside speed restriction signs to remind drivers of permanent speed limits
● The provision of speed recorders rather than simple speedometers on trains
● The relaying of the curve through Sutton Coldfield to eliminate the 'elbow'
● The elimination or modification of the timing at Sutton Coldfield for diverted expresses as it was too tight for practical purposes and may have led the conductor driver to drive too hard

Norton Fitzwarren 1940

A combination of stressful wartime conditions and the anomalous siting of the signals between Taunton and Norton Fitzwarren led to the driver of the 9.50pm Paddington – Penzance train mistaking his position – a fatal error that led to the deaths of 27 people.

The original main line of the Great Western Railway (GWR) from Paddington to Bristol continued to Bridgwater, Taunton and Exeter on its way to the South West. A glance at a map shows that this route is very indirect. In July 1906, passenger trains began to use a more direct route from Reading, through Westbury to Taunton, meeting the old line at Cogload Junction. However, by then, the old route from Bristol was carrying trains from the North and Midlands, so both flows of traffic used one double track line, west through Taunton, to Exeter and beyond. Taunton was also a junction for the branch to Chard, and the next station to the west, Norton Fitzwarren, was the junction for branches to Minehead and Barnstaple.

On summer Saturdays in the 1920s and '30s the train service was intense, with holiday expresses all competing for a path through Taunton. A few left the main line at Norton Fitzwarren towards Minehead and Barnstaple, but this meant turning off to the right across the up line, and often trains on the down line had to stop to let an up train pass before they could reach the branches, delaying the following down trains.

Signalling arrangements

In the early 1930s, the GWR undertook to widen the section between Cogload Junction and Norton Fitzwarren to four tracks. This would give much more flexibility and, if trains were waiting on the down main to turn on to the branches, other trains heading for Exeter could be signalled along the down relief line and back on to the down main line ahead of the standing train.

The area continued to be signalled from local signalboxes with lower quadrant semaphore signals. GWR engines were laid out for the driver to

▼Having been signalled to continue further than usual along the relief line from Taunton in order to allow the newspaper to run through on the main line, the driver of the sleeping-car train mistook his position and ploughed off the end of the relief line into grass and soft ground. This land was bounded by a ditch to the left, just inside the post-and-wire fence separating the railway from the surrounding fields. On the left of the photograph can be seen a set of lower quadrant signals for the up main line.

be on the right (unlike most other railways). The signals were on the left of the line, placed so as to be seen from the right-hand side of an egine, taking into account the fact that a signal on the left of the line would become obscured from the driver by the boiler as his engine approached.

Some signals – because of obstructions – were on the right of the line, or bracketed out from the left, to be seen from the right. This was so at Taunton, where the down relief line signals at the Exeter end of the down relief platform were on a bracket with its supporting post to the left of the track, the bracket itself extending over the track. Thus both sets of signals – the left-hand mast with those for a train continuing on the down relief line, and the right-hand signal for a train crossing from the down relief to the down main – could be seen from the right-hand side of the cab.

A few yards on from the bracket signal, on the rifht of the down main line, was the down main signal; all these signals were controlled by Taunton Station West signalbox. Underneath the stop arms were the distant arms for Taunton West Junction signalbox. At that box, the home signals for the relief and main lines were carried on a gantry above and to the right of the line. But at Silk Mill Crossing, 1¼ miles on, the signals were on individual posts, to the left in the case of the down relief signals, while those for the down main line were on the right-hand side of the down main line. Nearly ¾ mile on, at Norton Fitzwarren, the relief and main tracks spread out either side of an island platform. At the Exeter end of the platform was a crossover from the down relief to the down main line giving trains on the relief line access to the branches going off to the right, and a further crossover from the relef to the main line beyond the branch connections. This was the end of the

relief line; immediately beyond the second crossover the rails stopped.

A dangerously distracted driver

In the early hours of 4 November 1940, the heavily loaded 9.50pm sleeping-car train from Paddington to Penzance was approaching Taunton at around 3.30am, just over an hour late. The driver had much on his mind, both in driving a train in blackout conditions, and in coping with the possibility of air attacks on the railways; his own house had recently been damaged by bombs. As was normal, the train was switched to the down relief platform at Taunton to make its booked stop. The train was routed via Bristol, and had already been

▲ In the right foreground is the overturned engine No 6028 *King George VI*. This locomotive was hauling 13 coaches, all well filled, largely with service personnel. Several soldiers can be seen in this photograph, and of the 26 people killed, 13 were in the navy.

Seconds from a double disaster

The driver of the 9.50pm Paddington – Penzance train misread the signals leaving Taunton, looking at those to the right of his train, which were showing clear for the 12.50am Paddington – Penzance newspaper train on the down main line. The signals he should have been looking for were mostly on his left. Only when the 12.50 newspaper train overtook him on the right did he realize his mistake, but by then it was too late. The automatic train control did not help. The 9.50's driver must have subconsciously cancelled a warning, having accepted the wrong signal at green. The 12.50 escaped a collision with the wreckage of the 9.50 by just a few seconds.

◄ To Penzance ◄

King class 4-6-0 hauling newspaper train

slight embankment

fourth carriage thrown across down main line

front two coaches ran past the engine

No 6028 *King George VI* overturned to the left

on the journey for nearly six hours. At the head was King class 4-6-0 No 6028 *King George VI*, and the train had 13 coaches.

Normally, once the right away had been given from Taunton, the train took the crossover from the down relief back on to the down main, but not this morning. Past Cogload Junction, five miles east of Taunton, the 12.50am Paddington – Penzance newspaper train of five vans hauled by a King class 4-6-0, was just ahead of its booked time. The Taunton West signalman decided to let it run through on the main line, and to send the passenger train forward on the down relief to Norton Fitzwarren. By the time it got there, the 12.50 should have cleared the section beyond.

Reading the wrong signals

The 9.50 train left Taunton on the down relief line, but in the darkness, and although the signals told the driver which way the train was routed, he somehow thought he had gone over the crossover to the down main, and looked for the signals to the right. Just before he left Taunton, the signals on the down main had been cleared to beyond Norton Fitzwarren for the newspaper train. So the 9.50's driver was looking at the clear signals for the 12.50 train. From Silk Mill the signals for the 9.50 were on the left. At Silk Mill was the distant signal for Norton Fitzwarren. It was at caution for the relief line, and the 9.50 duly picked up a caution 'horn' on the cab automatic train control. But its driver, seeing a clear distant signal to his right, thought it was a false alarm, and cancelled the warning.

As the 9.50 approached Norton Fitzwarren at about 45mph, the driver became confused, seeing that the main line signals were not where they should be if he was on the main line. The down relief line home signal was at danger, but cleared as the 9.50 approached, the signalman intending to stop it at the next signal. But at the same moment, another engine was fast coming up behind, on the right of the 9.50, and soon the King Class 4-6-0 on the newspaper train was level with the 9.50's driver, and going ahead in the darkness at nearly 60mph. The 9.50's driver now realized his mistake, but had only 350yd of track left.

No 6028 ran over the end of the rails, ploughed into the soft ground and overturned, killing the fireman. The front six coaches piled up, and with about 900 passengers on board (mainly service personnel), casualties were high – 26 were killed and 56 badly hurt.

The newspaper train had a lucky escape: its back coach had just passed as the 9.50 was derailed. A broken rivet from the leading bogie of No 6028 shot through a window into the guard's compartment, and the guard stopped the train at the next signalbox to examine the damage. But in the darkness the crew could see little, and stopped again at Wellington four miles on to have a better look. Only then were they told of the accident to the 9.50. When the train arrived at Penzance, a few hours later, daylight showed scrape marks on the left side of the last coach of the newspaper train, probably as the wreckage from the 9.50 had spread towards the down main line.

Only now did those involved realize how close the 12.50 train had been to disaster. If it had been seconds later, wreckage from the 9.50 would have either been thrown across the down main line right in its path – which would have brought the King class 4-6-0 crashing through the remaining coaches of the 9.50 – or hit it sidelong, which would inevitably have derailed it. Equally, if the 9.50 had accelerated just a little quicker, the 12.50 would have been involved.

The driver takes the blame

The two inspecting officers thought the evidence of the 9.50's driver at the subsequent inquiry was inconsistent, both in thinking he had received an Automatic Train Control warning on leaving Taunton and in saying he did not receive a caution at Norton Fitzwaren distant signal.

The inspecting officers felt there had been an unaccountable lapse on the part of the 9.50's driver, but the strain of wartime conditions undoubtedly played a part. The report was critical of the erratic siting of the signals; had they been consistent, the 9.50's driver might have realized his mistake earlier.

Recommendations

The report of the inquiry blamed the driver of the 9.50 for the accident, but spared him excessive criticism because of the stress of driving in war conditions. The inspecting officer rejected calls to give drivers verbal advice when switched to a different line in four-track areas, saying that it was all too common, and the signals were there for that very purpose.

But the report did criticize the variation in the positioning of the signals between Taunton and Norton Fitzwarren on the down relief line, and suggested that positioning should be standardized. He made little comment on the driver's right-hand position on GWR locomotives, but in later years BR standardized left-hand drive on new locomotives.

Key to trains

■ 9.50pm Paddington – Penzance passenger train

■ 12.50am Paddington – Penzance newspaper train

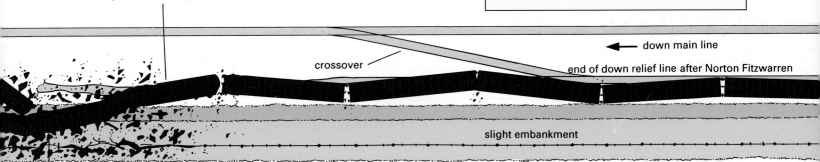

fifth carriage telescoped against third

To London →

down main line

crossover

end of down relief line after Norton Fitzwarren

slight embankment

third carriage telescoped against tender

Harrow 1952

**One of the most perplexing and tragic
of all rail crashes left engines and coaches from
three trains piled up in a mass of twisted metal and 112
people dead. Investigations soon revealed what
happened but no one knows why – even today.**

October 8, 1952. A typical autumn morning – cold, with mist and fog lying over the countryside bordering the north-west approaches to suburban London.

South of Watford and neighbouring Bushey was a green belt of fields and woodland interspersed with newly developing housing estates before the outskirts of Harow were reached. After that it was houses and industry almost all the way for the 11 miles to London Euston.

On that October morning the mist and fog were delaying trains and fog signalling procedures were in operation. As the sun rose it was burning off much of the mist and normal signalling was resumed as soon as visibility had improved. But the poor weather was to play a major part in the tragedy that unfolded and leave forever unanswered the question, 'Why did it happen?'

Collision course

Just before 8am the Harrow signalman accepted the overnight 10.20pm train from Glasgow. Once

▼In the aftermath of the Harrow crash, rescuers surround the wreckage. The force of the first collision, combinded with the effects of the second, meant that the toll of dead and injured was high. Fire hoses snake over the track and platforms while ranks of stretchers (top left) wait to carry away the victims.

it was accepted by North Wembley, further up the line, the signalman cleared all his fast line signals for it.

A few minutes later he accepted the 7.31 suburban train from Tring on the slow line from the signalman at Hatch End. By what was to turn into a strange quirk of fate, this train carried many office workers from the railway's own departments at Euston station.

At about this time the fog had thinned sufficiently for the Harrow signalman to resume normal block working. Once the Glagow train had passed Harrow at 8.11, he replaced his fast line signals to danger and the distant to caution and could accept the following train, the 8.15pm overnight sleeper from Perth, on the fast line.

The Perth train had left Crewe 32 minutes late and had lost further time. The Harrow signalman decided to run the 7.31am from Tring in front of it and set the crossover for the 7.31 train to cross from the up slow to the up fast line, which it was booked to do, and make its scheduled stop at the fast line platform.

The 7.31 train was due at 8.11 but was running a few minutes late and arrived in the platform at about 8.17. It was a nine coach train hauled by a 2-6-4 tank engine. Normally the outer suburban

Fog signalling

During fog, special train signalling arrangements were brought into use. Each signalbox had a fogging point and at Harrow this marker was the up slow line home signal 300yd from the signalbox.

If the signalman could no longer see this he introduced fog working. This usually meant double block working – two block sections had to be free ahead of the train before the signals could be cleared. At certain signals fog signalmen used hand signalling lamps or flags, and detonators were sometimes placed on the rails.

During the 1930s the LMS introduced colour light distant signals in semaphore signalled areas because the intense beam can penetrate fog. These signals did not have fog signalmen during poor visibility. Distant signals acted as a warning of the indications given by the stop signals on the same line at the next signalbox ahead.

When the stop signals were at danger – meaning stop – the distant signal showed caution with a yellow light. This gave a train approaching at speed time to slow down after passing the distant signal, ready to stop at the danger signal ahead.

▶Looking from the wreckage of the footbridge above platforms 4 and 5 gives a view of Harrow No 1 signalbox. The crossovers which transferred the local Tring train on to the up fast line. so that it could make its scheduled stop at the up fast platform before the run into Euston, can also be seen.

trains were formed of seven coaches with the end coaches having guard's compartments, but as usual this train had two extra third class coaches, both old and timber bodied, behind the guard's van. Because of the large number of passengers waiting to board the already well loaded train, the guard allowed some to stand in the guard's van.

As he watched the loading and was getting ready to give the right away to his driver, the 7.31's guard suddenly became aware of an express approaching behind him at high speed on his line.

Danger signals

The Perth sleeper, hauled by one of the most powerful locomotives in the country, had passed the two home signals at danger and slammed into the back of the standing 7.31 train. The force of the impact punched a two-and-a-half inch depression into the track at the collision point and shattered the back three coaches of the 7.31. The sleeper's engine, Princess Coronation (Duchess) class No 46242 *City of Glasgow*, veered to its right and almost immediately there was a second collision.

While the up trains were approaching Harrow,

Build up to disaster

Just before 8.20am, the Perth-Euston express (red) smashed into the late running 7.31 Tring-Euston train (blue), standing on the up fast line at platform 4. The express had passed two stop signals and made a full brake application only seconds before the crash.

The Perth train's locomotive No 46242 *City of Glasgow* turned to its right directly into the path of the 8am Euston-Liverpool express which had already passed the signals protecting the platforms and so could not avoid the debris. A serious accident suddenly became a terrible tragedy.

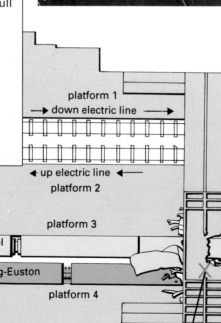

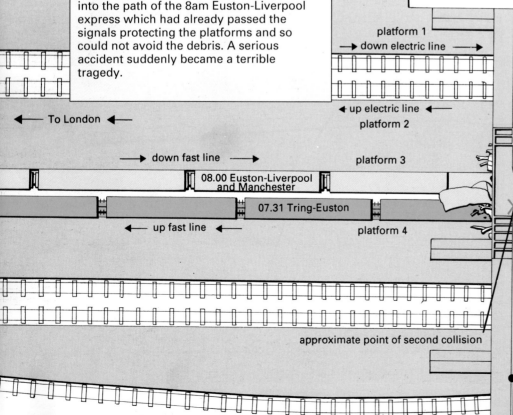

No 46202 *Princess Anne*

tender

platform 1
→ down electric line →

← up electric line ←
platform 2

← To London ←

→ down fast line →

platform 3

08.00 Euston-Liverpool and Manchester

07.31 Tring-Euston

← up fast line ←

platform 4

approximate point of second collision

No 46242 *City of Glasgow* buried beneath debris

footbridge

◀ No 46202 *Princess Anne* lies on its side with the first three carriages of the Euston-Liverpool express piled up behind it. In the background, the stopped clock on the footbridge lift tower poignantly records the time, 8.20, when the bridge was almost demolished.

the signalman had accepted from North Wembley the 8am express from Euston to Liverpool and Manchester. This was hauled by two locomotives, Jubilee class 4-6-0 No 45637 *Windward Isles* piloting 4-6-2 No 46202 *Princess Anne*.

As the first collision occurred these two locomotives with their 15 coach train were approaching Harrow from the south at nearly 60mph and had passed the signal protecting the platforms.

Horrified onlookers dived for cover as *Windward Isles* hit *City of Glasgow* almost head on, reared up over it, went through the station footbridge followed by *Princess Anne*, and over-

turned across the down fast platform on to the up local electric line. Coaches from three trains were now piled up in a twisted mass of metal and smashed woodwork.

Rescue work

Rescue services, including a medical team from the US forces based near by, were quickly on the scene. But their job was horrific. Inevitably, casualties were high. In all, 112 people were killed, including three of the enginemen. Over 150 people were injured, more than 80 seriously.

Despite the number of fatalities, rescuers were

Failing to stop

The driver of the Perth-London express had three signals set against him but failed to take any action. The error cost the lives of 112 people.

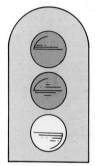

The up distant signal showed a yellow light meaning caution. The driver should have begun slowing down 2102 yards before the first impact.

At 628 and 188 yards before the impact, the up fast outer home and inner home semaphores were set at stop. But the driver didn't respond until making a full brake application just yards before he was killed.

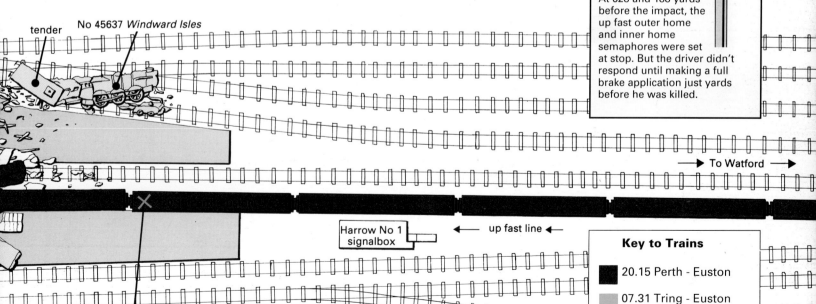

tender

No 45637 *Windward Isles*

→ To Watford →

Harrow No 1 signalbox

← up fast line ←

approximate point of first collision

N

Key to Trains

■ 20.15 Perth - Euston

▨ 07.31 Tring - Euston

▢ 0800 Euston - Liverpool and Manchester

thankful that none of the engines or carriages had caught light. Had they done so, the death toll would have been far higher. It was fortunate that an electric train was not involved as well, but it was stopped short of the wreckage of the two locomotives of the Liverpool/Manchester train.

In terms of casualties, Harrow was one of the worst railway accidents in Britain. Some of the casualties were not on the trains – people were caught walking over the footbridge when girders were swept away, and others were waiting on the up electric line platform shared with the down fast line.

A roll call of railway offices at Euston showed that some of the departments there lost their entire staff, for no fewer than 64 of those killed were in the 7.31 from Tring which carried many railway personnel.

The wreckage at Harrow took several days to clear away. The slow lines were reopened on October 9 but the fast lines remained closed until October 12.

What went wrong

How did such a catastrophe happen? We shall never really know. It was proved that the Perth express failed to slow down and stop at the Harrow signals after passing the distant signal showing the caution yellow light. But because the driver and firemen were killed, it was impossible to establish why they hadn't stopped.

Had the driver missed the distant signal? The morning sun was just breaking through at an angle which would have been in his eyes as he searched for the signal in the mist. Was the crew asleep, or was there some calamity in the cab of *City of Glasgow*?

There was no evidence of any of these things. all that's known is that right at the last minute the driver made a full brake application. But by then it was too late.

Lucky escape

The bookstall manager on platform 3 was one of the lucky ones on that tragic day. Just as the 7.31 from Tring ran into the up platform a newspaper blew off the counter on to the platform. The manager went out to retrieve it, but as he picked the paper up he saw the up Perth train hit the back of the 7.31.

The man was rooted to the spot as the locomotive rose up and came towards him, followed by a twisting mass of steel and splintered wood as the coaches broke up.

Seconds later the two locomotives of the Euston-Liverpool/Manchester express passed him and rammed the engine of the Perth train, adding to the huge pile of wreckage. Some of the pieces even fell against the door of the bookstall.

Had he not gone to pick up the newspaper, the manager would have been caught by the debris. As it was, he was uninjured as three trains came to rest in a tangled heap with broken glass and smashed carriages all round him.

▲ Just 24 hours after the crash No 45637 *Windward Isles* lurches drunkenly after being righted by a steam crane. Unlike No 46242 *City of Glasgow* which was repaired and continued in service for a decade following the crash, *Windward Isles* and *Princess Anne* were scrapped.

Action taken

The Chief Inspecting Officer of Railways, who chaired the Harrow inquiry, recommended the further development and adoption of what was then called automatic train control (ATC) – today called the automatic warning system (AWS).

The Great Western Railway had started trials with ATC in 1906, and eventually installed the system on most of its principal lines.

ATC consisted of a ramp between the rails, located usually at the approach to distant signals, which engaged a shoe under the locomotive. If the signal was at caution a horn warning sounded in the cab. For a clear signal a bell sounded. If the driver took no action to acknowledge a caution warning, the brakes were applied automatically.

The LMS had installed a similar system, known as the Hudd, but using magnetic links between track and train, on the Tilbury line to Southend. At the time of the Harrow

collision British Railways were conducting trials with a new standard ATC system combining the best features of both the earlier patterns. The design wasn't quite perfected when the Harrow accident occurred.

British Railways was soon able to evolve plans to install ATC – or AWS as it became on all principal routes. But even today, about 40 years on and over 80 years after the first GWR trials, AWS is installed on little more than 60% of the system. Now there are criticisms of AWS on lines with colour light signalling since repetitive cancellation of warnings can lead to drivers unconsciously cancelling a warning of a signal at danger and passing it.

Undergoing trials is a more positive form of control known as automatic train protection (ATP), which prevents a driver from passing a danger signal by actually bringing the train to a complete standstill if the system detects it is necessary.

Weedon 1951

A difference of about 20 thousandths of an inch in the clearances between axleboxes and the guides in which they worked could make for a safe journey or disaster. At Weedon in 1951, it was the lack of that clearance that led to an axlebox jamming, and 15 people being killed.

The 8.20am express from Liverpool Lime Street to Euston on 21 September 1951 was running well, after passing through Rugby. However, it was running 16 minutes late, following signal checks between Liverpool and its first stop at Crewe and further checks between there and Rugby. It was a heavy train of 15 coaches, typical of West Coast main line trains at that time. Like most of the Liverpool – London services it was hauled by one of the Stanier Pacifics. On that morning the engine was Princess class No 46207 *Princess Arthur of Connaught*.

After reaching the summit of rising gradients from Nuneaton, at the London end of Kilsby Tunnel, five miles south of Rugby, the line fell for seven miles through Welton to Weedon on fairly gentle gradients, no steeper than 1 in 350. Robert Stephenson's London & Birmingham line, built in 1837-38, which now forms part of the West Coast route, was well laid out with few gradients steeper than 1 in 330 after the initial climb from Euston to Camden. Nor were there many sharp curves to slow trains, especially steam trains, down.

Approaching Weedon was a left-hand curve, followed by a right-handed curve beyond the station, and then another left-hand curve leading to a straight length for more than a mile. On the straight section is the 492yd (450m) Stowe Hill Tunnel.

Flat-bottomed rail was used in many parts of Europe and widely in other parts of the world. It was only just coming into experimental use in Great Britain. The LMS had laid a section of very heavy flat-bottomed rail weighing 131lb to the yard on the last of the Weedon curves leading to the straight section and ending almost at Stowe Hill Tunnel. Beyond it was almost half a mile of what became standard flat bottom rail weighing 109lb per yd through the tunnel and there then followed conventional 95lb per yd bullhead rail in chairs.

No 46207 entered the curves at Weedon at about 65mph. It was riding well with the regulator just open to give a breath of steam on the falling gradient. It continued like that on to the straight and passed through Stowe Hill Tunnel.

▼An aerial view of the wrecked train. Although in a state of shock, the fireman of the train carried out protection duties. Fortunately, however, the signalman at Heyford signalbox had seen and heard the crash and put all his signals to danger. He was just in time to halt the Royal Scot which was approaching fast on its way from Euston to Glasgow.

Suddenly, the driver felt the engine shaking at the front end. He called across to his fireman that he thought something was wrong with the front bogie and shut the regulator and applied the brake straight away. It was too late. Almost immediately the whole engine was derailed and swerved to the left down a 12ft embankment to come to rest with the tender on its side.

The abrupt derailment of the locomotive, which was brought to a stop from more than 60mph in less than 100yd (91m), caused mayhem to the coaches. The leading coach, a brake third, was still coupled to the tender, but ended up on its side down the bank, while the second was thrown into an adjoining field upside down. The third and fourth were completely wrecked and ended up as a heap across both tracks.

The fifth passed over them and finished up on the bank above the locomotive and was not too badly damaged. The sixth overturned on top of the first and second, the seventh, a kitchen car, was demolished and finished up on top of the third and fourth, while the eighth stopped diagonally across the tracks, but upright. The ninth was partly

thrown down the bank and was leaning, and having been crushed at the front. Behind it the rest of the train had only minor damage, although all but the last two coaches were derailed.

Inevitably there were casualties. The coaches were typical LMS vehicles of the 1930s with steel panels on timber body framing carried on steel underframes. They did not stand a chance of resisting the forces as the train came to a rapid stop and one coach piled into another. The timber body frames broke up, and the steel panels were ripped apart. In some cases the steel underframes were badly distorted.

Seven passengers and one of the dining car staff were killed in the crash and seven more passengers died later in hospital. A further 26 passengers and nine dining car staff were injured and needed hospital treatment.

Lucky escapes

The driver and fireman had lucky escapes. The driver on the left side was buried in coal, but was not seriously hurt, while his fireman clung on to the right of the cab as the engine overturned to the left and was miraculously uninjured.

Despite suffering severe shock, the fireman carried out protection

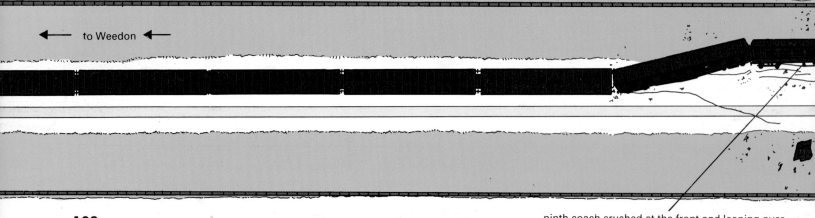

← to Weedon ←

ninth coach crushed at the front and leaning over

▲The coach in the foreground is an example of 'porthole stock'. These carriages got their nickname from the circular toilet windows and were some of the most modern in use in 1951. Nevertheless they had many old fashioned features, such as screw couplings, and stood up poorly in collisions.

◄The force of the derailment is graphically shown by the way that the 159ton 3cwt locomotive has been half buried by the momentum of the train as it derailed and fell down a 12ft embankment. Of the 15 carriages in the train, 13 were derailed, killing 15 and injuring 35 people. Another 25 people suffered minor injuries.

duties and partly running and partly walking got to Heyford signalbox half a mile ahead to warn the signalman who stopped the Royal Scot train.

Rescuers were quickly on the scene. A passing Metropolitan Police car crew had seen the accident and summoned the local police, fire and ambulance services. Army medical services also helped and voluntary organizations provided emergency canteens. Some of the passengers from the wrecked train who did not need medical treatment were taken on board the halted Royal Scot train. It then reversed back to Blisworth to take the branch to Northampton where it stopped to let the London-bound passengers off before continuing on the Northampton – Rugby line. This route also carried passenger trains normally routed on the main line while the wreckage was cleared.

The investigators soon got to work to find out what had happened. Normally in a derailment of this sort, if vandalism can be ruled out, it is likely to be caused by a defect on either the track or the

train, or possibly a combination of both. A close examination was made of the track and it was found that there were marks of a wheel flange riding on top of the right-hand railhead 1597yd (1460m) before the final derailment.

This initial derailment mark stretched for about 37ft (11m) on top of the rail and ran parallel with the edge for about half that distance. There was no groove on the rail suggesting that there was little weight on the wheel, nor were there any marks suggesting severe side thrust.

The mark was just towards the end of the final left-hand curve. This was on the transition towards the straight length on the 131lb rail, as the cant dropped from the average 5½in through the curve to nothing on the straight over a distance of 110yd (100m).

From the driver's evidence, it was clear that the first thing to derail was the leading bogie, but it was obvious that it derailed while still on the curve and had run for about 1200yd (1100m) off the rails before the driver felt the front end shaking as it reached the bullhead rail. There were marks on the rail fastenings on the flat bottom rail sections, and the track with the 131lb rail had been moved out of line by as much as 7in, although this had not been noticed by the driver.

Witnesses in the train had felt rough riding as the train approached Stowe Hill Tunnel, but not through the tunnel itself. The track gauge and alignment were checked on the curve and so too was the cant. Generally speaking the track was found to be in good condition. The right-hand rail was worn which produced gauge widening of around ¼in. On the transition from the curve to the final straight the cross levels, particularly at places with wet soft spots under the sleepers, were found to vary from the designed cant by ¼in in places to as much as ½in in 5yd about 10yd before the point of initial derailment. While these variations needed attention, they were not dangerous in themselves and any train with the springing and

A jammed axlebox

Locomotive No 46207 was on its first trip out after its bogie wheelsets had been swapped round. This was done because the flange on the leading bogie wheels would wear more quickly than those of the trailing wheels. The axleboxes which the front bogie axles ran in moved vertically between the horn slides. When the axles had been swapped round, the fitter at Edge Hill shed had checked the gap, but because he misread his callipers he believed there was enough clearance when there was really too little.

As the locomotive travelled at speed over the superelevated curves near Weedon, the right-hand leading axlebox jammed in the horn guides. This derailed the bogie, and then the whole train, as the bogie struck the join between flat-bottomed and bullhead track.

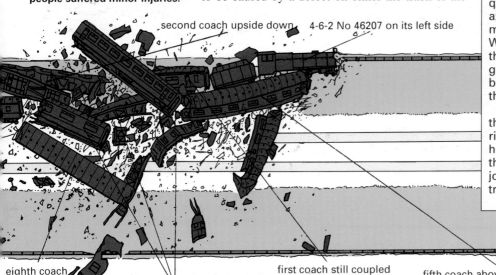

second coach upside down   4-6-2 No 46207 on its left side

eighth coach

wreckage of intermediate coaches

first coach still coupled to the locomotive

to Blisworth and London Euston

fifth coach above locomotive

▲Fortunately a police car was passing when the derailment occurred and was able to summon the emergency services straight away by radio. Soldiers from Weedon barracks nearby were also able to help. The carriages were mostly timber framed, and were smashed as one piled into another.

Transition curves
Although curved track is designed to have an even radius for the location so that speed limits, if needed, can apply right through a curve, the entry and exit to and from a curve is not sudden. If it were, trains would leave the straight and lurch into the curve with severe side thrusts at speed. Normally a transition curve is used between the straight sections and the main circular curve, and between curves in different directions. This is a length of track which begins to curve from the straight very gently, but with the radius decreasing until the circular curve is reached. At the exit from the curve the radius increases and the curve becomes much more gentle until it runs out into the straight beyond. This gives a much smoother ride and prevents a sideways movement. The cant is related to the line speed through the curve.

suspension in good condition could have taken them at full line speed in safety.

As the engine lay on its side and the debris was removed from the wheels, examination confirmed that the front bogie wheels had been the culprits in leaving the track at the initial point of derailment. The flanges had marks where they had struck the track clips and spikes. But no other wheels appeared to have derailed before the break-up of the bullhead track under the engine caused the final catastrophic pile up.

The engine was recovered and given a temporary bogie for it to be towed to Crewe Works for a detailed examination. First it was established that all the springs were in good order so that no wheels were unladen because of a broken spring. Then the front bogie was stripped down and every piece examined in detail.

What went wrong?
The detective work began to shed light on what had happened. The axleboxes of the leading wheels were tight in their horn slides. This is the assembly in the bogie frames between which the axlebox slides up and down, governed by track levels and the weight it is carrying through the springs. The axleboxes must have freedom of movement between the horn guides in order to slide.

Normally the clearance between the axleboxes and horns is about 10 to 17 thousandths of an inch (by comparison, 40 thousandths is approximately 1 millimetre and 20 thousandths is about half a millimetre). But the axleboxes of the leading wheels were actually larger than parts of the horn faces into which they were fitted. The horn faces were worn and varied by up to 25 thousandths, but despite this the axleboxes were minutely larger than the distance between the horn slides into

which they had been fitted.

The engine had run more than 980,000 miles since it was built in 1935 and over 81,000 after the wheels had been reprofiled in May 1950. But during a regular examination in September 1951 it was found that the left-hand leading bogie wheel flange was wearing to a sharp edge near the tip of the flange. During a visit to Liverpool Edge Hill shed on 19 September it was decided to exchange the front and back sets of bogie wheels. This was regular practice since it evened out the wear on wheel flanges and kept the engine in traffic for longer periods between wheel turning.

After the wheel sets were removed it was customary for the fitter to check the distance between the horn slides and compare them with the outside measurements of the axlebox to ensure that they had freedom of movement.

The fitter told the inquiry inspecting officer, Lt Col G R S Wilson, that he had done this. He thought he had clearance in all four horn slides of about 1/64in (16 thousandths). But at one point he said that he had clearance between the *inside* callipers measuring the horn faces, and the *outside* callipers measuring the axlebox slides. This meant that he had reversed the measurements and, rather than having clearance, the axlebox was larger than the distance between the horn slides. Even so, the bogie frame and horns dropped down on to the axleboxes which seemed to have freedom of movement when the bogie was reassembled. But they did not have that vital clearance. After the accident it was found that the left-hand front axlebox was 13 thousandths tight and the right-hand front axlebox was 17 thousandths tight.

The back axleboxes in contrast were very slack with the right-hand no less than 105 thousandths of an inch (2½mm) clear.

Lt Col Wilson was in no doubt about what had happened. As the engine rode round the left-hand curve, the leading right-hand axlebox had at some point risen in the horns and jammed. As the right-hand rail dropped when the cant decreased on the transition to the straight, the wheel-set remained raised. Therefore it could not follow the rail and rode over it, possibly affected by the variations in cant.

Having derailed, the wheels dropped and started to damage the track and broke up the chairs when the bullhead rail was reached, and the general derailment took place. The disaster had been caused by a mere 17 thousandths of an inch too little clearance.

Recommendations
Although placing some blame on the fitter at Edge Hill shed, Lt Col Wilson felt that supervision should have been better in carrying out such precise work in dark and dingy steam running sheds. He also recommended that better methods of measuring axlebox and horn dimensions should be evolved to prevent such minor mistakes, with such disastrous consequences, occurring in the future.

Doncaster 1951

On a March morning in 1951, an up East Coast express was accelerating away from Doncaster at about 20mph (32km/h) over a crossover when eight coaches were derailed. A massive bridge pier lay in the path of the third coach, which wrapped itself around the pier, killing fourteen passengers.

Doncaster has always been a major rail junction, comprising cross-country routes joining and leaving the principal East Coast main line between London and the north, several marshalling yards, carriage sidings, a locomotive depot and large workshops. The track layout was complex, with multi-track running lines and many sets of points and crossovers. Four principal passenger lines existed to the south of the station, the down slow and down main on the west side, and the up main and up slow on the east side.

Bridge Junction

Coming from the up slow platform 4 at Doncaster, there were two routes by which an up train could reach the up main line for the onward journey to the south. Near the platform end was a crossover from the slow to the main line, and about 600yd (550m) further on – at Bridge Junction – was another crossover, forming half of a scissors crossover, that is, with connections both from the slow to main and main to slow lines superimposed. By this point, the route, which was quite straight through the station, had entered a left-hand curve as it passed under Balby Bridge (carrying a principal road junction over the railway).

To provide a smooth passage for express trains running through the curve, the main line was canted by up to 4in (10cm), thus the outer (right-hand) rail was four inches higher than the inner (left-hand) rail, so trains leaned into the curve like motor cyclists taking a bend. However, the scissors crossover tracks from and to the slow line were not canted as their outer rails crossed the left-hand rail of the main line. Instead, after passing through the crossing gap with the left-hand rail of the main line, the right-hand rail of the slow to main crossover rose fairly quickly to meet the right-hand rail of the main line, before the two met at the switch blades. Because of this change in cross levels, in a short distance (most of the cant of about 3in/7.6cm occurring in about 11yd/10m), there was a strict 10mph (16km/h) limit through the crossover.

▼At Balby Bridge at Doncaster on 16 March 1951 the fourth coach of the express is just visible under the bridge, on the left. The photograph also shows the next three coaches derailed, with two of them partly on their sides.

The *Cock o' the North*

On 16 March 1951, the 10.06am up express from Doncaster was at platform 4, on the up slow line. It had just been made up from two other trains, the six-coach 8.45am from Hull to King's Cross, now at the front and, behind, the eight-coach 9.15am York to King's Cross, making 14 coaches in all, with a horse box at the back. It was hauled by a locomotive built in 1934 – one of the notable Gresley express engines of the 2-8-2 type, partly streamlined, and carrying the name *Cock o' the North*. In its youth, its ultra-modern appearance made it almost as famous as the Gresley Pacific *Flying Scotsman*. However, by 1951 it had lost all its glamour, for in 1943 – after Gresley's death – it and its few sisters had been rebuilt as Pacifics, rather ungainly in appearance, and now classed as A2/2, with No 60501, as it had become, still carrying its original name.

At 10.06 the train was signalled away from Doncaster, two minutes late. It was sent along the up slow line, because the signalman had accepted another train from the north along the up main line, and could not infringe the added clearance beyond his home signals by crossing the 10.06 over the crossover to the main line at the platform end. So it was up to the Bridge Junction signalman to switch the train to the main line through the scissors crossover 600yd (550m) ahead. The driver accelerated *Cock o' the North* along the up slow, and although aware of the 10mph (16km/h) speed limit through the crossover, he took it rather liberally – at nearer 20mph (32km/h), as he had done on previous occasions.

The train separates

The engine and the first two coaches negotiated the scissors crossover successfully, and the driver opened the regulator fully to increase speed now that he was on the main line. However, as the engine went under Balby Bridge, the vacuum gauge of the brake system went suddenly to zero, causing the brakes to come on automatically. When the engine crew climbed down to see what had happened, they met a scene of devastation.

The train had uncoupled behind the second coach, but of the third coach there was little left, for its steel underframe had bent into a U-shape around the pier supporting Balby Bridge, and the timber-framed body had disintegrated. The engine and first two coaches on the up main line had gone to the right of the pier, initially taking the leading end of the third coach the same way. But the back end of the derailed third coach and the fourth coach had gone to the left of the pier, propelled by the weight of the following train, so that for a short period the third coach had been dragged and then pushed broadside on to the bridge. The fifth and sixth coaches had followed the fourth, the seventh had overturned and the eighth and ninth coaches were also totally derailed, together with one axle of the tenth coach. Most of the casualties occurred in the third coach, with 14 passengers dead, 12 seriously hurt and 17 with lesser injuries and shock.

The response by staff trained in first aid was rapid, and the first casualties were brought out of the third coach in a few minutes; indeed, the first ambulances were on their way to hospital little more than half an hour after the accident. Breakdown cranes arrived at the scene about an hour after the incident and, once the dead and

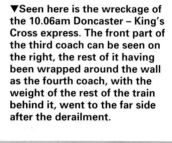

▼Seen here is the wreckage of the 10.06am Doncaster – King's Cross express. The front part of the third coach can be seen on the right, the rest of it having been wrapped around the wall as the fourth coach, with the weight of the rest of the train behind it, went to the far side after the derailment.

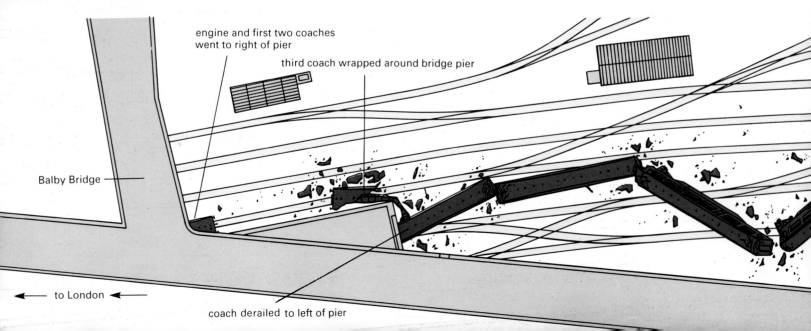

engine and first two coaches went to right of pier

third coach wrapped around bridge pier

Balby Bridge

◄— to London ◄—

coach derailed to left of pier

lowed by marks on the wooden sleepers of the trailing points of the crossover, where wheels had been derailed to the left of the rails. A little beyond the crossover was a diamond crossing over the up main, trailing from the down main and going to the left to join the continuation of the up slow line, now forming the up fast goods line. The derailed wheels were diverted to the left by this intersecting track, and had taken the derailed coaches to the left of the bridge pier, while the third coach, still coupled to the second, was trying to go to the right of the pier, and as a result met the pier side on. The problem for the inspecting officers was whether the wing rail at the crossing nose had caused the derailment, or whether it had been damaged by the derailment.

Looking for evidence
The driver admitted that he might have gone through the scissors crossover at about 20mph (32km/h), even possibly 25mph (40km/h) on other occasions. Thus, although he estimated he was travelling at only about 15mph (24km/h) on the day of the accident, the inspecting officers wanted to assess just how fast the train might have been

▲The sixth and seventh coaches of the express were left lying on their sides. The third to sixth coaches had timber-framed bodies with steel outer panels, and the seventh a teak body.

injured had been removed, started to clear the wreckage. The main lines were reopened at about 11.00pm the same night and the scissors crossover was restored by 7.00am the following day. Meanwhile, the detective work started, to find out what had gone wrong and why so many coaches had derailed at what was basically a very low and safe speed.

The investigation begins
The inquiry was undertaken by two inspecting officers, Lt Col G R S Wilson, and Brig C A Langley. They soon found that the trailing vee crossing nose and the wing rail assembly where the right-hand rail of the crossover met the left-hand rail of the up main line were damaged, with broken bolts and damaged supporting cast-iron chairs. The running-on wing rail had burst open, so the train's wheels had dropped into the gap of the crossing. This was all on the right of the train.

A few feet further on there were clear wheel marks going over the top of the left-hand rail, fol-

How the derailment happened
The inquiry found that the vee of the crossing nose and the wing rail assembly, at the place where the right-hand rail of the crossover met the left-hand rail of the up main line, was inadequately held in position. One bolt through the entire assembly was missing, two other bolts had newly fractured and the cast-iron chair supporting the vee of the crossing and the wing rails had broken.

Shortly after the accident, while the inspecting officers were watching a train – travelling faster than it should have been – pass through the scissors crossover, they saw a wooden block (or key), normally wedged between the rail and the side of the chair, fall out. The officers had already concluded that the derailed train had gone too fast through the crossing, but said that without a speedometer it was difficult for drivers to judge speeds exactly. The permanent way staff had not maintained the crossover properly for the traffic it was carrying. The inquiry concluded that the wing rail had been displaced, wheels had dropped into the gap and the opposite wheels had risen and ridden over the left-hand rail.

wheels dropped into gap

down main

up main

up slow

→ to Doncaster →

← direction of train ←
10.06am up express

▲The fourth coach, No E1032, was diverted to the left of the bridge support wall and took the back of the third coach with it, crushing and destroying it in the process. Little was left of the third coach, which can be seen this side of the wall, on the right.

Modern track layouts

Today's track layouts are much simpler than even ten years ago. Most junctions are formed of single points, and diamond and scissors crossings are used sparingly. If canted junctions are unavoidable, multi-level base plates are used to support the rails if varying rail heights are needed on the same sleeper.

In a few locations, where crossovers link multi-track layouts on a curve, the entire layout is canted to overcome the problems of joining some tracks with cant and some without.

travelling. They organized speed trials with a train of the same number of coaches and weight, hauled by the same engine, No 60501, and leaving from the same platform, but using the crossover to the main line at the platform end in order not to risk excessive speed through the Bridge Junction scissors crossover.

They found that if the engine had been worked steadily – as claimed by the driver – it would have reached 17mph (27km/h) by Bridge Junction, but if it had been driven hard, its speed could have reached 25mph (40km/h). Later on, while the inspecting officers were at the site, they saw another express go through the scissors at about 20mph (32km/h), so it was not unusual for trains to exceed the 10mph (16km/h) restriction.

Next, the inquiry held derailment trials on a specially laid length of track with all the cant and features of the actual crossover, and using old coach underframes on bogies similar to the derailed third and fourth coaches. Obviously they could not reproduce the speed; the trial was done to confirm exactly where each wheel was, and how it might have behaved in relation to the derailment marks on the actual track – reproduced on the trial track by being painted on.

The inspecting officers then tried to assess the effect of the steep rise of the right-hand rail as it reached the cant of the main line. They concluded that at 25mph (40km/h) the sharp lift of the right-hand wheels on the increasing cant would produce a dangerous condition, but they could not see how this would have damaged the trailing vee of the crossing nose and the wing rail, which had clearly been forced out of line.

Poor maintenance

The chairs holding the rail were supported on oak packing pieces inserted between the sleeper and chairs to provide the cant through parts of the crossover. One of these pieces had split, and was giving inadequate support, so the cant may have been rendered steeper than was intended. Also, some sleepers had voids or spaces underneath, and were not fully supported by the stone ballast. As part of the investigation, details of 13 previous derailments in 50 years at trailing vee crossings were examined to see if there were any similarities. Although the inspecting officers felt that the previous examples should not be taken as a pointer to what happened at Doncaster, the derailment was similar to others.

They concluded that the displaced wing rail to the right of the crossing nose had initiated the derailment, rather than being a result of the derailment. One bolt holding together the vee and wing rail assembly was missing, and two others fractured. In addition, while the inspecting officers watched a passing train go through the scissors, a wooden key or block was seen to fall out from the very chair holding the wing rail close to the vee, and it is quite possible the same thing had happened before.

Although the inquiry report did not think that excessive speed was a major factor, it must be considered, and the derailment might not have happened at 10mph (16km/h). While the driver was at fault for exceeding the speed limit, the engine had no speedometer. The broken bolts had fractured at a fatigue flaw, which could not have been seen, but clearly the permanent way staff had not paid sufficient attention to the maintenance of the crossover, as evidenced by the worn-out packing piece, the pumping sleepers with spaces beneath them, and the missing bolt.

The inspecting officers thought the crossing assembly in 95lb/yd (43kg/m) bullhead rail was adequate with good maintenance, but they felt that bolts should be examined and changed regularly, and commented that the 109lb (49.4kg) flat bottom rail just coming into use would be much stronger.

They recommended that crossovers on lines with cant should be examined to see if they could be remodelled with simpler constructions, or relocated to sections without cant. Finally, they suggested that all new and existing express locomotives should be fitted with speedometers.

Recommendations

Crossing assemblies should be examined and tests conducted on bolts at regular intervals to see whether they needed renewing.

The layout and design of crossovers intersecting canted track should be examined to see whether layouts could be simpler, or whether the crossing could be re-sited to a position where the cant was less, or even non-existent, thus avoiding the steep rise in rail level as one track without cant joined one with considerable cant.

All new locomotives should in future be fitted with speedometers, and existing locomotives being used on the major passenger services should be fitted with them as well.

Winsford 1948

**Just after midnight, a soldier going home on leave
pulled the communication cord to stop an overnight express
between stations so that he could take a short cut home. But it
turned to disaster when a signalling error let another train
into the same section and 24 people died in the collision.**

In 1948, several important and heavily used sections of the West Coast main line to Weaver Junction, where the Liverpool route branches off, and on to Warrington, Wigan and Preston, were only double track. There were four tracks from Crewe over the seven miles to Winsford station, but only two tracks from there past Winsford Junction 1½ miles to the north.

The 5.40pm train from Glasgow to Euston was the successor to the long established Scotch mail. (The word Scotch was always used in railway parlance rather than the more correct Scots.) This train carried passengers and the overnight mail from Scotland to England. Its passengers arrived at Euston just before 4am.

By 1948 the 5.40pm train no longer carried mail, or not in any quantity at least, as the mail had for many years been carried by the West Coast Postal, the Night Mail featured in the famous 1930s film, which was run exclusively for the Post Office. It did not carry passengers but had a large crew of Post Office staff sorting mail on the journey, despatching it and collecting it in strong leather pouches, set down or picked up from lineside exchange equipment as the train passed at speed. The southbound Postal left Glasgow at 6.25pm.

North of Crewe, after leaving Carlisle at 8.35pm, it called only at Lancaster (for passengers to change on to a connection back to Carnforth and the Barrow line), Preston and Warrington before running the 24 miles on to Crewe non-stop.

A lethal short cut

This did not suit a soldier who was travelling on the train on 16 April 1948. He was going home on leave and presumably lived near Winsford, for, as the train passed Winsford Junction, he pulled the communication cord – the alarm signal as it is called today – in one of the toilet compartments of a corridor coach.

▼Two steam cranes work to clear the wreckage of the trains involved in the Winsford crash. The nature of the flat north Cheshire countryside made it easy for the soldier who pulled the communication cord to slip away into the darkness to get home.

Nobody saw him do it, but as the train came to an unscheduled stop between Winsford Junction and Winsford station, a soldier was seen to open a door and jump from the train on to the track.

Although it was, and still is, forbidden to pull the communication cord to stop a train except in an emergency, it was not unknown for servicemen to pull the cord to stop a train out in the country, if it meant a more convenient way for them to get home on weekend or longer leave periods. The proper connections by train, bus or hitch-hiking, could sometimes add hours to a journey and the men only wanted to have a few extra hours with their families. Although the war was over, conscription for military service continued.

Normally, stopping a train like this between stations meant no more than a short delay to the train, and inconvenience for all the other passengers, while the fireman and the guard searched the train to find where the cord had been pulled and the guard made enquiries: 'Right, then, who did it?' Then he would get details of the culprit in his notebook for possible prosecution and a £2 fine.

The guard, or the fireman, would reset the alarm signal brake valve, the brakes would be released and away they went. If there was going to

be more than a minute's delay, the train crew had to think about protecting the train to the rear with detonators and a flag or hand lamp signal.

But this meant that whoever was going to carry out protection had to walk back for three-quarters of a mile and this could cause further delay. Normally the block signalling system would provide the primary protection by the principle of not more than one train being on one line in a block section at one time. But this time it was different.

Where was the train?

The signalman at Winsford Station box had put all his signals to clear for the 5.40pm Glasgow to Euston train at about midnight. It had been offered to him by Winsford Junction and he had offered it to Minshull Vernon and had had it accepted.

Quite what the Winsford signalman did after that was not entirely clear. Had he nodded off for a few minutes and then become confused? Had the train passed? Certainly the train had not reached Minshull Vernon, because the signalman there telephoned to Winsford Station box to ask where it was.

Then the signalman at Winsford Junction telephoned to Winsford Station box to ask why the 5.40pm train was such a long time in the section and whether it had passed since the Postal was not far away.

The signalman at Winsford Station signalbox had not actually seen the train pass, but thought that it must have done so. He then made a fatal mistake, for he sent the 'train out of section' bell signal to Winsford Junction for the 5.40pm train from Glasgow and cleared the block indicator. Winsford Junction immediately offered the Postal.

It had left Glasgow at 6.25pm on the Friday evening and was composed of 13 coaches, including Post Office sorting vans and stowage coaches. It was hauled by one of the largest of the LMS express passenger locomotives, Coronation class 4-6-2 No 6251 *City of Nottingham* and was making good progress southwards at express speed. As it approached Winsford Junction, the signals were clear.

Unknown to the driver, standing about a mile ahead, right in its path, was the 5.40pm train from Glasgow, headed by Princess class 4-6-2 No 6207 *Princess Arthur of Connaught*.

The fireman of No 6207 and the 5.40's guard were having difficulty in finding the location of the pulled communication cord. After the 5.40 had been standing for several minutes while they

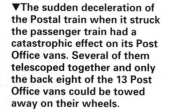

▼The sudden deceleration of the Postal train when it struck the passenger train had a catastrophic effect on its Post Office vans. Several of them telescoped together and only the back eight of the 13 Post Office vans could be towed away on their wheels.

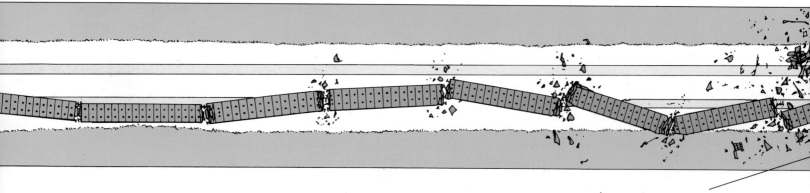

◄── to Winsford station ◄────────

last coach completely demolished

searched the coach with the tell-tale indicator showing where the cord had been pulled, they decided that the train ought to be protected. The guard went back to his van, picked up some detonators and started walking back along the line ready to put down one detonator on the rail at a quarter of mile. But he did not make it.

He had just about covered 400yd when he heard the Postal train approaching at speed and soon saw its two headlights coming round the gentle curve from the north. He managed to clip one or two detonators on to the rail, held his oil hand lamp showing a red light towards the oncoming train and stepped to one side as No 6251 swept past him, not knowing whether its driver had seen his warning.

The detonators exploded under the leading bogie wheel of No 6251 and the driver's hand went straight to the brake handle to make a full application of the vacuum brake and to shut the regulator. There was hardly time to wind the reversing gear into reverse and open the regulator to get added braking force from the engine in reverse, before the massive engine of the Postal rammed the back of the standing 5.40pm train at between 40 and 45mph.

Many casualties

The heavy Pacific demolished the rear coach of the 5.40 train and pushed the whole of it forward. Fortunately it was standing with its brakes released after the alarm signal valve had been reset. But other coaches were badly damaged and some of the passenger coaches of the 5.40 were pushed to each side by the impact.

The sudden stop of the Postal train caused telescoping between several of the Post Office vans. All the coaches had timber body framing and,

while some had all timber body construction, even those with steel body panels could not withstand the severe force of the collision. It was so destructive that only the front five of the ten passenger train coaches could be towed away on their wheels after the accident, and only the rear eight of the 13 Postal coaches could be drawn back, clear of the wreckage.

Inevitably casualties were high and no fewer than 16 passengers died on the spot. Eight more were so badly injured that they died later in hospital.

The collision happened at 12.27am, early on the Saturday. It took several minutes before the train crews could get to the nearest signalbox to report the accident and also to make sure that the wreck was protected by detonators on both up and down lines. By 12.45am the breakdown trains with cranes had been alerted at Crewe and Liverpool Edge Hill and the first doctor was on the scene by 1.15am.

Radio communication for the emergency services was very much in its infancy at that time and calls to doctors, the police, fire brigade and the ambulance service had to be made by telephone.

The breakdown trains could not get to the site

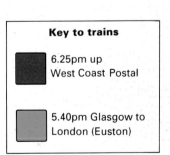

▲The remains of the last carriage of the passenger express struck by the postal train looked like a pile of spare parts. Locomotive No 6251 *City of Nottingham* was in the 1946 LMS passenger livery. The basic engine colour was black and the all over maroon of pre-war years had shrunk to a 2¹/₂ inch maroon band along the footplate angle.

A short cut to disaster

A soldier returning home on leave pulled the communication cord when the train on which he was travelling reached a convenient spot. As he slipped away the crew could not find where the cord had been pulled in the coach.

While the guard set off to protect the train, the signalman assumed that the stopped train had cleared the section and signalled another train into it. The second train thundered into the back of the first and 24 people were killed.

Key to trains

■ 6.25pm up West Coast Postal

■ 5.40pm Glasgow to London (Euston)

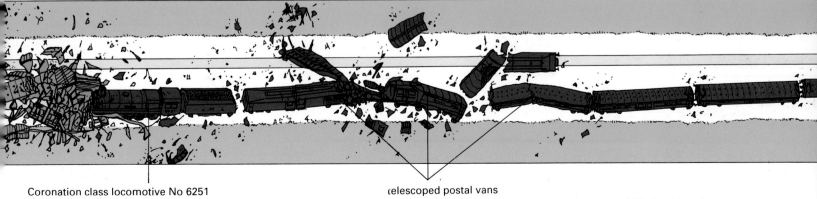

Coronation class locomotive No 6251

telescoped postal vans

➡ to Winsford Junction ➡

train. Had the guard gone back a few minutes earlier the severity of the accident would have been reduced or even avoided altogether. Although there was a berth track circuit at Winsford station home signal, the standing 5.40 train had not reached it and was undetected.

The accident was like that at Welwyn Garden City in 1935 all over again. Although Welwyn control, introduced on the LNER after the 1935 collision, would have prevented the Winsford disaster, the LMS had not adopted it, and war conditions had not allowed the widespread provision of extra signalling safety devices. Winsford happened just four months into the new BR era of nationalization, and in later years Welwyn control was fitted more widely but not universally.

As for the soldier who pulled the communication cord he was later traced and fined for improper use and nothing more. He had to live with his conscience. He had stopped the 5.40 train and, had he not done so, the accident would not have happened. But the prime responsibility for the collision lay with the Winsford station signalman because he had not carried out the rules and regulations. Had he actually seen the 5.40 train pass him before he gave train out of section for it and accepted the Postal there would have been no disaster. The railway rules had been framed to cover out of course stops and this time they failed.

The communication cord

To provide some means for passengers to raise the alarm, the railways in Victorian years adopted what was known as the communication cord. Usually the cord or chain was outside the coach in a tube with gaps above the doors. Passengers reached out to pull it, if necessary.

In 1892, the Great Western Railway connected the communication chain on each coach to a valve at the coach end which was linked to the vacuum brake. When the chain was pulled, the brakes were partially applied and the driver, noticing the drop in the vacuum, would stop the train. From then on the communication system acted directly on the brakes, although to prevent trains being stopped by passengers in awkward places – in tunnels or on viaducts for example – the brake application was always slight and the driver could keep control and stop in the best place. Each coach had an indicator at one end on each side so that the crew could see in which coach the chain had been pulled. They had to look in each compartment to see the dangling chain since from the 1890s the chain was inside the coach running in a tube between compartments.

▲Rescuers are seen here struggling to free the injured and dead from a wrecked carriage in the light from the headlamps of a fire engine. The inspecting officer commented on how the all steel carriages in the train had withstood the crash better than the timber framed ones.

straight away because the accident happened on the double track section and both lines were blocked. To make matters worse, there were two trains already on the down line between Crewe and Winsford, and six on the up line south of Warrington, or Runcorn, and they had to be stabled in loops and sidings, or worked back, to free the line for the breakdown gangs.

Despite the damage, the breakdown and repair gangs worked non stop and the line was reopened, with a severe speed limit, soon after 8pm the same day – 20 hours after the collision. During the period of the total blockage of this important route, some long distance passenger trains were diverted from Crewe, either via Chester and Frodsham or through Manchester.

What went wrong?

As for the cause of the accident, it was not hard to find. The inquiry inspector Lt Col G R S Wilson held the Winsford station signalman responsible for the collision. He had sent the train out of section signal to Winsford Junction and accepted the Postal train without having seen the 5.40 train. The signalman had not even claimed to have seen the train but had assumed it must have passed despite the fact that the signalmen at the boxes on each side of him had enquired as to the whereabouts of the 5.40 train.

The 5.40's crew could not at first find out where the communication cord had been pulled and time was lost while they searched, with consequent delay in carrying out the rules to protect the

Recommendations

The collision occurred because the Winsford Station signalman had given the train out of section bell code to Winsford Junction and had cleared the block indicator without actually seeing the 5.40pm train pass his signalbox.

The signalboxes in the area were equipped with what was known as Class C block controls. This meant that if a train was occupying a berth track circuit approaching the home signal, the block indicator would automatically be held at 'train on line'. This in turn meant that the starting signal at the previous signalbox, normally released by 'line clear' on the block instrument, would be held at danger.

But the 5.40pm train had not reached the track circuit when it stopped, so there was no safeguard against the improper release of the block indicator.

Lt Col Wilson, the inspecting officer, observed that the LNER Welwyn control, which was adopted by the company after a crash at Welwyn in 1935, would have prevented the premature clearance of the block indicator.

Under this control system the berth track circuit approaching the home signal had to be first occupied and then cleared in order that the block indicator could then be cleared in turn.

He made no positive recommendation that Welwyn control should be adopted, but just mentioned that the Railway Executive had been considering making it standard everywhere.

South Croydon 1947

On a foggy morning in October 1947, two electric trains collided near South Croydon on the busy London – Brighton line, killing thirty-two people. The signalling included lock and block controls to prevent errors, so how did it happen?

The London – Brighton line is one of the most intensively worked routes on what was known – until recently – as the Southern Region of British Railways, and before 1948 was called the Southern Railway (SR). It carries the suburban services from Coulsdon, and the Tattenham Corner and Caterham branches, which diverge at Purley. In addition, since electrification in the 1930s, there have been frequent express, semi-fast, and stopping trains, not only to and from Brighton, but also Eastbourne and Hastings to the east, and Worthing and Littlehampton to the west. At South Croydon, the Oxted branch leaves the main line, and further north, between East Croydon and Norwood Junction, there is an absolute maze of junctions and flyovers.

Due to the heavy traffic, which in the 1940s still included some trains between Charing Cross and Dover via Redhill and Tonbridge, the line south from East Croydon had been quadrupled by the end of the nineteenth century; this work included a new Coulsdon to Earlswood line, avoiding Redhill, which opened in April 1900.

With the intensive train services, signalmen on much of the Brighton main line were helped by safety equipment, which was linked to the block instruments, but controlled by the trains themselves. It was known as Sykes lock and block, and was the invention of William R Sykes, who was originally employed by the London, Chatham & Dover Railway (LCDR) from 1863. In 1865, he devised an electrical signal repeater, and by 1875 had patented lock and block railway signalling, which was tried out between three signalboxes on the LCDR. It was later adopted by the LCDR and a few other railways, including the London Brighton & South Coast Railway (LBSCR). It was not used universally on the LBSCR, but was installed on parts of the Brighton line, including the stretch between East Croydon and Purley.

The basis of the system was that the signals and the block instruments were locked and released by the passage of trains, which operated treadles alongside the rails by pressing them down with

▼Just three compartments on the leading coach of the Tattenham Corner train survived, although they were damaged. The rest of the coach was flattened as it hit the Haywards Heath train (left). The leading unit of the Tattenham Corner train was composed of old LBSCR wooden-bodied coaches. The Haywards Heath train coaches had steel-panelled bodies on timber framing, but the rear coach was wrecked in the collision.

their wheel flanges. As a train depressed a treadle, the treadle opened or closed electrical switches, these switches in turn operating circuits in the signalboxes.

In the offering signalbox, the block indicator for the forward section consisted of a small semaphore arm in a circular glass-fronted case. A lowered arm indicated that the section ahead was available for the signalman to offer a train to the next signalbox. Below the block indicator was the rest of the instrument, comprising two apertures: the top one – relating to the signal controlling entry to the section ahead – displaying either 'locked', or 'free'; and the lower one – relating to the block section to the rear – being either blank, or showing 'train on'. If the signalman in the forward section was able to accept the train offered to his signalbox, he would operate a plunger on his instrument. This put the semaphore indicator at the offering box to the horizontal position, meaning the section was occupied, or to be occupied, and the top aperture changed from 'locked' to 'free', thus releasing the lock on the starting signal into the section ahead. If the train was already in the rear section, the bottom aperture displayed 'train

on' until the treadle was operated.

The essential feature of Sykes lock and block was that once a train was signalled, a second train could not be signalled until the first had passed through the section and operated the treadle. The signalman at the offering box could then clear his starting signal into the section ahead, but after he had pulled the lever, the top aperture in the Sykes instrument again showed 'locked'. He could replace the signal to danger in an emergency, but the Sykes locking prevented him from restoring the lever fully to release the interlocking until the train had passed the signal, and operated the trea-

Key to the disaster
The collision was caused when the Purley Oaks signalman, inexperienced and working for the first time in fog, mistakenly thought that the locks on the block instruments and signals had failed, when they were actually correctly held by a train at his signals hidden in fog. He used a release key to unlock and clear the rear section block instrument, and accepted the following train, clearing the signals for it. The first train moved on, but the second, seeing clear signals, caught up and ran into the back of it, killing 32 people. With around 1800 passengers on the two trains, it is astounding that so few died.

← to Purley North and Brighton ←

Key to Trains

7.33am Haywards Heath – London Bridge

8.04am Tattenham Corner – London Bridge

leading coach of 8.04am train completely smashed

rear coach of 7.33am train badly damaged

dle that turned the top aperture to 'free' again. However, as soon as the signalman put the lever back to danger, it became locked once more, and could not be cleared until the whole procedure had been repeated, and then only when the first train had cleared the treadle at the signalbox ahead. It was foolproof – or was it?

Because of the locking between the treadle, the block instruments, and the signal levers, if anything failed, such as a treadle not making the proper contact between the electrical switching (perhaps because of dirt), the whole thing was locked up, the signal could not be cleared, and the train service was seriously delayed. To avoid this, each instrument had a release key, which in the event of a fault could be inserted into the instrument and turned several times to release the lock. However, the release key was usually sealed, and instructions were quite precise that it was to be used only in genuine cases of a fault, after careful consideration by the signalman, and that the incident had to be recorded in the train register. But it was known that in a few places (those with very frequent services) the signalmen sometimes broke the rules, and used the release key to avoid delaying peak-hour services, because they gained a few seconds more by doing this than by waiting until the train operated the treadle.

Thick fog causes delays

The morning of 24 October 1947 dawned very foggy in south London. Fogs around London during the autumn and winter were exacerbated by the coal fires burnt in most houses before the Clean Air Act of 1956. At South Croydon, the morning rush hour was in full swing, but trains were being delayed because drivers could not see the semaphore arms of the signals through the fog until they were right up close to them.

Resignalling of the Brighton line through the London suburbs with modern colour lights was long overdue. Colour lights had been in use at London Bridge from 1928, and Victoria from the mid-1930s; the SR planned to extend them down the Brighton line to meet the existing colour-light signals south of Redhill, but World War II had delayed progress. So, in the Croydon area the old signalling was still in use.

All went well that morning until the signalman at Purley Oaks accepted the 7.33am from Haywards Heath to London Bridge on the up main line from Purley. This train comprised four-coach sets of SR semi-fast stock built in the 1930s, mostly non-corridor, but with one coach in each set

with a corridor. The coaches were on steel under-frames, and had steel body panels on timber framing. The train was not booked to call at Purley Oaks, but because the previous train had not cleared South Croydon – the next station to the north – the signalman was unable to clear his starting signal for the Haywards Heath train to run through, and the train duly stopped at the signal at Purley Oaks. However, the fog was so thick that the Purley Oaks signalman could not see the train. He did not have a track circuit to remind him of where it was standing, but because the train had not yet operated the treadle to free the section to the rear, it was protected by the Sykes lock and block system.

Fatal mistake at Purley Oaks

The Purley North signalman started to wonder how things were moving in the fog. He had not received train out of section for the Haywards Heath train, so, as he had other trains approaching, he telephoned to Purley Oaks asking how things were looking on the up main. The Purley Oaks signalman realized that he had not cleared the rear section instrument from Purley. This was indeed so, but quite correctly, since the Haywards Heath train had not passed the treadle to release the lock on the rear section controls. The signalman tried to

▼The evening after the collision, breakdown gangs right the back coach of the Haywards Heath train, revealing that the side panels had been ripped away.

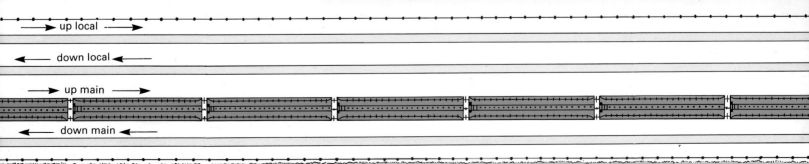

up local

down local

up main

down main

▲The rear coach of the Haywards Heath train lies on its side having been flung to the right by the collision. The wrecked rear cab and guard's compartment can be seen clearly. Just in front of the camera is all that was left of the leading coach of the Tattenham Corner train.

train, running at about 45mph (70km/h), caught it up. In the thick fog, there was no chance of avoiding the collision, even if the driver of the Tattenham Corner train had seen the Haywards Heath train.

The Tattenham Corner train rammed the back of the train ahead with such force that its leading coach was smashed to matchwood, and the rear coach of the Haywards Heath train was badly damaged. The driver of the Tattenham Corner train was killed, together with 31 passengers, and many more were injured. Both trains were crowded, with around 800 on the Haywards Heath train, and about 1000 on the Tattenham Corner service, and it was remarkable that there were not more fatalities. The front of the Tattenham Corner train was so badly damaged that it was impossible to ascertain whether or not the brakes were applied before the accident.

After the accident

The inquiry was chaired by inspecting officer Colonel Sir Alan Mount. It was soon clear that the accident had been caused by human error, arising from a deliberate act by the Purley Oaks signalman in using the Sykes release key. The Purley Oaks man was a porter-signalman, whose duties were partly on the station, and – following training – partly in the signalbox. He had been working in the signalbox on a part-time basis for about four months, but at the time of the accident, because of the illness of one of the regular signalmen, he was working the box full-time. The morning of 24 October was the first time he had worked in fog.

Col Sir Alan Mount concluded that the main cause of the accident was the use of the release key. Sir Alan commented that he knew 'of no other instruction which gives warning that improper use of apparatus may cause dismissal'. The signalman thus lost his job. The inquiry recommended rapid completion of resignalling with track circuits and colour-light signals.

Sykes's system
The semaphore arm at the top was a repeater for the forward section. Below, the upper tablet showed the status of the lever connected to the track treadle system, and the lower one related to the section behind. When allowing a train to come into his section, the signalman operated a plunger which put the semaphore indicator at the offering box to horizontal.

semaphore indicator

signal ahead is locked or free

keyhole for release key

FREE

TRAIN ON

plunger

switch hook

rods linking levers and block instrument locks

clear the block instrument, but found it was locked, and immediately jumped to the wrong and fatal conclusion that it had failed. He used the release key, gave train out of section to Purley North, and immediately accepted the following 8.04am from Tattenham Corner to London Bridge.

Simultaneously, South Croydon cleared the section back to Purley Oaks, the Purley Oaks signalman offered the Tattenham Corner train forward, and it was accepted. With his forward section instrument showing 'free', the Purley Oaks signalman cleared his starting signal, which was then relocked in the clear position. On seeing this signal, the Haywards Heath train – still hidden in the fog – started away, and operated the treadle that released the lock on the starting signal, ready for it to be put back to danger. The signalman thought this odd, but even then did not realize that the lock had been released by the Haywards Heath train. Instead, he cleared the home and distant signals for the Tattenham Corner train.

The Tattenham Corner train, like many SR suburban units of the time, was made up of coaches with all-timber bodies. It accelerated away from Purley, and its driver – seeing the Purley Oaks distant signal at clear – naturally assumed the line was clear at least as far as South Croydon. But approaching South Croydon, the Haywards Heath train had encountered the distant signal at caution, and slowed down just as the Tattenham Corner

Recommendations
Col Sir Alan Mount, the inspecting officer, held the Purley Oaks signalman responsible for the accident. He criticized the use of the release key before the signalman had satisfied himself beyond all measure of doubt that it was safe to do so. But the signalling was already 50 years old, and was long overdue for replacement. Colour-light signals and track circuits controlled from power signalboxes, which helped to prevent signalmen's mistakes, had already been provided at London Bridge and Victoria, and had been planned in the 1930s to be extended down the Brighton line through Purley, but progress had been delayed by World War II. The inspecting officer recommended that the scheme should be resumed as soon as possible, but it took another eight years before the resignalling was finally completed on the section of track between East Croydon and Coulsdon in May 1955.

Bourne End 1945

**After passing a colour-light distant signal showing a
special caution indication, a driver traversed a 20mph (32km/h)
crossover at speed and wrecked his train, losing his own life
and causing the deaths of 42 others, the worst accident in
the history of the London Midland & Scottish Railway.**

Four-track routes, with two tracks in each direction, carrying a mixture of fast and slow trains, can be laid out in one of two ways: by direction, in which the two tracks for trains in the same direction are side by side; or by use, in which the up and down lines for the faster traffic are together, and the two tracks for the slower trains are a separate pair. Pairing by direction allows easy transfer from the fast to the slow line, or vice versa. A crossing move over tracks paired by use means that a train switching from the fast to the slow track has to cross the line for trains running in the opposite direction.

The arrangement chosen depends on the history of the line and the type of traffic it handles. On routes with the four tracks paired by use, the crossovers had to include a diamond crossing over the intermediate track. As a result, speeds through the crossovers from one track to another were very restricted until the simplification of such crossovers in the 1960s.

The four-track West Cost main line out of Euston to the north had pairing by use as far as Roade, the junction for Northampton. Double crossovers, one for up trains and one for down, were situated at most principal stations. Large stations, such as Willesden, Watford and Bletchley, had crossovers running in both directions, from fast to slow and slow to fast. Some stations had them running in only one direction (that is, with the two crossovers parallel to each other), down fast to slow, and up slow to fast, or vice versa.

At Bourne End, between Hemel Hempstead and Berkhamsted, there was no station, but the signalbox controlled crossovers in all directions: up fast to slow and from down slow to fast; and from down fast to slow and up slow to fast, each pair end-on to each other. The signalbox had originally been provided to split the 3½ miles (5.6km) between Hemel Hempstead and Berkhamsted into two block sections. Because of the reverse curves at Berkhamsted, it was not feasible to have

▼ **The day after the derailment of the 8.20am Perth – Euston express, the three cranes continued with the task of removing the wreckage. The roof of Bourne End signalbox can just be seen at the bottom right-hand corner of the photograph. Temporary plain track has replaced the up slow facing points on the left-hand track.**

▲ This photograph shows the two double crossovers at Bourne End. The Perth – Euston express hurtled over the distant crossover, travelling from the up fast (second track on the left) to the up slow (fourth track on the right) – the latter hidden in this shot below the wrecked coaches. The cab and wheels of engine No 6157 can be seen clearly under the coach on the right.

Berkhamsted towards Watford, Bourne End's up fast distant had to be moved to about 1¼ miles (2km) from the first up fast home signal, instead of the one mile (1.6km) previously needed. A mechanical lever with 1½ miles (2.4km) of wire to a semaphore arm would have been too much for a signalman to pull. While the distant arm could have been worked by an electric motor, the LMS instead replaced many of its semaphore distant signals on the West Coast route with colour-light signals, but retained mechanical semaphore stop signals for home and starting signals.

Introduction of the double yellow

Originally, junction distant signals had been provided to give drivers a positive indication of whether the signals at the crossover were clear for the through fast route or clear through the slow speed diverging track of the crossover. But the new colour-light signals were not only being installed at distant signals on the LMS: in some places they were being used as stop signals, one after another. When colour-light signals were first seen on main lines in the 1920s, a new double yellow indication was introduced, in addition to the single yellow meaning caution, and green meaning clear.

The potentially ambiguous meaning of the double yellow at that time on the LMS might have led the driver to make his fatal error. The rule said that in some cases colour-light signals will display two yellow lights, meaning pass the next signal at restricted speed, and that 'At a junction this indication *may* denote that the points are set for a diverging route with a speed restriction'.

On the morning of Sunday 30 September 1945, shortly after the end of World War II, the railways were still run down and engineers were trying to catch up. That morning they were working on the fast lines in Watford Tunnel, so up trains were being crossed from the fast to the slow line at Bourne End, with a speed restriction of 20mph (32km/h). The work was in the weekly notice, so the driver of the overnight 8.20pm Perth – Euston express train should have known of the diversion.

crossovers there, so Bourne End had an important role in train operation on the West Coast route.

The other factor in this accident was that of the signals. Because of increasing train speeds in the 1930s, particularly arising from London Midland & Scottish Railway (LMS) competition with the London & North Eastern Railway (LNER) for Anglo-Scottish traffic, and with the Great Western Railway (GWR) for the Birmingham – London traffic, braking distances were becoming longer. This meant that drivers needed more advanced warning of whether signals were clear ahead, so distant signals had to be re-sited further out from the stop signals to which they applied. On the 1 in 335 falling gradient from Tring Summit through

Going too fast

The Bourne End derailment was caused when an overnight Perth – Euston train, driven by an experienced man, failed to slow down to take the 20mph (32km/h) crossover from the up fast to the up slow line.

The driver should have seen the colour-light distant signal showing double yellow, warning him that the train was to be diverted off the main line at low speed. Instead, the train continued at 60mph (97km/h) and was wrecked when it was derailed passing through the crossover, the engine then rolling on to its side in a field. Forty-three people died in the accident, including the driver and his fireman; 60 or more were injured.

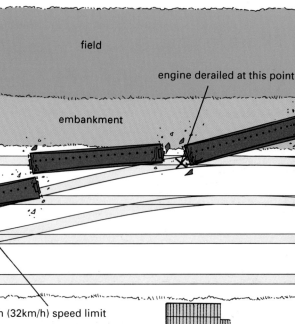

field

engine derailed at this point

embankment

up fast home 2 signal clear to up slow line

three coaches not derailed

crossover — 20mph (32km/h) speed limit

signalbox

← to Berkhamsted and the North ◄─

The Bourne End signalman accepted the Perth train from Berkhamsted, and having passed on the bell signal to Boxmoor (the signalbox at Hemel Hempstead) and had it accepted, he cleared his outer home signal (home 1) and then the up fast to up slow inner home signal (home 2). The distant signal would then have shown double yellow; there should have been no misunderstanding of its meaning. There were not many options for a train at Bourne End: if all the signals were clear for it to proceed on the up fast, the distant signal would show green; if the signals were at danger, the distant signal would display a single yellow.

The overnight Perth train, hauled by Royal Scot class 4-6-0 No 6157 *The Royal Artilleryman*, was travelling at around 60mph (97km/h), on the falling gradient after negotiating the Berkhamsted curves. It was still travelling at this speed as it approached Bourne End, but it did not slow for the crossover. The large engine rolled as it swung to the left. Initially it managed to stay on the track, but then encountered an equally sharp curve to the right as the crossover trailed into the up slow line. With the engine still recovering from the left-hand jolt, the right-hand one was too much: it rolled to the left, with its right-hand wheels lifting off the track. The engine became derailed, and still travelling fast it went further to the left and rolled over on its side down a 15ft (4.5m) embankment into the fields below, coming to rest a little way from the line. Six coaches followed the engine and were almost totally destroyed; only the last three coaches of the 15-coach train were not derailed. All four tracks were blocked by the wreckage.

Casualties were heavy: 38 people, including the driver and the fireman, were killed on the spot; five more died later. Over 60 people were injured to some degree. In terms of casualties, it was the worst accident to befall the LMS in its 25-year existence from 1923 to 1947.

What did the driver see?

Fast to slow diversions were commonplace on this route, particularly on Sundays when engineering work meant that one pair of lines was often closed, entailing crossover moves. With an experienced driver, how did this occur? The use of the double-yellow aspect on the distant signal had no ambiguity at Bourne End, since it was used only when the route was set through the crossover. But what the driver actually saw as the train passed the distant signal, 1½ miles (2.4km) from the crossover, was never known, for he and his fireman were killed in the crash. Did he see the signal, and did he see the double-yellow lights?

By the time the overnight Perth – Euston express reached the outer London suburbs, at around 9.00am, the sun was rising into the south-east skies of a clear autumn morning. Through this part of Hertfordshire the LMS West Coast main line runs in a north-west to south-east direction, with variations as curves take it more to the south or the east. Approaching Bourne End, a driver looking forward from the left of his cab had the sun full in his face just to his left and upwards, causing light to glare into his eyes just as he was

▼ After the Bourne End disaster coaches were left piled on top of one another. Although most of the leading coaches had steel body panels with timber framing carried on steel underframes, they did not stand a chance in this high speed derailment, in which the engine came to a halt from 60mph (97km/h) in little more than 60yd (55m).

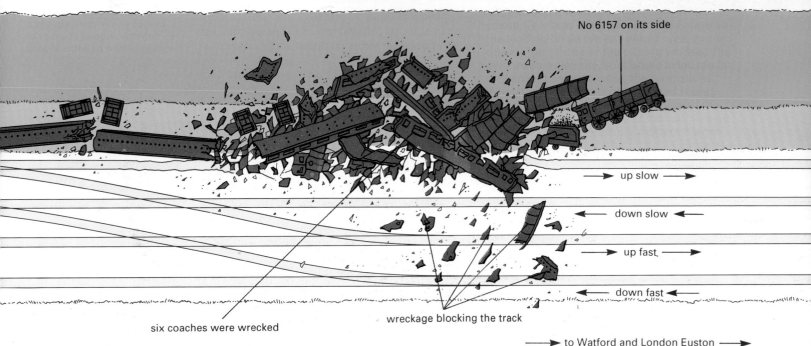

No 6157 on its side

→ up slow →

← down slow ←

→ up fast

← down fast ←

six coaches were wrecked

wreckage blocking the track

→ to Watford and London Euston →

looking for the distant signal. Perhaps the sun affected his perception of the colour shown by the signal, although it ought not to have done, since the signal was showing two yellow lights when normally only one was displayed. Or did he relax concentration and miss the signal altogether?

Lt Col Sir Alan Mount, the inspecting officer, could only speculate as to why the driver failed to slow down. He criticized the wording of the rule applying to double-yellow indications, which at junctions 'may' mean that the route is set for a low speed junction. Whatever the rule meant, the use of double-yellow aspects at colour-light distant signals leading direct to semaphore stop signals, as on the West Coast main line, was discontinued. From then on, trains signalled over the crossovers were given the normal indication of single yellow meaning: caution, prepare to stop at the next signal ahead at danger. Also, when trains were to be switched over the crossovers from fast to slow lines in unscheduled moves, the signals were to be kept at danger until the signalman could see that the train was slowing down.

Salvaging the engine
The engine had finished up on its side, several yards from the bottom of the embankment. Although the wreckage of the coaches was removed within two days, the engine remained in

▼ When night fell, rescuers were still hard at work amid the wreckage. Here a crane raises the shell of an open third class coach, consisting of no more than the sides and the roof, which were ripped away from the floor and underframe.

the field for four weeks. Everything that could be removed from it was removed, until just the boiler, frames, cylinders and wheels were left. The embankment was strengthened with piles and timber, and a timber deck of sleepers was laid alongside the overturned engine. Then, cables from two cranes standing on the up slow line on the top of the embankment were attached to the engine. The most difficult job was to pull the engine upright, but gradually it came up, and rolled on to its wheels on the sleeper bed at the foot of the bank. The two cranes then lifted the engine back on to the track. It was later repaired and returned to service.

Castlecary 1937

**In heavy snow, a signalman thought a train that had
run through his signals at danger was going to collide with
a goods train ahead. Instead of checking, he accepted another
express; that also passed his signals at danger and rammed
the back of the first train, killing 35 people.**

The Edinburgh – Glasgow main line of the former North British Railway (NBR) runs
through the Forth-Clyde valley, with its many
towns and strong manufacturing industry. From
1923, this section was part of the newly formed
London & North Eastern Railway (LNER), effectively becoming an extension of the East Coast
main line from King's Cross. A few express services ran between Glasgow and London by this
route, competing with the rival West Coast line
from Glasgow to London Euston, through Carlisle
and Crewe.

The Glasgow – Edinburgh line carried (as it
still does) considerable traffic between the two
Scottish cities, as well as trains between north-east
Scotland and Glasgow over the Forth Bridge. With
so much industry in the area, there were many
goods trains collecting and distributing products,
not just within the industrial belt, but with through
services to and from England, north-east Scotland
and a few services to the West Highlands that
came within the domain of the LNER.

Severe snow creates delays

On the afternoon of 10 December 1937, heavy
snow showers, some prolonged, were causing
problems for the railwaymen. At Gartshore, a
goods station about 10 miles east of Glasgow, the
snow was thick enough to block points on the
down main line (from Edinburgh). The switch
blades would not close tightly against the stock
rail and the facing point lock bolt would not go
into the slot to lock the points.

Trains could not pass over the points until the
snow had been removed by the permanent way
staff, helped by a signal lineman. But first the staff
had to be called to the points, and that took time.
Meanwhile, a goods train had to be held back at
Dullatur, waiting for the snow to be cleared before
it could proceed towards Gartshore. The goods
train was standing on the down main line, and thus
occupying the section from Castlecary.

The Castlecary signalman knew from the block
indicator for the section ahead that it was occupied, and that he would have to stop the next train
to await the onward move of the goods train at
Dullatur. He had restored his down line distant,
home and starting signal levers to normal after the
goods train had passed. He was therefore convinced there was nothing to stop him from accepting the next train, a Dundee – Glasgow express,
when it was offered to him by the next box to the
east, Greenhill Upper Junction.

Snow continued to fall heavily as darkness fell

around 4pm, but the Castlecary signalman could
still see his signals, and thought he could see the
white back light of the down distant signal at caution. Rules said that in fog or falling snow additional precautions should be taken, such as calling
out fog signalmen for stipulated distant and stop
signals to repeat the signal indications by hand-
lamps, and to put down detonators when the signal
was not at clear, or that the signalman should
adopt double block working.

The snow did not seem to be that bad, and the
Castlecary signalman did not think of taking any
extra precautions. However, as he watched for the
Dundee express, having received the 'train enter-
ing section' bell signal from Greenhill Upper
Junction, he suddenly saw its two headlights in the

▼ When the Edinburgh –
Glasgow express hit the back
of the Dundee train, the force
threw the leading coaches over
the top of Class A3 4-6-2
No 2744, seen here beneath
one of them.

(most of the platform track was out of sight, hidden from the signalbox not only by the footbridge, but also by a goods shed) he would have seen that the line was still occupied.

The Dundee express driver had indeed seen the signalman's red lamp and heard the shrill whistle. He made an emergency brake application and pulled up just beyond the starting signal, but he had not sounded the engine whistle or made any other acknowledgement. The Castlecary signalman knew nothing of this. He sent for the stationmaster to tell him he thought there was an accident at Dullatur, and in the intervening minutes telephoned the Greenhill Upper Junction signalman to ask what action he should now take, as he knew the 4.03pm Edinburgh – Glasgow express was due.

The two signalmen went through the procedure: had the Castlecary signalman seen the tail lamp of the Dundee train; were his signals at danger; was the line clear for a quarter mile beyond the home signal? The Castlecary man answered yes to each of these questions. There was just one final requirement: detonators should be put down. The Castlecary man said he would do so, and accepted

▲ A breakdown crane starts to lift debris from the wrecked brake third on top of the express engine. The remaining coaches have been removed already.

darkness. He realized it was travelling fairly fast and not slowing to stop at his home signal.

The Castlecary signalman grabbed his handlamp and checked that the red shade was turned in front of the oil lamp. He yanked open the signalbox window as the train swept by, showed the red light towards the engine and blew his whistle. But the red tail lamp of the express disappeared through the station and was hidden by the footbridge at the Edinburgh end of the platform. The express had seven bogie coaches and a six-wheeled fish van at the back, and was hauled by one of the NBR Scott Class 4-4-0s, No 9896 *Dandie Dinmont*.

Without a moment's hesitation, the Castlecary signalman sent the 'train running away on right line' bell signal – *4 pause 5 pause 5* – to Dullatur East box, expecting to hear very shortly that the Dundee train had run into the back of the standing goods train. Had he looked at his track circuit indicator covering the down line through the platform

Key

■ Edinburgh – Glasgow express

□ Dundee – Glasgow express

A telephone call to disaster

When snow blocked points at Gartshore on the Edinburgh – Glasgow main line, a goods train was held at Dullatur awaiting clearance, and occupying the section from Castlecary. The signalman at Castlecary accepted a Dundee – Glasgow express from Greenhill Upper Junction with all his stop signals at danger and the distant signal at caution.

When the Dundee train approached at speed, the signalman showed its driver a red handsignal and blew his pea whistle, but thought the train had gone on towards Dullatur. The signalman telephoned to Greenhill Upper Junction and asked what he should do. The two signalmen agreed that a following express from Edinburgh could be accepted by Castlecary. But the Dundee train had managed to stop just a few hundred yards out of sight of the Castlecary signalman.

Then, in the falling snow and darkness, the Edinburgh train swept by, ignoring the danger signals, and ploughed into the back of the Dundee train, killing 35 passengers. Both drivers claimed the distant signal was showing a good clear indication. Had it stuck at clear in the falling snow?

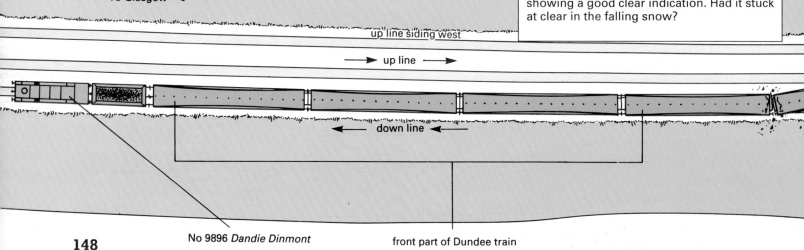

To Glasgow

up line siding west

up line

down line

No 9896 *Dandie Dinmont*

front part of Dundee train

the Edinburgh – Glasgow express.

At that moment, the stationmaster arrived with the fireman of the Dundee train. The signalman now knew the Dundee train had not gone on in the darkness into a collision with the goods train.

Then, two beats on the block bell from Greenhill Upper Junction alerted all three men to the fact that the Edinburgh – Glasgow express was now in section. They had just a minute or two to get some detonators down to give added protection to the standing Dundee train. As the three men left the warmth of the box the headlights of the Edinburgh train came into sight. Like the Dundee train, it was not slowing down, but rather speeding towards them at about 70mph. The stationmaster had time to get just one detonator clipped to the rail before jumping back out of the way of the oncoming train. The signalman again turned his red lamp towards the driver.

No time to stop

This was no local train. It had nine bogie corridor express coaches and was hauled by one of the Gresley A3 Pacifics, No 2744 *Grand Parade*. The driver heard the explosion of the detonator, shut the regulator and made an emergency brake application. But, with less than 300yd to the back of the Dundee train, there was no hope of stopping. Still travelling at about 60mph, the Pacific ploughed into the fish van and the rear passenger coaches of the Dundee train, totally demolishing them, before coming to an abrupt halt, partly overturned and with the front three coaches of its train hurled over and beyond the engine.

The Edinburgh train was composed of modern LNER stock, timber bodied, but with heavy steel underframes. All coaches were equipped with buck-eye automatic couplers, which held the rest of the train more or less in line. There was a mound of wreckage, but fortunately it did not catch fire.

Casualties were heavy: 35 passengers killed and 179 injured. It was the worst accident since Quintinshill (1915), and the worst ever in terms of casualties on the LNER. Amazingly, the driver and fireman of *Grand Parade* survived, the driver being hardly scratched, and the fireman suffering

just slight injuries. They had been saved by the massive steel body of the tender, which had remained behind the cab of the locomotive, and had not jack-knifed. The high sides and the surround of the cab sides and roof had protected the men from the wreckage flung on top of the engine.

In contrast, even the driver of the Dundee engine was injured as the standing engine was hurled forward together with the front of the train when the Pacific ploughed into the back. But why did two trains run through signals at danger, and had the snow prevented the drivers from seeing those signals?

Colonel Sir Alan Mount, who chaired the inquiry, had a puzzle to solve. Both train drivers were positive that Castlecary down distant, lower quadrant signal was clear and showing a green light. It was not drooping, but giving a good clear

▼ The third coach of the Edinburgh express broke its back as it was thrown on top of No 2744. The Pacific's crew escaped serious injury as they were protected by the large cab roof and the high sides of the tender. The surrounding wreckage is all that remained of two coaches and a fish van from the rear of the Dundee train.

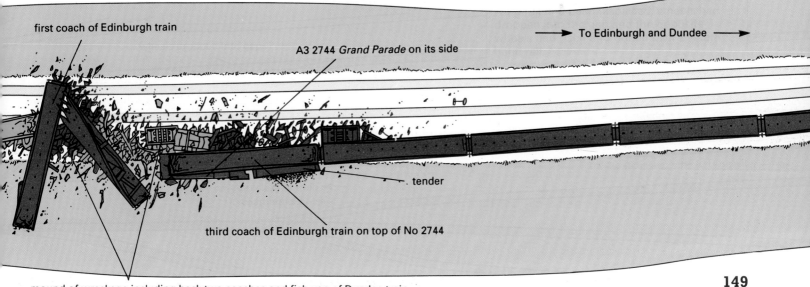

first coach of Edinburgh train

To Edinburgh and Dundee

A3 2744 *Grand Parade* on its side

tender

third coach of Edinburgh train on top of No 2744

mound of wreckage including back two coaches and fish van of Dundee train

▲ **LNER Class A3 4-6-2 No 2744 Grand Parade,** seen here after the coaches had been removed, lay on its side after the collision. Part of the front bogie can be seen between the middle and rear driving wheels. The engine was repaired and lasted in service until October 1963.

have operated double block working. Equally, the two express trains were travelling too fast for the limited visibility.

To prevent a recurrence, Colonel Mount recommended not just a repeater for the distant signal, but complete block interlocking between signals, block instruments and track circuits. This would ensure that signals could not be lowered for a second train until the first had been proved to have left the section, and the signals replaced to danger and caution behind, with the signal arms proved to have responded. This was the Welwyn control, first recommended two years earlier after the Welwyn Garden City collision. Finally, the inspecting officer recommended the development of automatic train control (ATC), which had been used by the GWR for nearly 30 years but virtually ignored by other railways.

ATC

By the late 1930s, the GWR had its own automatic train control (ATC) system, but other railways – despite pressure from inspecting officers – had done little towards its implementation.

After Castlecary, they started trials with an induction ATC system known as the Strowager-Hudd type, using permanent and electro magnets on the track. World War II delayed progress, and although the Hudd system was installed a decade later (on the London, Tilbury & Southend line) it took the devastating Harrow disaster in 1952, with 112 deaths, to push the by now nationalized British Railways to install an AWS system over many of its routes.

indication. Both drivers naturally assumed they had a clear road until the Dundee driver saw the red hand signal displayed by the signalman and the Edinburgh driver heard the detonator.

The signalman was equally positive that he had restored the signals to danger and caution after the goods train passed and that he had seen the backlight of the distant signal showing white through the dusk and snow – in the clear position the backlight is obscured and invisible. But the signalman also said that the track circuit indicator must have failed, since it was showing clear after the Dundee express had passed. Yet that train had come to a stop on the track circuited part of the line. When the signalman made the telephone call to Greenhill Upper Junction he looked at the track circuit indicator and was positive it was clear.

There was no suggestion that the signals had been left at clear after the goods train had passed, yet somehow the two drivers, both known to be highly responsible, had taken the distant signal as being clear. Had the arm somehow remained lowered, jammed by snow, or with its wire weighted down by snow, even though the lever had been put back to normal in the signalbox?

Colonel Mount could not find a positive answer. Having been to the signalbox he concluded that, in the failing light and the weather conditions, the signalman could not have seen the signal go back to danger after the goods train, nor could he have seen the backlight.

After the Dundee train ran by the home signal, the signalman's actions were irresponsible. His first duty was to find out why the train had not stopped, and then to protect the line. The track circuit indicator was tested after the accident and found to be in order. It should have shown the signalman that the Dundee train was still within his signals. But the signalman panicked: in accepting the Dundee train when he could not have seen the distant signal his action was wrong; he should

Welwyn Garden City 1935

Three late night expresses running closely together, and a serious error in their signalling, led to one running into another in a huge collision at Welwyn Garden City on the main line out of King's Cross. Thirteen people died.

In the 1930s, Welwyn Garden City, 20 miles north of King's Cross on the East Coast main line (ECML), was a developing new town. It was situated south of the Mimram Valley, amid low hills at the eastern end of the Chiltern ridge. Further south, near Barnet and Potters Bar, was another ridge of hills. This meant that ECML trains were faced with an almost continuous climb, largely at 1 in 200, from King's Cross to the first summit at Potters Bar, then, after six miles of falling gradients through Hatfield, a further six mile climb through Welwyn to the summit at Woolmer Green.

There were four tracks from Potters Bar, through Hatfield and as far north as Welwyn Viaduct. Between Hatfield and Welwyn Garden City there were two more, one on each side of the four main lines. These carried the branches west to Luton and east to Hertford.

Signalling in the area was controlled by mechanical signalboxes at Hatfield (where there were separate up and down boxes), Welwyn Garden City (South) and Welwyn North. All were equipped with three-position block instruments, with a few track circuits, mainly at home signals.

A busy night

In the late evening of 15 June 1935, three express trains left King's Cross closely behind one another. The first left at 10.45pm, bound for Newcastle; the second, also for Newcastle, departed at 10.53, and the third, a passenger and mail train to Leeds, left at 10.58. The second Newcastle train was formed of 11 coaches hauled by 4-4-2 No 4441, a type more suited to lighter loads, but adequate for the job. The Leeds train, also with 11 coaches, was headed by Class K3 2-6-0 No 4009, a much more powerful class. Most of the coaches were LNER or Great Northern (GN) timber-bodied types with steel underframes, although some, including vans on the Leeds train, had timber underframes.

The 10.45 express had a clear run and passed Welwyn Garden City at 11.20. The following 10.53 train was going well on the climb from Hatfield a few minutes later, when the driver saw the Welwyn Garden City South distant signal at caution. He shut

▶ An aerial view of the track just beyond Welwyn Garden City station shows clearly the devastation. The point of impact was just at the far end of the signalbox, but the 2-6-0 K3 locomotive, travelling at almost 70mph, didn't come to a halt until a point beyond the road bridge.

off steam and braked to 20mph; then he saw the home signal arm move from danger to clear. He thought that he had caught up with the 10.45 train so he let his train roll on slowly, thinking he might have to stop at the signals ahead. As he approached the station, he saw the starting signal at clear and so he opened the regulator to accelerate again. But hardly had he done so when his train was pushed forward by the impact of a violent collision at the back. The third train had run into the back of his train at about 70mph.

The heavy 2-6-0 of the Leeds train totally demolished the rear coach of the Newcastle train. None of the passengers in the coach survived. The underframe actually folded itself round the front of the 2-6-0 locomotive. The bogies of this coach and the one ahead were pushed forward for 140yd. But the coach ahead suffered less damage and the body held firm. The buckeye couplers, with which the train was equipped, remained tightly coupled keeping the coach upright and in line. Not one of its passengers was seriously hurt. The older coaches of the Leeds train suffered severe damage, and two were telescoped.

In all, 13 passengers were killed (the crews sur-

vived) and 81 injured, 20 of them seriously.

What went wrong?

Suspicions immediately fell on the actions of the signalman in Welwyn South signalbox. He had only recently been passed to work the box and hadn't gained much experience. It was a busy signalbox with six lines to control; the four track East Coast route and the two single lines, one on each side. There were no fewer than 11 block bells and 16 block indicators to look after. In addition, the signalbox was used as an enquiry office for missing parcels. Late at night the principal traffic was on the four main tracks with local and slow goods trains on the up and down local lines and express passenger and fast goods trains on the centre up and down main lines.

On the night of the accident, the Welwyn South signalman had accepted the 10.45 train from Hatfield, and it had duly entered the section and passed Welwyn Garden City at 11.20. But from then on his actions were confused. He must have

A fatal distraction

The accident arose when three down expresses were running north on the LNER main line out of King's Cross a few minutes apart. The signalman at Welwyn South, who had just been dealing with an up train, was distracted by a call from the station about a missing parcel.

The first of the expresses passed safely. The second was delayed approaching Welwyn as the signalman had not cleared the signals while answering the parcel enquiry. He then cleared the signals, but for some unknown reason sent 'train out of section' to Hatfield while the second express was still in his section, and accepted the third express.

The second express approached slowly, its driver thinking he was catching up the first, only to be rammed by the third which ran into the back of his train at full speed. The signalman was blamed for the collision.

▲A night-time photograph, taken soon after the collision, shows the little-damaged engine of the 10.58pm Leeds express, a K3 class 2-6-0, No 4009, which came to a halt entwined with the wreckage of the rear coach of the second Newcastle train. It was able to steam away later on.

▶ One of the wrecked coaches of the Leeds express which partially telescoped under the force of the impact. Behind are the starting signals and the Welwyn Garden City signalbox from which the fatal acceptance of the Leeds express came.

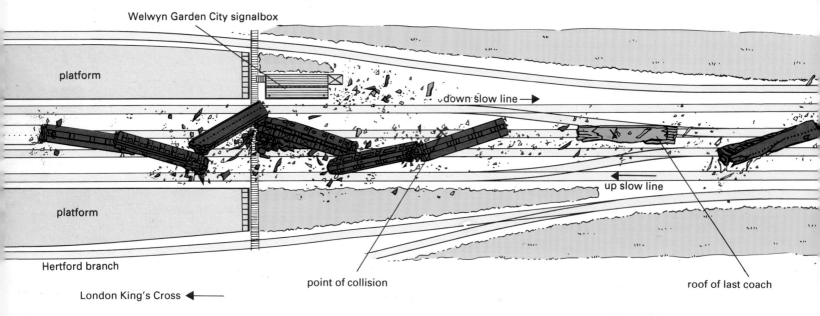

Welwyn Garden City signalbox

platform

down slow line →

up slow line

platform

Hertford branch

London King's Cross ←

point of collision

roof of last coach

given the 'train out of section' bell signal and cleared the block instrument for the down main line from Hatfield for the 10.45 train and accepted the 10.53 train, because the Hatfield signalman had received 'line clear' for it and cleared his signals. But then, for some unknown reason (although just after a goods passed on the up main), the Welwyn South signalman gave 'train out of section' and cleared the block indicator for the down main section from Hatfield. The 10.53 Newcastle train was still in the section.

The Hatfield signalman thought it was rather quick for the 10.53 train to have passed Welwyn Garden City, so he telephoned the Welwyn South signalman and asked him if he really meant to have sent 'train out of section'. 'Yes' came the reply, so the Hatfield signalman immediately offered the 10.58 Leeds express which was accepted by Welwyn South. The Hatfield signalman now cleared his signals for the Leeds train. These were signals to disaster as the 10.53 train was still in the section ahead and running slowly.

It was ironic that although there was a track circuit leading to the Welwyn South down main home signal, the 10.53 train hadn't reached it when the signalman cleared the block section from Hatfield. Otherwise it would have reminded him that there was a train approaching the home signal.

The driver of the Leeds train opened up his K3 2-6-0 on the long climb towards Welwyn and he was powering up steadily at well over 60mph. The signals approaching Welwyn were clear, but then in front of him was the back end of the second Newcastle train, its oil-lit tail lamp dimly visible against the lighting of the station ahead. It was too late. He couldn't avoid a massive collision with the Newcastle train.

The inquiry

The inspecting officer, Colonel Mount, had a mass of conflicting evidence to sift through. The signalmen at Welwyn North and Hatfield told the inquiry what actions they had taken, and they disagreed with the evidence given by the signalman at

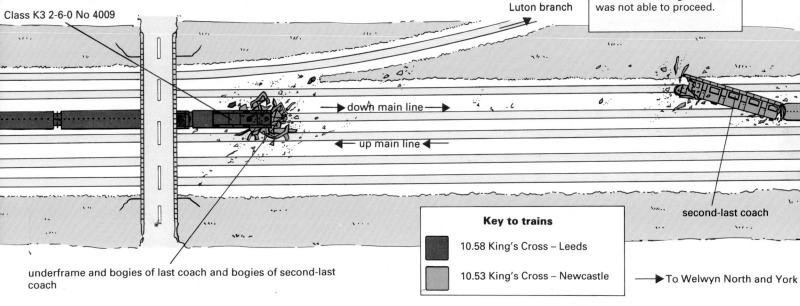

Class K3 2-6-0 No 4009

Luton branch

→ down main line →

← up main line ←

second-last coach

underframe and bogies of last coach and bogies of second-last coach

Key to trains

10.58 King's Cross – Leeds

10.53 King's Cross – Newcastle

——▶ To Welwyn North and York

Welyn South. It all seemed to point to the fact that the Welyn South signalman had become confused between all the trains.

Colonel Mount concluded that the Welyn South signalman had wrongly given 'train out of section' to Hatfield for the 10.53 Newcastle train and accepted the Leeds train. It could have been because he used the wrong set of block bells and block indicators. An up train had just passed and if, instead of clearing the up line section from Welyn North, he had cleared the down section from Hatfield, that would have accounted for his error.

As for the telephone call from the Hatfield signalman regarding the rather quick 'train out of section' bell signal for the 10.53 train, the Welyn South signalman thought they were talking about the 10.45 train, even though he had already cleared that one, and had accepted the 10.53.

Colonel Mount criticized the use of the signalbox as an enquiry office in respect of missing parcels which were nothing to do with the signalling. (Such an enquiry had come through just before the collision and probably distracted the signalman.) He also suggested that the various block instruments for the different sections should be painted in distinctive colours. But his main recommendation – for automated add-ons to the block system to prevent signalmen's mistakes – was revolutionary and brought a new safety dimension to railway signalling from then on. This has lasted right up to the present day on principal lines retaining mechanical signalling.

The system, which eventually became known as

▼One of the central coaches of the 10.58 Leeds express, brake van No 492, is hoisted away. There were several such wooden-bodied mail vans in the train, all over 30 years old, and most suffered severe damage.

▲The twisted remains of the underframe of the rear coach from the Newcastle express shows the huge force of the collision. The roof was left about a hundred yards behind. In the background lies the upturned second-last carriage whose wooden body remained largely intact.

Welyn control, was gradually installed on many of the LNER and LMS principal routes. It was not adopted universally on all mechanically signalled routes, however, although some features such as the 'line clear' release and the inability to give 'line clear' to the rear with signals still at clear, gave some protection against errors.

The signalman at Welyn South had little automation to help him and, in his confusion, he made a fatal mistake. But the recommendations by Colonel Mount to add safety devices to the block signalling system marked a major step forward in signalling procedures and safety, just as the accidents at Abbots Ripton in 1876 and Armagh in 1889 had done before.

Recommendations
Colonel Mount recommended the installation of track circuits, linked to the block instruments and the signals. This would impose some form of control on the signalman's actions, both in accepting trains and in clearing the rear section block instrument. It would prove that trains had actually passed through the section. What was developed as a result added a comprehensive system of checks to the existing equipment.

He also recommended that block instruments be painted in distinctive colours for each section, and that improved tail lamps be introduced. However, neither of these were implemented and, indeed, until recently the basic oil-lit lamp is still in use on some trains.

Abermule 1921

**Single line railways operate under strict
safety regulations, making it impossible for two trains
to be on the same section at the same time. At Abermule in
1921 a catalogue of human errors caused the impossible to
happen, resulting in a head-on collision and 17 deaths.**

On 26 January 1921 the 10.25am up express from Aberystwyth to Manchester left Newtown on time, heading the four miles north-east towards Abermule in rural mid-Wales. Driver Prichard Jones was in possession of a Newtown – Abermule tablet, which meant that no other train could legitimately be on that section of line at the same time. His Cambrian 4-4-0 No 95 hauled a train consisting of a six-wheeled van behind the tender and six wooden-bodied bogie coaches.

As he accelerated down the falling gradient he reached around 50mph. Then, about 1½ miles before Abermule, the gradient steepened to 1 in 123 and Driver Prichard Jones shut off steam ready to slow to about 10mph through Abermule for the hand exchange of the tablet pouches.

Suddenly, to his horror, he saw the smoke of another train coming towards him no more than 300yd away. He immediately made a full applica-

tion of the vacuum brake and sounded the whistle. Then he and his fireman climbed out on to the steps ready to jump.

The two engines met head-on at a combined speed of about 60mph. The other train was the 10.05am down slow from Whitchurch to Aberystwyth, composed of six coaches hauled by Cambrian 4-4-0 No 82. Both engines and tenders were wrecked in the collision, together with the first four coaches of the up express train and the leading coach of the down slow train.

Fourteen passengers were killed in the accident and so too were the driver and fireman of No 82 and the guard of the express. Over 30 passengers were injured, including two railwaymen travelling as passengers. The driver and fireman of No 95, who managed to jump off just before the collision, were also seriously injured, as was the guard of the slow train.

▼The disaster at Abermule was the only major single line head-on collision in Britain this century. Seventeen died in the accident, most of the fatalities occurring in the fourth coach of the express train, pictured below. The third coach telescoped right through it, sweeping the entire contents of the fourth coach – including the passengers – into a mass of wreckage at the rear end.

Single line safety

The Cambrian Railways' principal route from Oswestry to Pwllheli/Aberystwyth was a typical rural main line, with many features in common with similar routes elsewhere in the more remote parts of Britain. Largely single tracked with passing loops at stations, it ran across mid-Wales, through the mountains, linking the English West Midlands and north-west areas to the coastal resorts of Cardigan Bay, chief of them being Aberystwyth. As an independent backwater, time tended to pass the line by and railway operating methods had changed little for decades.

During the latter part of the nineteenth century a number of pioneering signal engineers had developed various forms of electrically interlocked instruments for working on single lines, using a variety of different shaped tokens. Cambrian Railways adopted Tyer's No 6 electric tablet system: two instruments were provided for every single line section – one at each end – each with about ten metal discs, called tablets, which were given to drivers as their authority to be on a single line section of track.

Each tablet, with the names of the stations between which it applied engraved on it, was kept in a vertical stack in the electrically interlocked tablet machines. When a tablet was drawn from one

instrument, both would become locked so that no more tablets could be removed until the first was reinserted into either machine. Both instruments showed if a tablet had been drawn out and whether it was for an up or down train. Thus at all stations with a passing loop there were two tablet instruments – one for the section on one side and one for the section on the other. It was a safe and reliable system, but unfortunately not one that was impervious to incompetence.

Abermule station

The layout and operation at Abermule station had remained unchanged for many years. The next station to the north-east was Montgomery, 3½ miles away. To the south-west was Newtown, 4 miles distant.

The signalbox was at the Montgomery end of Abermule station and controlled a level crossing.

▲The first coach of the slow train was totally destroyed and the two leading compartments of the second coach (pictured above) were also wrecked, with the bogies knocked away backwards.

Key to trains

⬛	10.05 Whitchurch – Aberystwyth
⬜	10.25 Aberystwyth – Manchester

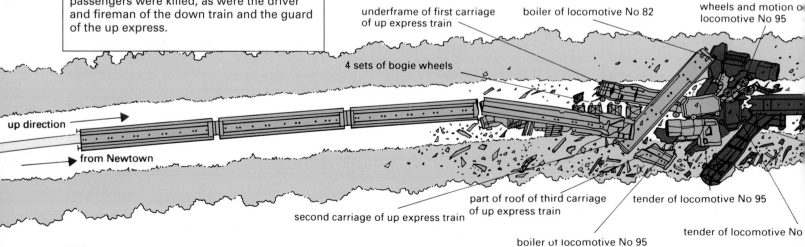

underframe of first carriage of up express train · boiler of locomotive No 82 · wheels and motion o locomotive No 95

4 sets of bogie wheels

up direction

from Newtown

second carriage of up express train · part of roof of third carriage of up express train · tender of locomotive No 95

boiler of locomotive No 95 · tender of locomotive No

Because of an old limitation by the Board of Trade on the distance at which points could be worked from the signalbox, the points at the Newtown end of the station, leading to the single line, were worked from a ground frame released from the signalbox.

The signalbox had a lever controlling the platform starting signal towards Newtown, but there was also a slot on the signal worked by a lever in the ground frame to make sure that the points were correctly set before the signal arm could be cleared. The tablet instruments were not in the signalbox – which was the usual position – but in a room in the station building near to the stationmaster's office, so that the stationmaster could personally oversee operations.

On 26 January 1921, a relief stationmaster was on duty at Abermule who knew the working well (the regular stationmaster was on holiday). Also on duty were one of the two regular signalmen, a young porter, and a junior clerk who did booking office work and collected tickets. Only the signalmen and the stationmaster were allowed to work the tablet instruments, and instructions had been issued to say that stationmasters had to watch over the signalling, particularly when express trains were involved.

The 10.05 from Whitchurch and the 10.25 from Aberystwyth were booked to cross at Abermule at about midday. The relief stationmaster was away from the station having lunch when Montgomery offered to Abermule the 10.05 train from Whitchurch on the tablet instrument bell. The signalman was in the office where the tablet instruments were located and correctly accepted the 10.05 train by working plungers on the machine to a prescribed routine, which gave Montgomery a release to draw out a tablet from the instrument there for the section to Abermule. The Abermule instrument then showed that a tablet was out for a down train.

The signalman telephoned to Moat Lane Junction beyond Newtown to find out how the express was running and was told that it was on time. The signalman passed on the details to the two juniors and went back to the signalbox to open the level crossing gates and clear the signals for the stopping train to enter the station.

At about the same time the relief stationmaster came back, but nobody told him about the stopping train or of the whereabouts of the express, so he went to the goods yard to check on some wagon movements. While he was gone, Newtown sent the 'Is line clear?' bell signal to Abermule for the express; as nobody else was near, the junior porter – who knew how to work the tablet instruments – accepted, allowing Newtown to draw a tablet for the Newtown – Abermule section to give to the express driver.

The junior porter went to the ground frame at the Newtown end to set the points for the express to run in, but he would have needed a release from the signalbox. At that moment the 10.05 train arrived at the down platform.

The junior clerk on the up platform crossed the line and collected the tablet in its pouch from the 10.05's driver and intended taking it to the tablet instrument to clear the section back to Montgomery. Instead, the relief stationmaster returned from the goods yard, saw the youngster with the tablet in his hands and asked where the express was. Whether the young clerk had realized what the porter had done or not, he replied that it was just past Moat Lane. Only the porter at the

▼The combined length of both trains was reduced by about a quarter in the collision. The two engines and tenders and five coaches (four of the express, one of the slow train), which would have covered about 115yd of track before the crash, were reduced to a 50yd mass of tangled wreckage.

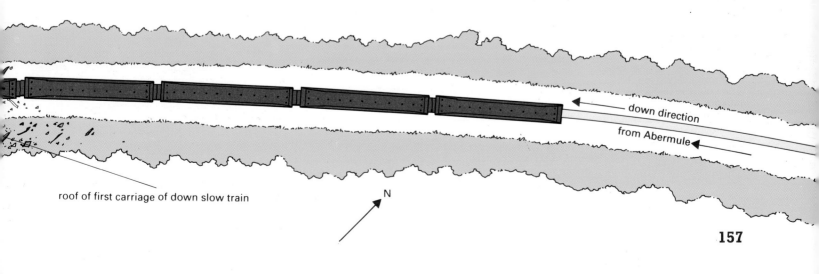

roof of first carriage of down slow train

N

down direction

from Abermule

▲An engine driver at Abermule station receives a leather pouch containing a tablet for the single line ahead, just as the driver of the fateful 10.05am down slow from Whitchurch to Aberystwyth did on 26 January 1921 – only he was mistakenly given the tablet for the line he had just covered. The hoop attached to the pouch allowed exchange on the move up to 10mph, the recipient putting his arm through the hoop to collect it.

ground frame at the far end of the platform knew that the express was actually in the section from Newtown.

What conversation then passed between the junior clerk and the stationmaster was never really discovered. The boy said he asked the stationmaster to change the tablet while he collected tickets from the stopping train. The stationmaster thought the boy had said the tablet had been changed and that the 10.05 train was going on.

Whatever was said, the stationmaster did not check the tablet he now held in his hands. Had he looked he would have seen 'Montgomery – Abermule'. Had he gone to the tablet instruments near his office he would have seen the instrument for the Newtown section showing tablet out for an up train – the express. He did neither. He handed the tablet in its pouch to the driver of the 10.05.

The porter correctly at his duties working the ground frame was trying to set the points for the express to enter but he did not have the lock on the ground frame released from the signalbox. Instead, he saw the stationmaster giving the right away to the 10.05 train. He thought that Newtown must have cancelled the express and that the stopping train was going on to cross the express at Newtown. The signalman had cleared his down starting lever and the porter cleared his signal lever, releasing the slot on the signal arm which went to clear. It was the signal to disaster.

There was just one last hope. As the stationmaster handed the tablet to the 10.05's driver, the driver should have checked it – as required by the rules – to see that he had been issued with the proper one for the section. He had actually been given the one he had recently surrendered to the junior clerk; had he looked at it the accident would not have happened. As it was, within five minutes both he and his fireman lay dead, together with fourteen passengers and the guard of the other train.

What went wrong?

Colonel Sir John Pringle, the railway inspecting officer who chaired the inquiry, found that the accident occurred from a combination of failures to adhere to working instructions and the rule book.

The juniors should never have been allowed to work the tablet instruments, nor to handle the tablets in collecting them and delivering them to the drivers. There was a lack of supervision by the stationmaster – and he himself had failed to ensure that he was being given the correct tablet.

Any one of the people involved, from the two juniors, the signalman, the stationmaster and the 10.05's driver, could have saved the situation had they either looked at the equipment or told those who should have known what they had done. It was a complete failure of communication.

Colonel Pringle criticized the fact that the tablet instruments were away from the signalbox, and that a separate ground frame was needed to control the west end of the layout.

Recommendations
Colonel Pringle recommended that the tablet instruments should be in the signalbox under the direct control of the signalman. He also suggested that the instruments should be interlocked with the starting signal leading into the single line section, so that the starting signal could be cleared only when the correct tablet (or key token or staff) had been drawn out. This would prevent clear signals from being displayed to a train which did not have the correct tablet for the single line ahead.

Had this form of interlocking been provided at Abermule, it would have prevented the signal for the 10.05 down slow train to proceed to Newtown from being pulled to clear.

Quintinshill 1915

**Two collisions within a minute or so,
involving three trains and two others standing alongside,
amounted to the worst ever railway accident in Britain. At least
227 were killed and 246 injured because the signalmen
disregarded a train that was in their full view.**

May 22, 1915. It was wartime, with Allied forces bogged down in France fighting Germany. At home, troops were on the move as they assembled at regimental bases for training before being sent to join their comrades in battle.

At 3.45am on that Saturday morning a battalion of the 7th Royal Scots Regiment left Larbert, in Stirlingshire, to travel to Liverpool. They were on a special train composed of old wooden non-corridor carriages, all but one of them lit by gas. Normally these coaches would not have been used for a long distance journey but in wartime every available vehicle was employed.

During the war all railways had come under government control so that it was not unusual for trains of one company to be used over the lines of another railway. The engine hauling the troop train as far as Carlisle was a Caledonian McIntosh 4-4-0 No 121, on home territory.

The train made its way towards Kirkpatrick and, three miles further south, Quintinshill, a small country block post just a mile and a half from the English border. Two overnight sleeping car trains from Euston station, the 11.45pm to Edinburgh and Aberdeen and the midnight to Glasgow, were booked to leave Carlisle at 5.50 and 6.05am respectively, followed by the 6.10 local train to Beattock.

Because the local train connected into an important commuter service from Beattock to Glasgow the authorities tried to keep it to time. If the sleeping car trains were late, the local left to time and was shunted out of the way along the line at Quintinshill or Kirkpatrick. Normally the local would simply be switched into the down loop at Quintinshill while the express trains overtook it.

Bending the rules

The Quintinshill signalmen worked two principal 10 hour shifts, a relief signalman filling in the remaining four hours, and they were supposed to change shifts at 6am. Both the men involved lived

▼Emergency workers direct their hoses on the wreckage of one of the rear coaches of the troop train, a Great Central 12 wheeler. The 15 GC passenger coaches were of timber construction, and most had wooden underframes. The combination of timber, newly recharged cylinders for the gas lamps and live coals spewed from the wreckage of three engines all added up to a calamity on an unimaginable scale. The inferno raged for nearly 24 hours, and 'brought with it such scenes as a man would remember with a shudder to the end of his days', reported *The Times*.

Wartime horror

The failure of the Quintinshill signalmen to protect a train standing in full view of the signalbox led to by far the worst catastrophe ever to occur on a British railway. The Larbert-Liverpool troop train, travelling fast on the falling gradient, collided with the engine of the standing local, No 907, a heavy 4-6-0. The head-on collision was of great violence, with the engine of the troop train ending up lying on its side and most of the wooden coaches smashed to pieces.

But worse was to come. The signalmen remembered too late the approach of the double-headed Euston-Glasgow sleeping car express. The crew of the coal empties and the guard of the local ran up the line to raise the alarm, but in spite of their frantic efforts, just one minute after the first collision all 600 tons of the express ploughed into the wreckage of the troop train. To add to the horrific chain of events, gas from the newly recharged cylinders on the gaslit troop train was ignited by coals spewing from the engine. The fire spread with nightmare speed. The result was carnage on an unimaginable scale.

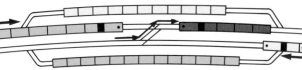

1 6.10 local shunted to make way for express. Troop train approaches.

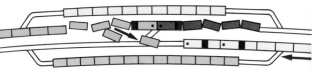

2 Troop train collides head on with local; sleeping car express approaches.

3 Double-headed express hits wreckage of the first collision.

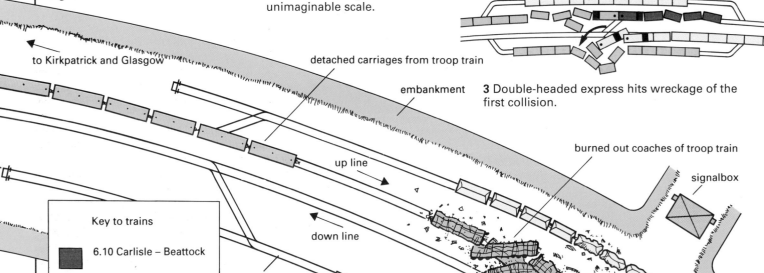

to Kirkpatrick and Glasgow

detached carriages from troop train

embankment

burned out coaches of troop train

signalbox

up line

down line

down loop

Key to trains

- **6.10 Carlisle – Beattock**
- Larbert – Liverpool troop train
- Euston – Glasgow Express
- 4.50 goods train from Carlisle
- Welsh coal empties

tender of troop train

locomotives of express

◀ No 121, a Caledonian McIntosh 4-4-0, hauled the troop train into disaster when all 550 tons thundered at 70mph into the standing local. While running, the engine and coaches of the troop train were 213 yards in length – after the collision the train was reduced to a 67 yard wreck.

▲A 4-6-0 McIntosh Cardean class was an enormous locomotive to be hauling the 6.10 local train from Carlisle to Beattock. It was wartime and any available motive power was used, however ill suited to the purpose.

To railwaymen this train was known as the Parly – a name taken from the days when railways were required by Act of Parliament to run third-class trains at low fares.

locomotive No 121 pulling troop train

locomotive No 907

up loop

to Gretna and Carlisle

at Gretna and walked or cycled to work. But it had become regular practice for the day man to use the local train from Gretna if it was likely to be stopped at Quintinshill.

On these occasions the day signalman used the local train and took up duty when it arrived at Quintinshill. But the local train arrived at Quintinshill half an hour after he should have taken over the signalbox. This was against the rules.

To avoid being found out, the night signalman would stop filling in the train register at 6am and record on a piece of scrap paper the times that bell signals for train movements were sent and received. The day shift man could copy them into the register in his own handwriting when he arrived to make it look as though he was there on the dot at 6am.

On 22 May Signalman Tinsley found out from Gretna Junction that the local train was stopping at Quintinshill. He joined it but when the train arrived at Quintinshill the down loop was already occupied by a goods train.

The local train was stopped on the down line and set back over the crossover on to the up main to leave the down line clear for the London trains to pass. At the same time an empty wagon train was arriving in the up loop so the troop special from Larbert to Liverpool could overtake it.

Signalman Meakin on the night shift handed over to Tinsley who at once started to copy into the train register the times of bell signals made by Meakin. Meakin sat back to read the morning papers brought by Tinsley.

The first of the down sleeping car trains had been accepted from Gretna as soon as the local train

was out of the way. The first sleeper passed safely at 6.38.

Neither signalman recalled giving the 'Train out of section' bell signal for the up goods and clearing the block indicator to Kirkpatrick to allow the troop train to be sent forward. Certainly neither sent the bell signal 'Blocking back inside home signal' to Kirkpatrick to protect the local train standing on the up main line right outside the signalbox.

Nor had they used a lever collar on the up home signal lever. These round metal rings would have reminded them not to pull the lever to clear because of the local train standing on the up line beyond it.

Tinsley accepted the second of the down sleeping car trains from Gretna and after acceptance from Kirkpatrick cleared his down line signals. Moments later Kirkpatrick offered the Larbert – Liverpool troop train.

Tinsley not only accepted it but offered it to Gretna and cleared the up line signals – disregarding the local train standing in its way right in front of him. The scene was set for a tragedy.

There was just one more chance of saving the situation. The fireman of the local train was in the signalbox to carry out Rule 55. Even now, with mechanical signalling on lines without track circuits, this or its successor Rule K3 is one of the most important rules in the book – to remind the signalman of the position of a train.

Certainly the fireman told the signalman where his train was – right outside the signalbox window. But he did not check that the signalman had taken steps to protect his train by sending the blocking back bell signal or using the lever collars. The last chance had gone.

Impact

The troop train was travelling at about 70mph on the falling grade with all signals clear. Suddenly, right in front of it, was the engine of the local, a big Cardean class 4-6-0, No 907. No 121 hit the standing locomotive head on with colossal force.

No 907 was badly damaged but No 121, hauling the troop train, was totally destroyed. The tender of 907 was thrown across the down line and so too was what remained of 121. But on top was a mound of wreckage from the coaches and vans of the troop train, some of which had been hurled right over the two engines.

The two signalmen were aghast.

'What have you done?' called Meakin to Tinsley. 'You've got the Parly standing there.' He was referring to the 6.10 local. Parly is an old railway term, dating back to the 1840s, for what were called Parliamentary trains – trains run originally at Parliament's insistence. 'And where's the 6.5?'

They rushed to the down line signal levers and put them to danger, but it was too late. The midnight sleeping car express from London, hauled by two 4-4-0 locomotives and travelling at about 60mph, hit the mound of wreckage and drove No 121's tender through the standing goods train on the down loop. Live coals from the engines were

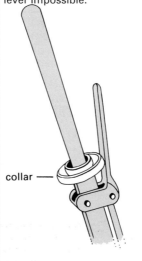
▶ Firemen from Carlisle took three hours to arrive at the remote scene of the disaster. Fanned by a stiff breeze, the fire spread rapidly – many passengers who escaped the worst effects of the collisions were caught in the blaze. The full horror became apparent at the tragic roll call of the troops – out of nearly 500 men, 446 were killed or injured.

thrown out and gas was escaping from the broken tanks under the old coaches of the troop train. The wreckage swiftly caught fire and burned right through the day and for much of the following night. Tragically, if they could not escape, those who were not killed in the collisions were caught in the fire.

The carnage was indescribable. Of the 500 or so troops on the special train only 53 answered a roll call after the accident. Some 215 of the troops were dead and 191 injured. The exact number killed was never known since the men's records were burnt in the fire. In addition to the troops, ten civilian passengers were killed, two in the local train and eight in the sleeping car train plus the driver and fireman of the troop train.

Called to account

The inquiry inspecting officer did not recommend the provision of new technology for added safety even though track circuits, which could have prevented two trains occupying the same section at once, were gradually coming into use. He felt it unreasonable to expect the Caledonian Railway to go to the expense of providing track circuits at locations such as Quintinshill where the layout was simple and the signalman had a good view of the trains.

The inquiry found that the accident was caused by inexcusable carelessness. Had the rules been correctly carried out the accident would not have happened. If the fireman of the local train had not left the signalbox to return to his train until he was satisfied that the safety procedures had been applied, the tragedy could have been avoided.

Convicted of culpable homicide at Edinburgh

What went wrong

The immediate cause was that the local train shunted on to the up line was forgotten by the signalman even though he had just arrived on it. He failed to carry out the regulations for its protection.

The signalmen's attention was diverted at crucial moments mainly because they changed duty times without authority. This led to Tinsley copying movements into the train register in his own handwriting.

The fireman failed to implement fully the requirements of Rule 55 by neglecting to see that the signalman followed the protection procedure.

The correct procedure

The signalman should have sent the 'Blocking back inside home signal' bell to Kirkpatrick and placed the block indicator at 'Train on line'. He should also have placed a lever collar on the home signal lever to prevent him pulling it clear with the local train standing on the track beyond the signal.

High Court (there was no offence of manslaughter in Scotland), Tinsley received three years' hard labour and Meakin was sentenced to 18 months' imprisonment.

Until the widespread adoption of track circuits and other automated safety features there were many accidents caused by signalmen's errors. But none had the tragic combination of factors which gave Quintinshill a place in railway history as the worst railway accident in Britain.

Baddengorm Burn 1914

On a June afternoon in 1914, storms raged over the Scottish mountains between Aviemore and Inverness. As a dam of debris burst, a wall of water swept down a burn and demolished a railway bridge just as a train was crossing, throwing the fourth coach into the torrent, and killing five passengers.

Railway civil engineers have always had to allow for the effects of wind and water when designing bridges, to ensure that they are strong enough to withstand exceptional weather. Bridges across streams, rivers or estuaries need good foundations, often taken down deep to bedrock under sand, silt and soil to make a firm foothold for the structure above. Large bridges and viaducts, particularly those made of steel (and originally iron), had to allow for wind pressure as well as water action, while the smaller masonry, and later concrete, arch bridges had to have solid foundations and abutments to prevent movement, which could weaken the arch.

Most Victorian railway bridges, particularly the masonry arches, were well built – indeed, often to far stronger standards than were really necessary in those early days of small locomotives and lightweight trains. This is evidenced by the fact that some of these bridges now carry trains many times heavier and at far higher speeds than were

originally envisaged – and they do so perfectly safely. This extra strength arose largely because the Victorian understanding of stress factors was rudimentary, and bridges were usually built with a generous safety margin. A few of the early iron bridges were not so successful, largely because the pioneer engineers did not allow for adequate strength to counter severe weather conditions, nor did they understand the behaviour of the materials they were using. The fall of the Tay Bridge, in 1879, was a prime example of poor design and workmanship leading to a downfall in a severe gale.

Getting across the Scottish mountains

On the Highland Railway (HR) main line, running north from Perth to Inverness, the civil engineers involved had to allow for the fact that the railway was being taken through mountainous country. It encountered peaks well over 3000ft (1000m) high on each side on its way through the Grampian and

▼Little was left of the wrecked Highland Railway (HR) brake third (left-hand side), which fell into the floodwater when the railway bridge over Baddengorm Burn collapsed. On the right is the second HR composite of the 11.50am Perth – Inverness train, which slid down the embankment as the bank subsided.

Aberdeen, Keith, Elgin and Forres. However, the considerable inconvenience associated with two unconnected stations (owned by different railways) at Aberdeen led the HR to build its own line to the south from Forres, through Aviemore and Blair Atholl. This opened in 1863, by which time locomotive power had developed so that engines were able to tackle the steep 1 in 60 gradients up to the summits, albeit slowly.

However, even this new route was not ideal. Aviemore lies about 30 miles (50km) south-east of Inverness in a direct line, but the rail route via Forres was closer to 60 miles (100km). So thoughts turned to making a more direct rail route from Inverness to the south, but it was not until 1898 that the new route, over Slochd Mhuic summit and through Carr Bridge to Aviemore, was completed.

Negotiating Baddengorm Burn

Just three-quarters of a mile (1.2km) north-west of Carr Bridge, this new section of the Highland main line had to cross the Baddengorm Burn, which came down from the mountains to the north of the line, running between the peaks at Carn Glaschoire and Carn nam Bain tighearna, both around 2000ft (610m). Just after leaving Carr Bridge station, the railway crossed the River Dulnain, heading north-east into Strathspey. Baddengorm Burn, coming steeply down the mountain slopes to the right of the line (looking towards Inverness), turned to run parallel with the railway through a deep gorge, with the line on an embankment for just over 200yd (180m), before turning sharply to pass under the railway, which was carried over the stream by a masonry arch bridge. The burn continued south on the south-west side of the line to join the River Dulnain.

The railway approached the bridge across the burn, initially travelling through a cutting in the hillside rising to the right, then emerging on to an embankment and the bridge. The bridge itself was not large, having an arch span of just 15ft (4.5m). After having crossed the bridge, the railway passed on to a further short length of embankment. About 200yd (180m) beyond was another embankment; here the line was carried over the former course of the burn (which had been divert-

▲This photograph was taken looking downstream through the gap where the bridge passed over Baddengorm Burn. The burn comes down from the mountains from the right and then makes a tight turn to the right just before passing under the railway. At its peak on the night of 18 June 1914, the floodwater was only just below track level.

Monadhliath mountains around Aviemore. The railway kept as much as possible to river valleys, but even so had to be taken up steep gradients to surmount the watersheds between river systems at Druimuachder (1484ft/452m high) after a 17 mile (27km) climb from Blair Atholl to the south (mostly at 1 in 70), and then to a second summit at Slochd Mhuic (1315ft/400m high) after a 10 mile (16km) climb from Aviemore (mainly at 1 in 70 and 1 in 60).

This was not the original route between Perth and Inverness; in the early days of the railways it was thought that the small locomotives of the time would be unable to tackle the steep gradients needed to carry the railway through the mountains. At first the link was along the relatively low ground near the coast, from Perth through

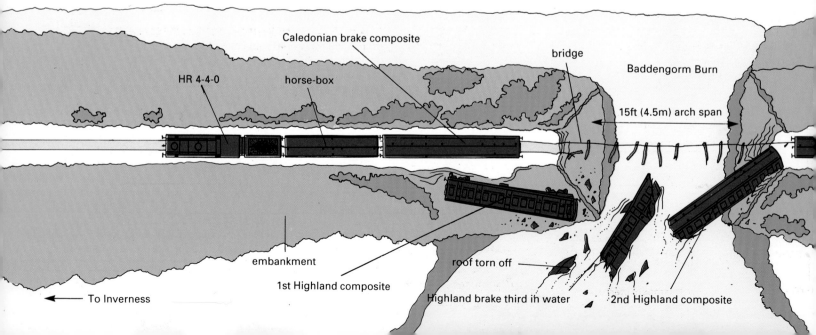

ed when the line was built so that it would pass under the line at the bridge).

There was no doubt that the railway was solidly built; this was no pioneering line, venturing into the unknown – like the railways of the 1830s, but on the contrary, one built with all the advantages of experience and 60 years of practice. The bridges were well constructed, a fact commented upon when the line was inspected by the Board of Trade officer Sir Francis Marindin before the line was opened just 16 years earlier. But the afternoon of 18 June 1914, just six weeks before the outbreak of World War I, proved that however good the construction, unforeseen circumstances could defeat the best engineers.

The 11.50am train from Perth to Inverness, including a through coach that had left Glasgow at 10.00am, was a few minutes late reaching Carr Bridge, the first station on the new line after Aviemore. It was booked to leave Carr Bridge at 3.15pm, but was actually away at 3.24pm, hauled by an HR 4-4-0. The train consisted of six vehicles: a Caledonian Railway four-wheel horse-box, a Caledonian bogie brake composite, and three Highland bogie coaches – composite, brake third and composite – brought up at the back by a six-wheel Highland brake van.

That nine-minute delay was possibly a critical factor in the accident that followed. Just about half an hour earlier the warm humid June day had been broken by a tremendous thunderstorm, which had moved north-east from the Monadhliath mountains towards the lower mountains bordering Speyside. Torrential rain fell, described by some witnesses as the worst they had ever seen. The storm reached the mountains to the north of the line at about 3.00pm, and the rain higher up in the mountains was so heavy that Baddengorm Burn and other waterways feeding into it developed quickly from placid streams into raging torrents. Just over half a mile (800m) upstream from the railway bridge was a road bridge carrying the road from Carr Bridge to Inverness. This bridge was swept away by the force of the water.

Just by the railway bridge was a farm. The burn was in such full flood that the farmer saw a wave about 18in (46cm) high tear down on to his property, covering an acre of his land and washing away much of the topsoil.

Uprooted trees and debris were carried downstream by the water and then trapped on the approaches to the railway bridge by the enormous volume of water, which simply could not pass quickly enough under the bridge.

An unsustainable pressure

As the burn entered the narrow gorge, water was at rail level. On the upstream side of the bridge the water depth was about 19ft 6in (6m) above the stream bed and 13ft (4m) below rail level, yet just 44yd (40m) downstream from the bridge the top of the water was 11ft (3.4m) lower. The resulting pressure on the bridge was enormous. The eddying of the water caused a vortex on the lower side of the bridge, washing away both the granite blocks forming the foundation, and the gravel on which they were bedded.

▼In the centre of this photograph, almost on its end, is the second Highland Railway composite, which came to rest on the Carr Bridge side of the bridge over Baddengorm Burn.

The most famous disaster involving a railway bridge is probably the Tay Bridge disaster of 1879, in which poor design and bad workmanship could not withstand gale force winds.

...ay Disaster, Carr Bridge, 18th June, 1914.   'Courier'

An unforeseeable catastrophe

Torrential rain caused a road bridge to be torn away and swept down the raging Baddengorm Burn towards a railway bridge, the burn carrying uprooted trees, soil and chunks of the road bridge on its way. The combination of this floating debris and an unprecedented volume of water were too much for the railway bridge's foundations, and an arch collapsed just as the 11.50am Perth – Inverness train was crossing it. The track had looked normal to the driver, but he soon realized that his train had split in two as the bridge collapsed, with the fourth coach falling into the water and drowning five of its nine passengers.

...rake van   embankment   To Carr Bridge and Perth ⟶

up what was left. It was in this coach that the casualties occurred, with five passengers drowned. Yet, remarkably, four people escaped from this coach, and survived. But the raging waters had not finished their work. The rest of the arch and abutments collapsed gradually, then the approach embankments on each side of the bridge were washed away, and the third and fifth coaches slid down to lie on what was left of the banks; fortunately, their passengers had time to escape.

No one to blame

Lt Col E Druitt inquired into the accident for the Board of Trade. He concluded that this had been no ordinary flood, but arose from 'an aerial disturbance of quite a phenomenal and unprecedented character'. There had never before been a flood like it in the area, and it had not occurred to the engineers who designed and built the bridge that it would ever have to withstand such a volume and force of water.

The bridge had a foundation of flat stones, each about 6sq ft (0.6sq m) in area, bedded in lime on mountain gravel, between 2ft 3in (69cm) and 4ft (1.2m) below ground level. The abutments were built in square blocks of granite as much as 6ft (1.8m) thick, and packed behind with heavy rubble. But this was not enough; the water carried the blocks away. Great chasms were washed out in the stream bed, to such an extent that one of the bogies from the ill-fated fourth coach was later found buried under the sand and gravel.

The question must be asked: if the train had been on time, just that few minutes earlier, would it have passed over the bridge safely, before the arch collapsed?

The bridge over the burn was rebuilt, but the new design allowed a longer span, of 26ft 6in (8m), and was constructed largely of concrete, with deeper foundations and a heavy invert all the way under the bridge, in addition to a curtain on each side, so that violent storm water could not scour the foundations.

▲Alexander Newlands (1870-1938) was Chief Engineer of the Highland Railway between 1914 and 1922. He was a principal witness at the inquiry into the Baddengorm Burn disaster, at which he was called upon to give a detailed description of the bridge's construction.

He stated that the bridge was destroyed by 'the quite abnormal volume of water which was the result of a cloudburst...that volume of water created a vortex [which] had the effect of tearing out the earth filling behind the wing wall, thereby exposing it and rendering it quite unstable in such a flood.'

Mr. Newlands.

Just then, the 11.50am train approached the bridge, working hard on the 1 in 60 climb. The rain had not been too heavy at Carr Bridge, and – viewed from the footplate of the Highland 4-4-0 – the track looked to be normal as the train left the cutting and ran from the embankment on to the bridge. But as the engine reached the arch the driver felt it tilt to the left. He kept steam on to keep the train moving, but the automatic vacuum brake came on and stopped the train. The driver got down, and to his astonishment saw that the section of the bridge over which he had just passed had disappeared.

The train had split in two, with its engine, the horse-box, the Caledonian brake composite and the first Highland composite beyond the northwest end of the bridge, and the second Highland composite and the brake van on the Carr Bridge side. The Highland brake third was just visible in the raging torrent downstream from the bridge. Its roof had been torn off, and part of one side demolished, while the force of the water soon smashed

Ais Gill 1913

Poor coal and inadequate motive power caused an express to come to a halt high up in the Pennines. As the crew of the 4-4-0 struggled to get their train going again, another train smashed into the back of the first, killing 16 passengers.

The Settle and Carlisle route of the Midland Railway formed a link from the south to the Scottish border, but in its progress from Leeds to Carlisle it had to cross the high Pennine moors. The summit of 1169ft (356m) was at Ais Gill, with long steep ascents from north and south at 1 in 100.

Once heavy corridor trains were introduced from about the turn of the century, many trains had to be double-headed. Late on the evening of 1 September 1913 two locomotives were being prepared at Carlisle to work two up overnight Scotch expresses to London St Pancras. A Class 4 4-4-0 No 993 was booked to work the 1.35am from Carlisle, formed of ten coaches, with portions from both Glasgow and Stranraer, and including three twelve-wheeled sleeping cars. The total weight was 243 tons, 13 tons over the limit for a Class 4 engine to handle on its own.

The second engine, Class 2 4-4-0 No 446 had a much lighter train of six coaches totalling 157 tons, and within the load limits for an unassisted Class 2. This train had the through coaches from Edinburgh and Inverness and was booked to leave Carlisle at 1.49am.

Poor coal

Both engines were taking on coal but their drivers were not very happy at its quality. Normally the South Tyne coal used at Carlisle was good and engines steamed well on it but that night there must have been a bad lot which had not been screened as there was a lot of dust, slack and small coal in it. For an engine to steam well it needed plenty of air to pass through the fire, but dust and small coal formed an almost impenetrable mass which restricted air flow. This meant that the coal did not burn well and gave off less heat than a good clean, bright fire so the boiler could not produce steam so easily.

A poorly steaming engine then suffered in other ways since other equipment relied on good steam pressure. The principal equipment was the live steam injector, which put water into the boiler.

▼Workmen survey the mournful remains of the wreckage at Ais Gill. Only metal parts remain as the largely wooden coaches were burnt when coals from one of the locomotives set light to gas escaping from the gas lighting cylinders. Several disasters had been greatly worsened by gas igniting after a collision and Colonel Pringle recommended the replacement of gas lighting by electric lighting. Despite this, however, gaslit carriages remained in use until the 1950s.

The injector was fed with live steam from the boiler, water in the tender was turned on to the injector and the steam carried the water at high speed into the boiler which maintained the water level.

Injectors did work over a wide range of boiler pressures, but once pressure dropped below certain limits injector operation became erratic. It failed to pick up the water which overflowed through a drain to waste on the track, or stopped working altogether. If this was not overcome it would lead to low water in the boiler and possibly a dangerous situation.

The other equipment which needed good boiler pressure on a steam locomotive was the vacuum brake ejector in which a steam jet was used to suck air out of the system. If boiler pressure dropped, the ejector became less efficient and could not maintain the vacuum. There would then be a risk of air leaking into the brake system and partly or even fully applying the brakes. A slow running train climbing a gradient with dropping steam pressure could be brought to a stop with the brakes leaking on.

The final factor was the speed of the train. An engine steaming well up a gradient would have a good exhaust blast through the chimney to draw air through the fire. This would keep it roaring away just when most steam was wanted. A poorly steaming engine losing speed would not have so much of an exhaust blast up the chimney, adding to the problems.

Steep climb

When No 993's driver was given the load details he asked for an assisting engine to Ais Gill, but was told that none was available. Eventually the train left Carlisle a few minutes late at 1.38am on 2 September. Almost from the start lay eight miles of climbing at 1 in 132, followed by 25 miles of slightly easier grades, climbing at between 1 in

Key to Trains

■ 1.49 Carlisle – St Pancras

▨ 1.35 Carlisle – St Pancras

← to Hawes Junction ←

Class 4 locomotive No 993

third class coach and sleeping car set alight

110 and 1 in 660.

Just south of Appleby, however, the climb to the Pennine peaks started in earnest with 15 miles more or less continuously at 1 in 100 to the summit at Ais Gill. It was a dark night with heavy rain and strong winds and, north of Appleby, No 993 was in trouble with steam pressure dropping back from the maximum.

The fireman tried to use the pricker to get air through the mass of coal, then the driver took a turn at firing and they managed to keep the train moving at a reasonable speed. But, once on the 1 in 100, pressure began to fall slowly but steadily from its maximum of 220lb.

After 10 miles of the steep climb, the train passed through Kirkby Stephen but speed was averaging less than 30mph instead of the 40mph needed to keep time. Three miles on, at Mallerstang, speed was down to 20mph, boiler pressure was down to 85lb and the driver had to put on the large vacuum ejector, normally used for releasing the brakes after a stop, to prevent the vacuum from dropping and the brakes rubbing.

Just three miles ahead was the summit, but the struggling engine eventually stopped half a mile from the top of the climb. The blower was hard on and the fireman was desperately trying to break up the mass of coal and slack to get some life into the fire. The guard was also told that the train would be only at a halt for a minute or two and nobody thought it necessary to go back and put down detonators to protect the stalled train.

Meanwhile, on the following 1.49am train, No 446 was progressing a little better with its light load but it too had steaming problems. It was gradually catching up on the 1.35 train. As the train approached Birkett Tunnel No 446's driver had climbed along the footplate towards the front of the engine to top up the oil reservoirs feeding the axleboxes. This was necessary on engines without mechanical lubricators. As the engine emerged from Birkett Tunnel the driver returned to the cab. He saw Mallerstang distant signal a few hundred yards ahead and thought he saw a green light.

Fatal distraction

But in the cab all was not well. The water gauge showed that water was low and getting near to uncovering the firebox crown, even though the train was climbing and the back of the engine was lower than the front. The right-hand injector would not work at all and the left-hand injector was spluttering. The boiler pressure was down to 130lb instead of the full 175lb. This was a crisis and No 446's driver had to help the fireman and act quickly to get at least one injector working properly.

By tinkering with the controls of the right-hand injector he got it to work, but at the same time the train was passing Mallerstang signalbox at about 30mph, with all signals at danger.

The Mallerstang signalman had thought that the

▼A train passes the scene of the crash at Ais Gill on 6 September 1913. Its locomotive is of the same class as that which had stalled so disastrously while hauling the 1.35 train. Ten of these Deeley 4P class locomotives were built from 1909, but they did not last very long; the last was withdrawn in 1928.

Poor steaming to disaster

Engine No 993 hauling an Anglo Scottish express train had stalled, but its crew did not carry out protection with detonators as they should have. The crew of the following up train were preoccupied by the poor steaming of their engine. Because of this they did not see the signals at Mallerstang at danger and continued at speed.

The Midland Railway management was blamed by Colonel Pringle for not providing properly graded coal for the two engines. They were also criticized for not providing large enough locomotives, which had indirectly caused the accident because the trains were too heavy.

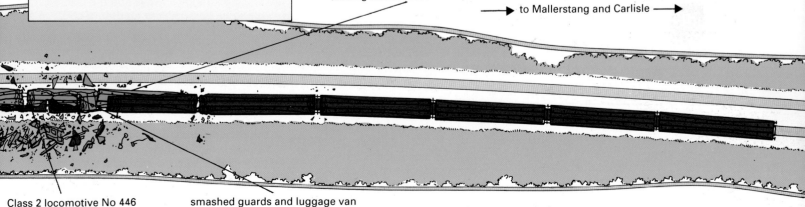

leading coach sliced into by roof

→ to Mallerstang and Carlisle →

Class 2 locomotive No 446   smashed guards and luggage van

▲The Ais Gill disaster was the second on the Settle to Carlisle line in just three years. The disaster at Hawes Junction had also been investigated by Colonel Pringle and had also involved the wreckage being incinerated because of the use of gas lighting. Therefore in his accident report he recommended the adoption of electric carriage lighting.

train was coming to a stop at his home signal so pulled it to clear to allow the train to run up to his starting signal at danger. He realized that the engine was still under steam and quickly put his home signal to danger. He grabbed his red hand lamp and waved it towards the engine.

Just over two miles ahead the 1.35am express had come to a halt as the 1.49 train roared past Mallerstang. There was just one means of preventing a collision. No 993's driver first saw the glare from an open firebox door reflected off the clouds above the moorland some way behind them and realized what it was. He sent the guard and fireman back to try to warn the oncoming express and sounded the whistle of his own engine. But it was too late.

A flaming inferno
No 446 crashed right through the rear guards and luggage van of the 1.35 train into the third class coach next to it. The clerestory roof of the luggage van went over No 446 and sliced into three compartments of the leading coach of the 1.49 train. Gas escaping from the lighting system of the 1.35's wrecked coaches was ignited by the fire of No 446 and the wreckage soon became a flaming inferno, engulfing the van, the third class coach next to it and the sleeping car beyond that.

In all 14 passengers were killed on the spot and two more died later. On the second train, 38 passengers were seriously injured even though they were spared from the fire.

What went wrong?
Colonel Sir John Pringle chaired the inquiry conducted by the Board of Trade. He concluded that the disaster was caused by the 1.49 express passing the red signals at Mallerstang and that its crew could not have seen the distant signal at green.

While accepting that the crew had severe diffi-

culties in running the engine, the crew of No 446, having realized they had missed the Mallerstang home and starting signals, kept going at speed rather than slowing down to run at caution. But he was also critical of the crew of the 1.35 train for not going back with detonators and a red light to stop any oncoming train.

The Mallerstang signalman was criticized for at first clearing his home signal without ensuring that the 1.49 train was actually stopping, although Colonel Pringle accepted that this action would probably not have made any difference.

It was recommended that all engines should have mechanical lubricators, so that the dangerous practice of oiling on the move could cease, and that detonator placer levers should be installed in signalboxes so that the signalman could give an audible warning to a train ignoring signals.

He also suggested that coal should always be screened to eliminate dust and slack. But apart from his recommendations for eliminating gas for lighting, a call which was to be heard several more times after train fires in 1915 and 1928, his primary recommendation was for some form of automatic stopping device to prevent trains from going past signals at danger.

The Great Western Railway had already introduced its automatic train control system, giving audible warnings at distant signals and an automatic brake application if the driver did not acknowledge a caution indication. Colonel Pringle thought that this system ought to be tried out more widely to see if it could be adopted as a future safety device. In the event two world wars and 40 years elapsed before a standard automatic warning system (AWS) was devised by British Railways.

Shrewsbury 1907

**The overnight Manchester to Bristol mail
and passenger express took the 10mph curve approaching the
platforms at Shrewsbury General on 15 October 1907 at 60mph. It
passed signals set to danger, making disaster inevitable.
The train was wrecked and 18 people died.**

At the turn of the century, Shrewsbury was a major railway crossroads with two principal main lines and two branches meeting at General station. Two of the lines ran into the station on very sharp curves with severe speed limits.

Shrewsbury was a border town in more senses than one. Not only was it the county town of Shropshire, bordering Wales, but it was also the meeting point of two principal main lines, each belonging to one of the major pre-Grouping railways.

From the south east came the Great Western (GWR) line from Paddington through Birmingham and Wellington, which continued north west to Wrexham, Chester and Birkenhead. From the north east came the London & North Western (LNWR) line from Crewe, which went on as a joint line with the GWR south to Ludlow, Hereford and Newport. But it was not quite as clear cut as that, since the early railways around Shrewsbury were part of the railway politics of the

1840s. They were the result of plans and counter plans traded between local companies and the already established larger railways.

The first railway into Shrewsbury was the line from Chester which opened in 1848. Other routes had already received parliamentary approval and were under construction by then, so that within three years the lines to Wellington and Hereford had been opened. The lines from Chester and Hereford had a fairly straight approach to what was to become Shrewsbury's main station, known for many years as Shrewsbury General. Its second station, Shrewsbury Abbey, was a small terminus, served only by an independent minor rural railway, the Shropshire & Montgomeryshire Railway.

Approaches to Shrewsbury

Whether a railway had a straight or easy approach to a station depended to a large extent on the geography of its route, whether there were any physical obstacles which it had to skirt and, at junctions,

▼Recovery operations were soon under way. Shrewsbury's locomotive tool van is on the right. Its unusual shape allowed the breakdown crane's jib to swing past it. The complexity and sharp curvature of the trackwork which the train had to negotiate can be seen. Most of the tracks here are check railed, as required for especially sharp curves.

another line, which came in from Crewe and was wholly owned by the LNWR. It was built a decade later than the other lines at Shrewsbury, opening in 1858, and it therefore had to be added on to what was already there. Coming in from the north east it approached the station on a very sharp curve, to reach the platforms on the east side. The radius of the curve was no more than 200yd (182m) and it had a severe speed restriction of 10mph.

Another hazard was the gradient, since the line crossed higher ground between Crewe, lying in the Cheshire plain, and Shrewsbury in the valley of the River Severn. The final four miles of the line from Crewe dropped almost continuously from Hardnall on gradients of 1 in 117 to 1 in 124 to within half a mile of Crewe Junction at Shrewsbury. That was the setting for a mysterious accident which occurred in 1907 and which has never been explained to this day.

With its own line as far as Shrewsbury and the joint line with the GWR on to Hereford, the LNWR had a thriving service from north west England to the south west and Wales by this route. It was not as direct as its Midland competitor which ran straight from Derby through Birmingham to Bristol, but it provided useful cross country links. From Hereford, over the Great Western, LNWR carriages reached South Wales, and through the Severn Tunnel, Bristol and the far south west.

Several portions

One of those trains was the overnight passenger and mail train from Manchester to Bristol. At Crewe, portions from Glasgow, York and Liverpool were combined into one heavy train leaving at 1.20am for Shrewsbury and Hereford. Through carriages or connections gave morning arrivals in South Wales, and onwards from Bristol to Exeter, Plymouth and Penzance which was reached after 1pm.

the angle of approach from a secondary route on to a main line.

When the Shrewsbury & Wellington line was opened in 1849, it soon formed part of the Great Western Railway trunk route from Paddington to Birkenhead, although it had been promoted as a local line. And, because of railway politics, it was jointly owned by the GWR and the LNWR. So too was the main line south to Hereford, and a branch to Buttington which joined the Cambrian line to Welshpool and, across Wales, to Aberystwyth. But the Wellington line, despite forming part of a main route, entered Shrewsbury from the south east on a sharp curve.

At the north end of Shrewsbury station was yet

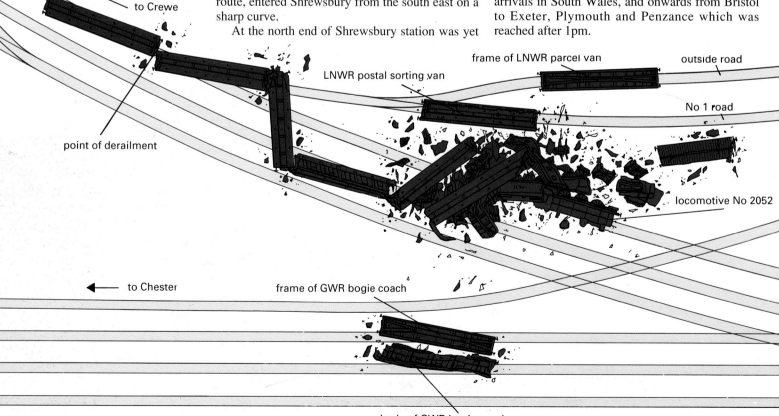

to Crewe

point of derailment

LNWR postal sorting van

frame of LNWR parcel van

outside road

No 1 road

locomotive No 2052

to Chester

frame of GWR bogie coach

body of GWR bogie coach

On 15 October 1907, the 1.20am train consisted of 15 carriages and vans, belonging to several companies, including the GWR, LNWR and West Coast Joint Stock (LNWR and Caledonian). It was hauled by one of the LNWR inside cylinder 4-6-0s of the Experiment class, No 2052 *Stephenson*. Many LNWR locomotive names and class names revived old names from the pioneer days of railways.

By the time station work was complete, the train left at 1.28am and the driver set about regaining some of the lost time straight away. He kept a steady pace up the eight mile climb between Nantwich and Whitchurch, but from then on to the approaches of Shrewsbury he regained five minutes on the easy gradients of this 18 mile section, averaging 60mph.

Quite what happened on the four miles of falling gradient into Shrewsbury was never established, but the train was undoubtedly travelling fast.

Approaching Shrewsbury the signalling was under the control of two signalboxes, Crewe Bank at the bottom of the descent from Hadnall, and Crewe Junction at the intersection of the line from Chester, immediately at the north end of the station. When Crewe Bank offered the 1.20am train

to Crewe Junction, the line was not fully clear into the station and Crewe Junction accepted the train under what was known as the 'warning' arrangement; meaning 'section clear, station or junction blocked'.

Under this procedure Crewe Bank would have had to stop the train and warn the driver that he could proceed, but must be ready to stop at the first of Crewe Junction's signals precisely, since there was no over-run distance beyond the signal, as in a normal acceptance. The Crewe Bank signalman thus kept his home signal at danger and distant signal at caution against the 1.20.

The distant signals would at that time have shown a red light at night, the same indication as a stop signal, since yellow lights for caution were not adopted generally until the 1920s.

The Crewe Bank signalman watched the train approach in the darkness. But, to his horror, it was not slowing to stop at his home signal. It swept by him at full speed and he realized that it was not going to get round the curve 600yd (550m) ahead. At once he sent the 'train running away on right line' emergency bell signal to Crewe Junction; but it was too late.

By the time the last beat on the bell had faded in Crewe Junction signalbox, the engine reached the sharp curve and nothing could prevent it from rolling to the right and falling on to its side. The momentum threw it across the adjoining tracks. In the darkness the Crewe Junction signalman saw the lights of the carriages continuing forwards over, and to the side of, the engine, splintering into matchwood as their wooden bodies crumbled into a mounting pile of wreckage.

The entire train was wrecked and inevitably casualties were heavy. The driver and fireman were killed, together with eleven passengers, two guards and three Post Office sorters working in the mail carriages.

The Experiment class 4-6-0s

The engine hauling the train wrecked at Shrewsbury was one of the LNWR inside cylinder 4-6-0s of the Experiment class, No 2052 *Stephenson*, built only ten months before. Although called the Experiment class they were anything but experimental. Effectively they were a 4-6-0 version of the Precursor class 4-4-0s of 1904 and both had been designed by the LNWR engineer George Whale. The Precursors were intended for heavy express haulage, while the Experiments, with slightly smaller driving wheels (6ft 3in against the Precursor's 6ft 9in), and more adhesion weight, were largely used on the climb over Shap between Lancaster and Carlisle. But they were also in use on the Crewe – Hereford route. But the newspapers of the day got it wrong, criticizing the use of an 'experimental' engine on the wrecked train.

▼ *Stephenson* lies on its side after the accident. No-one saw the crew at the time of the accident. It could not be ascertained whether they did not heed the signals because they had fallen asleep, or were attending to some other matter on the engine, unaware of where they were.

Passing the signals

Before the 1920s, both distant and home signals displayed a red light when at danger. On the night of 15 October 1907, the signalman at Crewe Bank signalbox in Shrewsbury had set both his home and distant signals to danger. This was to protect the junction ahead at Shrewsbury station, which was approached over a curve with a 10mph limit. But the overnight train from Manchester to Bristol approached Shrewsbury at about 60mph. It passed the red light of the Crewe Bank distant signal and then the home signal without slowing down. The 15 carriage train was meant to pass round a sharp curve and negotiate two sets of points but never made it. The locomotive turned over and the carriages piled into one another, strewing wreckage everywhere.

Shrewsbury station island platform

No 2 road

to Ludlow →

▲Eight locomotives were coupled together in an attempt to pull *Stephenson* from the rest of the wreckage. Precedent class 2-4-0 No 381 *Patterdale* is at the head of the ensemble. The chain can be seen attached to the 4-6-0. After two attempts the chain broke and more conventional recovery methods were used.

The warning arrangement

In normal mechanical signalling practice, the line must be clear before a signalman can accept a train from the preceding signalbox; not only through the block section, but also for a quarter of a mile beyond his first stop signal. This is known as the clearing distance and the quarter mile is the clearing point. It is provided just in case a driver misjudges his braking and over-runs the signal at danger. It does not give enough margin for a driver to ignore the signal altogether. To avoid delaying trains unnecessarily, a special signalling instruction, known as regulation 5, the warning arrangement, allowed signalmen to accept a train, provided the block section itself was clear, without the quarter mile clearing point also being clear. Regulation 5 was often used at junctions.

The train should have passed through two sets of facing points, the first to switch it off the main track from Crewe to the left (on to what was called No 1 road) and then a second set of points on a very sharp left-hand curve on to what was known as the outside road.

The derailment took place just before the second set of points and the engine was flung across the main track from Crewe; two tracks from where it ought to have been. Most of the train followed the engine but the carriages and vans at the back just managed to take the correct track.

One GWR carriage was actually thrown right across the engine and finished up totally wrecked on the Chester tracks, while another ended up on top of the mound of wreckage. When the rescue gangs arrived, they tried at first to pull the locomotive clear by using a steel cable attached to no fewer than eight locomotives, to get to the bodies of the driver and fireman. After two unsuccessful attempts the cable snapped, and eventually the engine had to be lifted by the breakdown crane which had come from Wolverhampton.

What went wrong?

How could such a disaster have happened? And why did an experienced driver, who must have known of the severe 10mph speed restriction into Shrewsbury station, not only fail to slow down in time, but also ignore the Crewe Bank signals at danger, which he passed at full speed?

It was a clear autumn night so that an experienced driver should have had no difficulty in knowing where he was. He should have been looking for signals and ought to have been expecting them from his knowledge of the route. After passing Hadnall, with four miles to go to Shrewsbury on falling gradients, he should have seen the signals at Harlescott and then the distant signal for Crewe Bank showing a red light.

As the gradient changed to a slight climb, the home signal would have come into sight, and would also show a red light, since the signalman intended to stop the train to warn the driver that he was to approach the junction signals ahead with extreme caution. Even after passing Crewe Bank signalbox there was still the starting signal to be seen with Crewe Junction distant signal beneath it. So two red lights were visible, one above the other. Had the driver fallen asleep – and if so what was the fireman doing? The crew should have been preparing to stop at Shrewsbury so the fireman was unlikely to have been firing, but he might have been checking the boiler water level or standing looking out.

Was there a problem with the train brakes and were they working at all? The train was equipped with the automatic vacuum brake system. This was one of the systems approved after the Regulation of Railways Act 1889 was passed. It required a fully automatic continuous brake to be fitted to all passenger trains following the Armagh accident of that year.

The automatic vacuum brake is simple in its equipment and operation. If the vacuum hoses between carriages, or the engine and leading carriage are uncoupled or broken, the brakes are applied or cannot be released from the engine. The pipes have to be coupled, and the air sucked out of the system, for the brakes to be released.

So at Crewe, if the vacuum brake hoses had been joined properly, when all the various portions of the train were coupled together, the brakes would work throughout the train.

If the hoses were not properly linked up, the brakes could not be released on the carriages behind and the driver would soon know if the engine was trying to start with brakes fully applied on some carriages. Furthermore, the rules said that a brake test had to be made when carriages or vans were attached or detached, with the rear guard checking that the brakes had been applied and released through the train. There was no suggestion that this had not been done at Crewe.

Nothing was found afterwards to suggest that the brakes were not in working order, nor was anything found that suggested a calamity on the locomotive, such as a broken steam pipe or a water gauge glass bursting. There was simply no explanation of what had gone wrong. Any suggestions could only be speculation. Theories seemed to point to the driver dozing off at the crucial moment with the fireman and the train guards unaware that the train was so close to disaster.

Recommendations

In view of the inexplicability of the accident the inspecting officer made no recommendations. The cause of the accident was that the driver of the train passed danger signals at 60mph and it jumped the rails on a sharp curve. In later years signals called outer homes were installed a quarter of a mile further out from what became the inner home signal.

Salisbury 1906

**Competition with the Great Western Railway in getting
trans-Atlantic passengers from Plymouth to London, a sharp curve,
and an ignored speed restriction were all factors which contributed to a
boat-train overturning at Salisbury in 1906 killing 28 people.**

Just before 2am on the morning of 1 July 1906, residents of Salisbury living near the railway were woken by the long continuous shriek of a train whistle approaching the station from the west and travelling fast. Train whistles in the night were not unusual, but this one was different; suddenly there was a tremendous crash at the east end of the station which was heard all over the town. The train had overturned hitting another one as it did so. Most of the coaches were smashed and in the wreckage 24 out of the total of 43 passengers were killed. The driver and fireman of the express, the guard of the empty milk train hit by the overturning train, and the fireman of a goods engine standing on the bay track on the other side of the milk train also died.

The express which had crashed was a boat-train run in connection with trans-Atlantic liners from North America. They called in at Plymouth to set down passengers who could reach London by train a day earlier than by continuing to sail in the liner to Southampton.

Two railways linked Plymouth to London, the Great Western Railway (GWR) and the London & South Western Railway (LSWR). The GWR had the longer route through Bristol and was hampered by speed restrictions and steep gradients over the hills of South Devon between Exeter and Plymouth. The LSWR route, although more direct, was steeply graded with sharp climbs to a series of summits between Salisbury and Exeter and the long steep climb round the north side of Dartmoor. An added complication was that the LSWR line crossed the GWR line on the flat at both Exeter and Plymouth with the Great Western signalmen controlling both stations and showing not a little bias.

Railway rivalry

Inevitably there was rivalry in running the ordinary express services, but the prestige trains which gave the railways international acclaim were the Atlantic liner services. At that time the GWR took the mail and the LSWR the passengers from the

▼Although the boat-train was composed of modern bogie stock, the carriages had wooden bodies on wooden frames and they disintegrated when the train turned over. By contrast, the locomotive of the train was so little damaged that it was towed to Nine Elms on its own wheels for repairs.

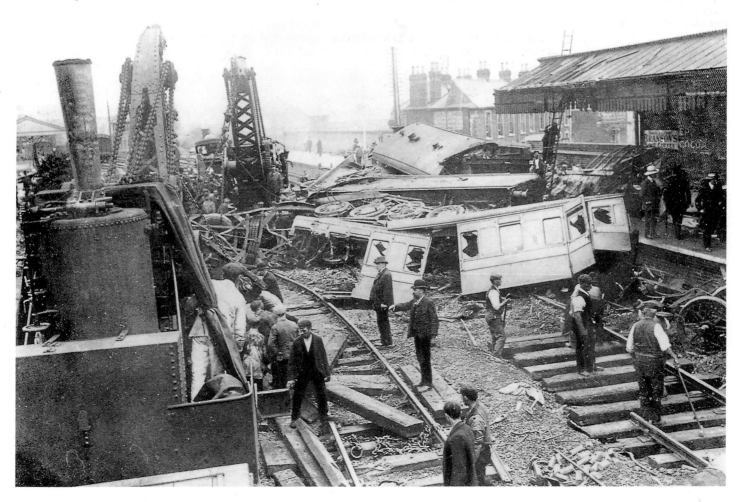

liners, and speed was of the essence. The trains were not regular or even frequent, as liners might be delayed by the weather. They generally ran weekly, but were usually arranged at short notice as soon as information was received that a liner was expected to arrive in Plymouth Sound.

It was on one of these trans-Atlantic mail trains that the GWR 4-4-0 *City of Truro* is credited with having reached 100mph on 9 May 1904 running down Wellington bank approaching Taunton. Two years later the quest for a fast run to London was still there. When the arrival of the liner *New York* was confirmed as it sailed towards Plymouth, the LSWR arranged for a connecting boat-train to leave the disembarking point, late on the evening of 30 June 1906.

The train was a light formation of five coaches. A passenger brake van conveying the luggage was leading, followed by three first class saloons and a kitchen brake van. Even though the train was running through the night and should have had no difficulty arriving in London in the early hours of the morning, it was a point of honour that the train should run as fast as possible. The inconvenience to passengers of arranging onward transport or finding a hotel at four in the morning was ignored. These boat-trains ran as soon after the arrival of the liner as possible.

Because there were neither precise regular

schedules nor regular crews for the boat-trains, they were fitted into the ordinary service in the best way possible, and the first available crew that knew the line and was qualified to run express passenger trains was picked for the job.

There was no need for any intermediate passenger stops between Plymouth and London, but the boat-trains were booked for an engine change at Templecombe. On the night of 30 June 1906, the boat-train had made a smart run from Devonport to Templecombe, arriving a minute ahead of the scheduled 1.22am on 1 July. The Class T9 4-4-0 No 288 which had brought the train from Devonport was uncoupled and replaced by the larger Class L12 4-4-0 No 421, driven by W J Robins. Although regularly employed on express trains to London, he had not driven one of the boat specials before, nor had he worked non-stop through Salisbury. He started from Templecombe but surprisingly, in view of the tight schedule to Waterloo, he drove too slowly and lost about four minutes over the first 20 miles towards Dinton.

Running to time

He knew the train had to run to time but equally he knew he was not to run too fast and arrive early; following complaints about excessive speed the feared locomotive chief, Dugald Drummond, had issued instructions that trains should not run

The American liner specials
The trans-Atlantic liners brought lucrative traffic to the railways serving the western seaports until air travel began to erode it after World War II. The GWR and the LSWR both ran boat-trains from Plymouth, and the LSWR had the developing port of Southampton to itself. The LSWR built a series of saloon coaches with open interiors, which had no gangways. Gangways were soon added so that meals could be served from a kitchen built into a guards and luggage van.

To the north Liverpool was served by the London & North Western Railway (LNWR) although, without direct competition, luxury rather than speed was their prime concern. The LNWR built a special set of coaches for the liner traffic which were quite the most luxurious vehicles ever seen in Britain other than those of the royal trains.

During the 1920s the GWR captured the Plymouth ocean liner traffic and built some special saloon coaches very much like Pullman cars internally, while the Southern Railway, as successor to the LSWR, concentrated on Southampton. But the ocean liner trains declined with the advent of long distance air travel and by the 1970s had all but disappeared. Today there are just one or two casual boat-trains running in connection with cruise liners, but the spirit of competition has gone.

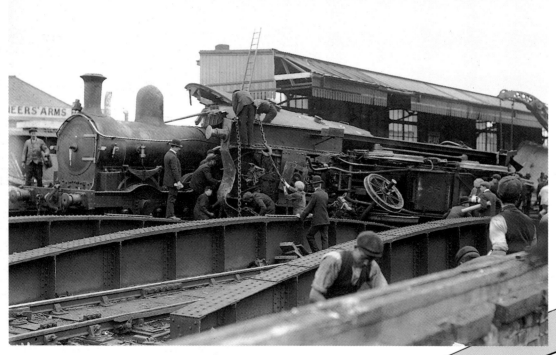

▲Breakdown crews work to recover the two locomotives involved in the accident. The overturning 4-4-0 rammed a milk van through the cab of a light engine standing in Salisbury station.

Class L12 4-4-0 No 421 and its tender lying on its side

To London Waterloo

▲The violence of the crash confirmed that the train had gone through the station at about 60mph. The coach on the left had been stripped of its body and the tender of No 421 jack-knifed into the locomotive crushing the crew.

than the inside to tilt the trains slightly as they went round the curve. But the cant lessened to almost nothing through the crossover, so that a train first leaned, then became upright and then leaned again as it went through the curve, giving it a sideways movement as it rolled.

At the normal maximum speed of 30mph there was little more than a gentle roll one way, and then the other. But as the boat special approached, its whistle blowing, the signalman at Salisbury West signalbox realized that it was travelling fast, too fast – at 60mph or more. The train swept on through the station and entered the curve at the east end. But it never made it. The big 4-4-0 overturned to the right. Coming the other way on the down line was a slow running train of milk vans. No 421 smashed into the vans, splintering them as it slid across the tracks and finished up against another engine, an old 0-6-0 goods engine standing on the bay track beyond the down line on the bridge across Fisherton Street.

The tender of No 421 jack-knifed and four of its five coaches with timber bodies and frames were completely wrecked. Only the rear van escaped destruction. The driver and fireman of No 421 were killed instantly, as was the guard of the milk train and the fireman of the goods engine. More than half of the passengers were killed – only 19 of the 43 survived and seven of those were severely injured.

too fast and gain time. Driver Robins even remarked to the station inspector at Templecombe that he dare not arrive in London too soon, otherwise he would be called upon to explain.

After Dinton, speed increased and the average over the six miles to Wilton was 70mph. On the approach to Salisbury from the west was a left hand curve into the station and another curve at the east end led right from the platform end. Both had a 30mph speed restriction. The one at the east end was much more tortuous, for in the middle of the 220yd radius left hand curve was a crossover to adjoining tracks. The curve was canted, super-elevation raising the outside rail higher

What went wrong?
How had such a disaster

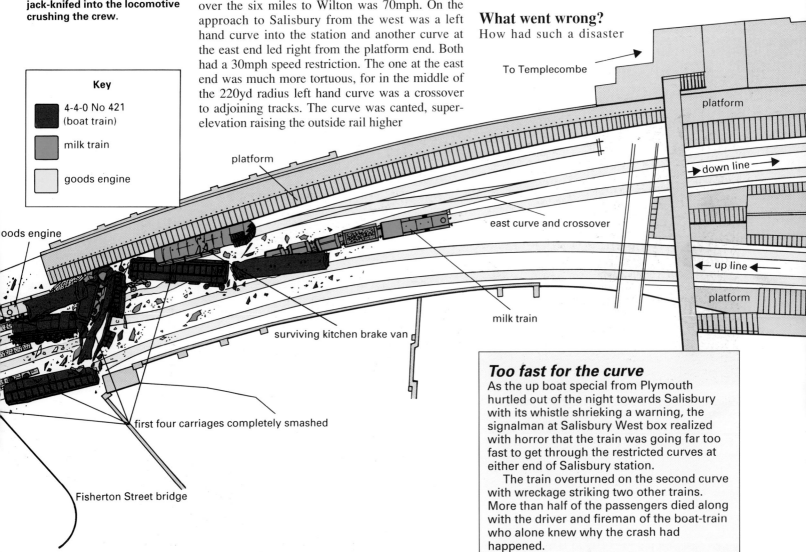

Key

- 4-4-0 No 421 (boat train)
- milk train
- goods engine

goods engine

platform

surviving kitchen brake van

first four carriages completely smashed

Fisherton Street bridge

To Templecombe

platform

→ down line →

east curve and crossover

← up line ←

milk train

platform

Too fast for the curve
As the up boat special from Plymouth hurtled out of the night towards Salisbury with its whistle shrieking a warning, the signalman at Salisbury West box realized with horror that the train was going far too fast to get through the restricted curves at either end of Salisbury station.

The train overturned on the second curve with wreckage striking two other trains. More than half of the passengers died along with the driver and fireman of the boat-train who alone knew why the crash had happened.

▲Crowds of sightseers came to watch workmen clearing up the aftermath of the disaster. Some of them, clinging to the bridge on the left, risked becoming casualties themselves. The condition of the carriages made it surprising that any of the passengers survived.

Was rivalry the cause?

At the time of the accident, the GWR was about to open its new Berks and Hants route between Reading, Westbury, and Taunton, which cut 20 miles off the route to Plymouth through Bristol. Was it possible that the crew of No 421 intended to show the GWR just what they could do?

A record breaking run the day before the new line opened would take some of the glory away from the GWR in favour of the LSWR. If that was what was intended then it went tragically wrong, causing the deaths of 28 people.

happened? Driver Robins was an experienced man and knew the line well. Yet he approached Salisbury with its 30mph speed restrictions at both ends of the station at well over 60mph, probably nearer 70mph. The whistle was sounded for several hundred yards as the train approached the station so the enginemen were not asleep. Had something gone wrong on the footplate of which the whistle was a warning?

Nothing was found afterwards to suggest that anything was wrong before the accident. But, although the regulator handle was found in the closed position and the reverser was in almost full forward gear, the brakes had not been applied before the engine overturned. It looked as though the driver had merely shut off steam to coast through the station and round the curves.

The driver could have misjudged his speed in the dark and it is also possible that he was quite confident of taking the 30mph curves at a higher speed. He probably knew that many drivers took the non-stop boat-trains through Salisbury at more than 30mph as part of the bravado which had become traditional. What he had not appreciated was the fact that although many of the LSWR 4-4-0s had small boilers with a low centre of gravity, the L12 was a more modern design with a large boiler and a higher centre of gravity. Excessive speed on a sharp curve was therefore more likely to cause overturning than it would on the smaller engines. The other boat-trains had small engines which probably just negotiated the curve without mishap, despite running faster than the limit.

The Salisbury derailment of 1906 remains a mystery, for as both driver and fireman died in the accident no-one ever knew why they were running

the train as they did. Certainly the inspecting officer, Major Pringle, could find no other answer than the recklessness of the driver in running through Salisbury station at about twice the permitted speed.

The damage to the train and the damage it wrought confirmed that it had been travelling at great speed. One or two of the survivors complained that it had been going very quickly earlier in the journey, and those who had been served with a meal said that some plates would not stay on the tables.

Yet despite the violence of the accident, No 421 was not as badly damaged as might have been expected. It had lost its chimney and safety valve cover, its front buffer beam was bent and there were other dents, but after rerailing it was towed on its own wheels to Nine Elms for repair.

Some of the passengers had remarkable escapes. One man had been hanging on to a strap attached to the coach side and was still holding it when the train left the track. He was thrown out as the coach disintegrated but hung on to the strap, which remained attached to the coach. This stopped him from being flung to his death.

Recommendations

Major Pringle, the inspecting officer, had few recommendations. The limited knowledge of the disaster could produce only a call for an even tighter restriction on the curves to 15mph instead of 30mph.

But the LSWR learned its lesson and from then on all express trains were booked to stop at Salisbury. The racing days were over.

Armagh 1889

**On 12 June 1889, 10 carriages of a Sunday
school excursion, with over 600 passengers on board, were
unhooked from their locomotive and careered out of control down
a 1 in 75 incline before smashing into an oncoming train.
It was Ireland's worst ever rail accident.**

Old operating methods dating back 50 years to the pioneering days of railways, an inadequate braking system, an engine not powerful enough to work a heavy train, and a staff argument led to Ireland's worst ever railway accident at Armagh in 1889. Parliament was shocked into making new rail safety measures compulsory by law.

The branch railway from Armagh to Warrenpoint on the east coast of Ireland was steeply graded as it climbed out of Armagh on the northern slopes of the ridge of high ground which further east became the Mourne Mountains. The line had been built in 1864 by an independent company, but in 1879 had been taken over by the Great Northern Railway of Ireland (GNRI). It was of single track, worked on the staff and ticket system in conjunction with time-interval operation, a method of working railways which had been in use since the 1830s.

On 11 June 1889, the GNRI traffic department in Dundalk had arranged for an excursion train to run from Armagh to Warrenpoint at 10.00am the next day. Around 800 passengers were expected and a 13-coach train was planned, including two brake vans, for which the locomotive department had booked a small 2-4-0 tender engine, No 86.

Even before the empty train arrived at Armagh, two more coaches had been added, and by the time loading began there were so many passengers that the stationmaster proposed to add two more. The driver of No 86 protested, and even threatened to take only the original 13. The stationmaster made some caustic comments but the driver, who was not very familiar with the line, insisted and said that he ought to have been provided with a more powerful 0-6-0.

A suggestion was made to transfer some of the coaches to the following regular train at 10.35am, which was a much lighter formation. Its engine could also have been used to assist the excursion up the 1 in 75 gradient to the summit just over 3 miles from Armagh. However, by now the excur-

▼The shattered remains of the last three vehicles litter the 70ft high embankment about 1½ miles east of Armagh. The coaches on the runaway were all light, wooden six-wheelers and two were smashed to matchwood on impact, as well as the rear brake van. The train behind the overturned 0-4-2 became uncoupled and ran down the incline before being brought under control with hand brakes.

◄ The 0-4-2 locomotive of the 10.35 train lies overturned on the top of the embankment after the crash. It was travelling at about 5mph when the runaway coaches smashed into it. The force of the collision dislodged it from the tender and train.

Thomas McGrath, and Elliot conferred on what best to do. They could have kept the train where it was, held on the vacuum brake and sent a man back down the line to warn the following train. This could then have been brought slowly up behind and used to push the stalled train.

Alternatively they could split the excursion so that No 86 could take the first part forward and park the coaches in the siding at Hamilton's Bawn (the first station, about two miles beyond the summit). The front guard told Elliot that the siding there already contained some wagons but that they should be able to get five coaches in. No 86 could then return for the rest of the train.

A fatal mistake

Elliot made the fatal decision to divide the train. He went back and told the rear guard to apply his handbrake and place stones under the wheels. The front guard also put a single stone under a wheel of the sixth coach while he unwound the screw coupling to lift the link from the coupling hook of the fifth coach.

Tragically, just as he did so the engine driver eased back and did just what the rest of the staff were trying to avoid – moving the rear ten coaches. The front portion moved back no more than a

Uncoupling the train
As the excursion did not have automatic continuous brakes, safety chains connected adjoining coaches on each side of the central screw coupling. The screw coupling allowed the buffers, which were sprung, to be held just in contact with each other.

As the train was stopped on the vacuum brake, some of the buffers may have been slightly compressed; the screw couplings were not absolutely tight because mixed lengths of buffer shanks made this impossible. The side safety chains were slack to allow passage round curves.

The guard said he undid the safety chains and vacuum pipe between the two coaches. This released the brakes, but, with the hand brakes applied and stones under the wheels, nothing moved. He was then able to undo the screw coupling without the need for the engine to set back to ease the couplings.

Tragically, just as he lifted the link from the hook of the fifth coach, the engine came back slightly and compressed the buffers. This pushed the rear coaches and started them back towards disaster.

sion driver was sufficiently annoyed at suggestions that he couldn't get his train to the summit to refuse any offers of help. He decided to take the 15 coaches.

Even so it was 10.15 before the train got away, with around 940 passengers on board, two-thirds of them children from a Sunday school. Many were standing, not only in the passenger coaches, but in the brake vans as well. As was customary at the time the passenger coach doors were locked to prevent 'unauthorized access'.

The engine was not short of steam and at first climbed the gradient well. Gradually it began to lose speed until, just short of the summit, it could make no further progress and stalled.

The train was equipped with the Smith's pattern non-automatic vacuum brake in which the brakes were applied by the creation of a vacuum in the system and released by letting in air. In addition there were screw handbrakes which operated only on their own wheels in the two brake vans. The essential feature of the simple vacuum brake was that if the continuous brake pipe through the train was either uncoupled or broken there was, in effect, no brake at all. Naturally the staff on the train knew this.

In charge of the train was the line superintendent's chief clerk, James Elliot. The driver,

A preventable disaster
The utter helplessness of the victims locked into the flimsy coaches and the preventability of the accident were what spurred Parliament to such sweeping actions with the Regulation of Railways Act 1889. The ten runaway coaches had quickly picked up speed from the summit of the 1 in 75 incline reaching 40mph by the point of impact. The collision was so powerful that the rear brake van and rear two coaches were completely destroyed. The engine of the oncoming train was thrown on to its side and the tender and vehicles behind became uncoupled to form another runaway. Only fate and the courage of the staff saved these coaches from a further accident. Automatic brakes, the absolute block system and interlocking controls, all of which survive to this day, were all made compulsory within 12 months.

point of impact

To Armagh (1½ miles)

detached vans and passenger coaches

detached tender and horsebox

overturned 0-4-2 tender locomotive

foot or so, but it was enough. The stone under the sixth coach was crushed to powder so there was nothing to stop the coaches rolling back, buffering up against the rear brake van and pushing it over its little pile of stones.

The driver tried to set back properly to catch up the slowly moving rear coaches while one of the staff tried desperately to get the coupling link over the hook again. But it was no use. On the 1 in 75 gradient the weight of coaches, crammed full of passengers, was too much for the handbrake and gradually the 10 runaway coaches speeded up.

At Armagh station the 10.35 train was ready to leave with no one aware of the drama developing three miles up the line. Behind the 0-4-2 tender locomotive was a horse box, two vans and three passenger coaches – a lightweight train. Under the time-interval rules the minimum 10-minute gap between following passenger trains had more than elapsed, the driver of the 10.35 had the wooden staff for the section (the excursion driver had been given a ticket authorizing him to occupy the single line) and, about four minutes late, he was given the right away.

The 0-4-2 was soon climbing the 1 in 75 gradient and was about 1½ miles from the summit when the fireman saw the runaway coaches hurtling towards him. The driver quickly applied the simple vacuum brake but he had not quite stopped when the runaways smashed into his train at over 40mph.

The coaches were all small, light, wooden six-wheelers. The brake van and first two coaches leading the runaways were destroyed, while the rest piled high up on the track and down the steep embankment. All those in the brake van (including 15 passengers) had managed to jump out, but in the other coaches the passengers were locked in.

And now there was another runaway train. The 0-4-2 engine had been knocked on its side by the force of the collision and the coupling bar to the tender had broken. The tender and the horse box began to run back. Meanwhile the two vans and three passenger coaches had also broken free from the horse box and they too were running back. Luckily the driver had been flung on to the tender and, despite being injured, he was able to screw on the tender hand brake, stopping that part. The guard also managed to apply his hand brake on the rear part of the train and stopped it about ¼ mile down the line.

Inevitably there were many casualties. Of the 600 passengers in the runaway coaches of the

▼A dramatic artist's impression of the immediate aftermath of the accident shows bodies strewn down the side of the embankment beneath the splintered remains of the rear three vehicles. Most of the fatalities occurred in the rear two coaches which were locked shut. Passengers and staff on the brake van had already jumped clear.

N

To Hamilton's Bawn/Goraghwood/Warrenpoint

to first five coaches and locomotive No 86 (1 mile)

surviving runaway coaches

...bris of rear brake van and rear two coaches

embankment (70ft high)

Key to trains

■ 10.00 excursion Armagh – Warrenpoint

▨ 10.35 regular Armagh – Warrenpoint

▼A large crowd gathered on the embankment after the crash. The tender on the right became dislodged from the locomotive of the 10.35, threatening to become a second runaway. However, the driver was thrown from the footplate on to the tender, and managed to apply the hand brake.

excursion, 80 were killed or died later, including 22 children. A further 262 were injured.

The inquiry

In the inquiry into the immediate causes of the accident, the inspecting officer, Major General Hutchinson found, after trials, that engine No 86 was able to take a 15 coach train to the summit in the hands of an experienced driver. He also found that a brake van similar to the one at the back of the uncoupled 10 coaches should have been able to hold a train of that size on the 1 in 75 gradient.

He could find no reason why the excursion was unable to get to the summit, despite the engine working near to its limit. As for the brake in the rear van, was it in full working order or had it been tampered with? There were 15 passengers crammed into the van and there were suggestions that some of them might have interfered with it.

Although Hutchinson concluded that the driver of the excursion should not have been rostered for the job as he knew so little about the line, he placed most of the responsibility on Elliot for authorizing the train to be uncoupled.

But Hutchinson's findings provoked much more. Even though only eight passengers were killed in other rail accidents in the British Isles in 1889, and fatalities had averaged no more than 28 a year over the previous 20 years (including the 80 lost in the Tay Bridge disaster 10 years before), Parliament decided it had had enough.

For years the Board of Trade (which supervised railways until the formation of the Ministry of Transport in 1919) had been urging the railway companies, through its railway inspecting officers, to adopt better safety standards.

Had the absolute block system been in force, which would have allowed only one train at a time on to the section, the 10.35 train could not have left Armagh with the excursion train already stalled. And if automatic vacuum brakes had been in use, the brake blocks would have been hard on the wheels of all the coaches when the train was divided. Given the horrific nature of the accident these issues were tackled by Parliament with uncharacteristic speed and decisiveness.

Abbots Ripton 1876

**A severe snowstorm and icy temperatures led
to signals freezing in the clear position and to a
collision between an up Scottish express and a goods train.
To make matters worse, a down express ran into
the wreckage and 13 people died.**

Late in the afternoon of 21 January 1876, the weather was bitterly cold with gale force winds. A belt of heavy snow swept in from the Bristol Channel across the south Midlands, disrupting services on the Great Western, London & North Western and Midland railways. It reached the Great Northern (GN) main line at around 6pm. The snowflakes were large – bigger than a two shilling piece, one witness said – and they stuck to pulley wheels, signal arms, track and buildings. Three to four inches of ice soon clung to telegraph and signal wires.

Abbots Ripton lies on the East Coast main line between Huntingdon and Peterborough, part way along a 1 in 200 hump on otherwise fairly flat country. To the north, in 1876, the next signalboxes were Woodwalton, 1³/₄ miles away, then Connington a further two miles on, and Holme almost two miles beyond. To the south of Abbots Ripton was Stukeley signalbox 2¹/₂ miles away and

then Huntingdon, two miles beyond.

The rules regarding snow provided for platelayers (permanent way staff) to take up duties at distant and certain stop signals to make sure that the signals were working, to repeat their indication by a hand lamp, and to put down detonators when the signals were at danger. But by the time the snow set in that afternoon, the platelayers had finished for the day and it would have taken some time to call them out again.

The first crash

Until the end of the afternoon the weather had not delayed trains unduly. The 10.30am Edinburgh – King's Cross Scotch Express, known unofficially as the Flying Scotsman, had left York about three minutes late and had lost another three minutes by the time it reached Peterborough. Ahead of it, from Peterborough, was a coal train, which was booked to leave the East Midlands junction at

▼A crowd of spectators braved the freezing conditions to gawp at the aftermath of the accident in which Stirling single No 48, the Leeds express (shown in the left foreground), ploughed into the Flying Scotsman, demolishing the third and fourth coaches, and killing 13 people in the process.

5.35pm but actually left at 5.53pm.

Peterborough telegraphed details of the progress of the Flying Scotsman forward to Holme, Abbots Ripton and Huntingdon. Many signalboxes on the GN line were equipped with the electric telegraph, in addition to the block system, for sending general messages, but the intermediate signalboxes at Connington, Woodwalton and Stukeley were not stations and did not have this facility.

The signalman at Holme planned to shunt the coal train off the main line to clear it for the Flying Scotsman. His signals were at danger. But the coal train did not stop, and ran on towards Connington. The Holme signalman could not 'talk' to the Connington signalman on the telegraph to tell him what had happened, so he merely signalled the train forward on the block instruments. But he was able to telegraph Abbots Ripton to tell them to shunt the coal train there.

From Holme to Abbots Ripton the coal train was signalled on the block instruments in the normal way. When the coal train approached Abbots Ripton all signals were clear, even though the signalman had placed the levers to danger. Fortunately, the coal train driver knew the working and was expecting to be shunted, and the signalman, unaware that his signals were working badly, used a red lamp to stop the train.

The Flying Scotsman was catching up fast and, as far as Woodwalton, was signalled correctly. The Woodwalton signalman had not received the line clear of goods train signal from Abbots Ripton and placed his up line signal levers to danger, but had done nothing more. On the footplate of the Flying Scotsman the driver saw clear white lights on the Woodwalton signals and, a mile or so on, a clear white light on Abbots Ripton distant signal.

The coal train was still backing into a siding when the Flying Scotsman came storming out of the blizzard at about 50mph. It hit the sixth, fifth and fourth wagons of the coal train, pushing the front wagons and the coal engine forward, with the engine, tender and some of the coaches from the express thrown across the down line.

The second crash

The Abbots Ripton signalman was in a state of shock, but other staff came to help, including some of the local platelayers, who had turned out again when they realized it was snowing heavily. The signalman tried to telegraph Huntingdon for help, and to tell them to stop down trains. But Huntingdon did not acknowledge the message.

It was obvious that signals were showing clear,

▼Taken from a sketch by one of the passengers, this illustration shows a working party removing the injured, hampered by the darkness and the falling snow. Behind them, in the centre, can be seen the six-wheeled tender, with a fire iron still firmly wedged into the coal.

Snow stops signals
Signals frozen in the clear position were to blame when the Flying Scotsman crashed into a shunting coal train at Abbots Ripton in the terrible showstorm of 21 January 1876.

A second collision between a down express and the wreckage of the Flying Scotsman, which caused 13 deaths, could have been avoided if signalmen had been more efficient.

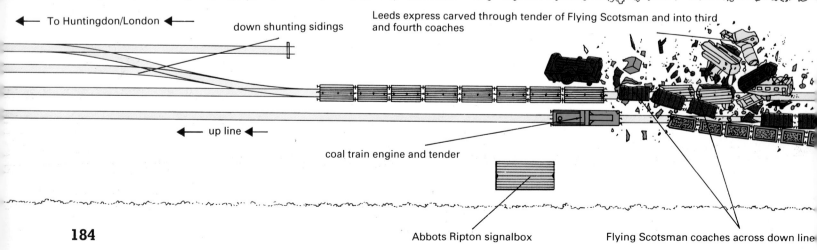

To Huntingdon/London ◄—

down shunting sidings

Leeds express carved through tender of Flying Scotsman and into third and fourth coaches

◄— up line ◄—

coal train engine and tender

Abbots Ripton signalbox

Flying Scotsman coaches across down line

even though the levers were at danger in the signalbox, so the fireman of the coal train, armed with detonators, set off running in the up direction to stop any trains on the down line. The rest of the crew, finding their engine was still in running order, started after him towards Huntingdon. It was still snowing hard.

The Abbots Ripton signalman had given up trying to call Huntingdon on the telegraph and, instead, at 6.52pm sent the five beat bell signal 'line blocked' to Stukeley. Just at that moment the 5.30pm King's Cross – Leeds down express was passing Stukeley. Had Abbots Ripton sent that bell signal straight away at 6.45pm, the Leeds train could have been shown a red light at Stukeley.

Meanwhile, the fireman had just fixed two detonators close to the Abbots Ripton down distant signal, about 1000 yards from the crash, when his own engine caught him up. As he climbed aboard, the down express approached. The coal train driver sounded a series of whistles and the crew showed a red light to the express, which was running at over 50mph on the falling gradient.

▲Three manually operated winches and a working party armed with levers were required to lift the derailed engine of the Flying Scotsman, 2-2-2 Single No 269, from its side. The lack of a brake on the engine is clearly visible from this angle.

Its driver responded by sounding an emergency whistle for brakes to be applied – like many trains of the time there was no continuous brake through the train, just the tender hand-brake and hand-brakes operated by guards in three brake vans – and himself put the engine into reverse. But it was no use. The Leeds express was still travelling at about 15mph as it carved through the tender of the Flying Scotsman and demolished the third and fourth coaches of the up train. It was in these coaches that most casualties occurred, with 13 passengers killed and 53 injured.

Acknowledgement from Huntingdon finally came through at 7.05pm, 10 minutes after the second collision.

The GN main line was equipped with what was then thought of as modern signalling, including

Signals old and new

Before the Abbots Ripton accident many railways were still using the old three-position slotted post semaphore, which was pivoted from inside the slot. After the accident, the Great Northern adopted the somersault signal instead, in which the arm was balanced. Snow was deemed to be evenly spread along the arm. Other railways evolved signal arms attached to the heavy spectacle casting, which automatically put the signal to danger if a wire or rod broke. The upper quadrant signal was a development of the 20th century, which was even better since any snow on the arm would weigh it down to the danger position.

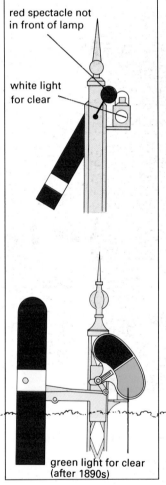

red spectacle not in front of lamp

white light for clear

green light for clear (after 1890s)

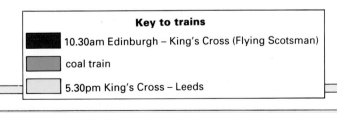

Key to trains

■ 10.30am Edinburgh – King's Cross (Flying Scotsman)

▬ coal train

▢ 5.30pm King's Cross – Leeds

→ down line →

→ To Peterborough →

up shunting siding

▲The scene of devastation on the night of Saturday, 21 January 1876, shortly after the crash between the Great Northern Scotch and Leeds expresses. The bottom arm of the Abbots Ripton signal can be seen in the centre of the picture frozen in the caution position.

Human error

Human error was partly to blame for both collisions. The Holme stationmaster, who had been told that the coal train was running against signals, could have made more effort to stop and warn the Flying Scotsman, as could the Holme signalman. He was blamed for not placing detonator signals on the line and failing to display a red lamp in his box. Either man might have prevented the first collision.

With regard to the second collision, the Huntingdon signalman was clearly at fault for not responding quickly to Abbots Ripton's urgent telegraph. The Abbots Ripton signalman was to blame for wasting time trying to contact Huntingdon when he should have sent the five beat 'line blocked' signal to Stukeley immediately. Both measures might have stopped the second crash.

the absolute block system. So how could one, let alone two, collisions occur?

The signals themselves were a legacy from the days of time interval working, when the semaphore arms showed three positions – danger (horizontal), caution (inclined down at 45°) and clear (arm vertical and invisible inside the slotted wooden post). But with the block system, only two indications were needed – danger and clear. The clear position was still with the arm almost vertical inside the slotted post.

Night indications were given by an oil lamp with coloured spectacles linked to the arm mechanism passing in front of the oil lamp. At that time only one colour was needed – red for danger – because the light indication for clear was white. When the signal arm was pulled to the clear position, the red spectacle simply moved away from the lamp and the direct light of the oil lamp was seen as white by a driver.

There were distant signals generally around half a mile, or a little more, from the home signals, to give drivers advance warning of whether they had to stop or had a clear run through, but they were little different in style, and at night showed the same red for caution and white light for clear. Drivers were expected to know the line thoroughly – which signals were distants and which were stops.

The main difference in train signalling by the block instruments at that time was that the line

was deemed to be clear unless a train was actually in the block section between two signalboxes. The block indicators showed two out of the three indications of today's instruments – 'line clear' and 'train on line'.

But a prime difference from today was that the block indicator needle was used to send messages in addition to the block bells, by being flicked from the centre to one side or the other. When a train was approaching a signalbox, the signalman called the attention of the signalman at the box ahead by one beat on the bell. When this was acknowledged the dial needle was used to send two beats to the left to show a passenger train was entering the section. The signalman at the far end then firmly pegged the needle pointing at 'train on line', which was displayed in both signalboxes.

When the train passed the signalbox ahead, the signalman there called back with a beat on the bell, and the block indicator needle was flicked twice to the right to mean 'line clear', whether or not another train was due. While the train was actually in the section, the signals at the entry signalbox were placed at danger, but as soon as the train was clear of the signalbox ahead, they were pulled to clear in the same fashion as automatic colour-light signals today.

Therefore the semaphore arms were normally at clear, unless there was a train in the section ahead. They could remain in this position for quite a long time. That day, the snow and ice had led to the arms becoming frozen in the clear position. This was a prime factor in the events leading to the Abbots Ripton disaster.

Recommendations

The Board of Trade inspector, Captain Tyler, made many recommendations after this accident, but the main ones that affected signalling from then on were that the block section should not be regarded as clear until a train was actually due. Therefore, signals would normally be at danger, and if they did stick it would be an error on the side of safety. Also, that signals be redesigned so that they could not be made inefficient by ice and snow and if they failed, this would be indicated in the signalbox. But whatever the failures that night, Capt Tyler remarked on the high standards of signalling which were normal on the Great Northern Railway at that time.

As for the second collision, this would have been prevented if the train had been equipped with continuous brakes and as in many reports he recommended their adoption.

Other recommendations included the use of hand lamps to supplement signals in poor weather; provision of telegraph instruments in all signalboxes; the building of an extra track for slow trains up Connington bank; the stoppage of less important traffic in severe weather and more guidance for and supervision of staff working in fog and snow.

He advised that in severe weather, fogmen with detonators should stand at the signals.

Penistone 1884

Accelerating downhill from Woodhead Tunnel, an express locomotive's crank axle broke, allowing the wheels to force apart the rails. Derailed carriages broke free from the train – which was not fitted with automatic brakes – and crashed down the embankment, killing twenty-four passengers.

The driving force for railway construction in England was from the North, and after the opening of the Liverpool & Manchester Railway (LMR) in 1830 further railways, radiating from Manchester, were planned. A route to the south was intended to give more direct access to Birmingham, but the most daring was an easterly route across the Pennines, with planners aiming to reach Sheffield, and thence the east coast Humber ports.

Despite the barrier of the Pennine moorland between Manchester and Sheffield, the promoters were undaunted, and took their line on a 21 mile (34km) climb from Manchester London Road (today Manchester Piccadilly), with gradients ranging from 1 in 200 to 1 in 100. At the top was Woodhead Tunnel, 3 miles 22yd (4.8km) long, and just a single line bore – the longest tunnel in Great Britain when it opened in 1845. The line reached its summit at the east end of the tunnel, after which it was downhill all the way from Dunford Bridge to Sheffield Victoria, with gradients mostly between 1 in 120 and 1 in 135. By 1852 a second bore had been added to Woodhead Tunnel, providing two tracks the length of the journey.

By the 1880s the route – by then the Manchester Sheffield & Lincolnshire Railway (MS&L) – was an important main line, linking west and east coast ports at Liverpool and Grimsby, and intermediate towns and cities. It also provided a through service to London King's Cross through Retford and the East Coast main line via Peterborough.

A routine trip for No 434

On 16 July 1884 the 12.30pm Manchester – Sheffield express had breasted the summit at Woodhead Tunnel and begun the descent to Penistone. It was hauled by a 4-4-0, No 434, designed by the MS&L's locomotive engineer, Charles Sacré, with outside frames carrying the bearings for the driving axles. It was a handsome

▼This sketch shows the view of the accident looking from Hazlehead signalbox along the line towards Sheffield. As usual on such occasions, sightseers came to inspect the wreckage.

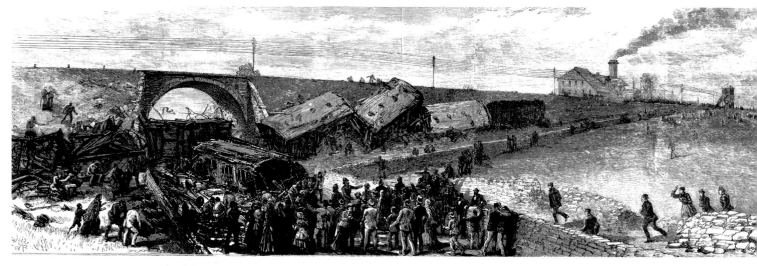

type, with curving frames over the axle bearings.

Between the 1850s and the 1870s, locomotive design had improved radically from the pioneering fashions developed by George Stephenson and his contemporaries. New materials were being used, such as steel to replace wrought-iron. Some engineers were reluctant to change, holding back until they could be sure of the same reliability they expected from high quality British wrought-iron. But by the 1870s steel was being used for axles, despite doubts on its use for crank axles.

Crank axles had cranked sections to take the ends of the connecting rods from the pistons of inside cylinders between the frames. They needed specialized manufacture, with forging and tempering to relieve any stresses. The axle was not continuous from wheel to wheel but cranked out and back twice to provide the drive for the connecting rods. And the points where the cranks were at right angles to the axle took the greatest forces, as the connecting rods pushed and pulled the axles round to convert the push-pull movement of the rods into the rotary movement of the axles and wheels. The Sacré 4-4-0s were built in the late 1870s for the Manchester – Sheffield line, with steel crank axles.

No 434 accelerated from Dunford Bridge, with clear signals, and had reached about 50mph (80km/h) as it approached Hazlehead signalbox, 2

miles (3km) after Woodhead Tunnel. Next to the engine was a horse-box, then six passenger coaches and three brake and luggage vans.

The train had entered a right-hand curve on an embankment at Bullhouse Bridge when the driver felt that the engine was running unsteadily. He applied the vacuum brake, but this was not like today's automatic vacuum brake. At this time the MS&L, like the Great Northern Railway, used the simple vacuum brake. When the brakes were off, the vacuum brake pipe through the train was at atmospheric pressure. To apply the brakes the driver had to put the brake handle into the position to create a vacuum (with a steam jet in the ejector sucking the air out of the brake system of the entire train). The process took a minute or two to become effective.

There was certainly not enough time for the brakes to take hold on the 12.30, for almost immediately there was a bang as the crank axle of the leading driving wheels broke. The wheels were no longer held together and, rotating freely, they pushed the rails apart, derailing the train behind. The tender and horse-box continued in line, but the coupling between the horse-box and first coach broke. Not being equipped with an automatic brake, there was not only a screw coupling holding the coach buffers against those of the horse-box, but also side safety chains. However, these broke too, and the passenger carriages and brake vans were now running loose, derailed on a curve on a high embankment, and with-

Inadequate brakes

The principal cause of the Penistone disaster in 1884 was the breaking of the crank axle on a 4-4-0 locomotive as it went round the curve at Bullhouse Bridge at about 50mph (80km/h). The leading driving wheels were no longer held together, and they pushed the track apart, derailing the rest of the train. The couplings behind the horse-box broke, and the passenger carriages and brake vans ran derailed, free of the locomotive and without any working brake, until they tipped over the side of the embankment to destruction. The train was fitted with the simple vacuum brake, which took a minute or two to become effective, and in any case lost any braking power as soon as the vacuum pipes broke when the train became uncoupled.

A black spot

Penistone saw four accidents in five years. Apart from the major disaster at Bullhouse Bridge (north-west of Penistone) in 1884, there was another major accident on New Year's Day 1885 at Barnsley Junction when a wagon axle broke and the wagon was thrown towards a passing passenger train. The passenger train was derailed, four passengers were killed and 45 injured.

In September 1886, after a through coach had been uncoupled and put on another train at the station, the engine backed on to the rest of the train, but the shunter failed to get the coupling link over the hook and the train went rolling back into a siding, only to collide with the buffers, injuring 20 passengers – another accident arising from the use of simple vacuum brakes.

Finally, in March 1889, a Liverpool – London excursion was derailed when the leading axle of an 0-6-0 fractured; one passenger was killed.

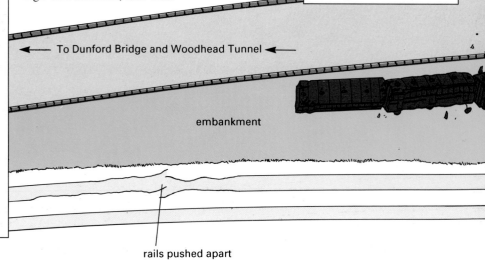

← To Dunford Bridge and Woodhead Tunnel ←

embankment

rails pushed apart

◄ The locomotive tender and horse-box remained on the track to the left of the bridge. The coaches, no longer coupled or restrained by brakes, derailed and went to the left of the curve and down the embankment.

▼More than half of the 25 fatalities were women, but also included in the dead was Massey Bromley, who, three years earlier, had retired as the Locomotive Superintendent of the Great Eastern Railway.

out braking power. The leading coach went to the left, and all the coaches cascaded down the embankment. Twenty-four passengers died instantly or soon after.

The hidden flaw is discovered

The inspecting officer, Major Marindin, did not have to look far for the initial cause of the accident; the evidence was visible underneath the engine between the frames. The crank axle, fitted in 1883, had a hidden flaw in the steel. It had run for 14 months, but the stresses from the cranks eventually found the weak spot and a crack developed, breaking right through as the express ran round the curve at Bullhouse Bridge. In the 1880s there was no way of finding such hidden flaws until they emerged on to the surface.

Major Marindin accepted that no one was to blame for the flaw. But comparisons were made between steel and wrought-iron. More long arguments between engineers concerned the relative merits of inside-cylindered engines with the cylinders between the frames – which necessitated the use of crank axles – against those of outside cylinders – which needed only plain one-piece axles.

The secondary cause of the disaster was the fact that the simple vacuum brake could not be applied with immediate effect. The vacuum had to be created to apply the brakes, thus losing valuable time, but as soon as the passenger carriages broke away from the horse-box the brakes would not work anyway because the vacuum was destroyed. Had the train been equipped with an automatic vacuum brake, the driver could have made an effective application as soon as he felt the strange movement of the engine. In addition, even if the carriages had become uncoupled from the horse-box, there would have been a full, automatic emergency brake application through the train as the vacuum pipe broke and admitted air to the system. This might have restrained the derailed coaches.

Major Marindin criticized the continued use of the simple vacuum brake despite recommendations to the contrary over the previous 20 years. Several railways used the simple form and the Board of Trade, which was responsible for railway safety, had no power to order the use of the automatic type. The chairman of the MS&L, Sir Edward Watkin, insisted that the simple vacuum brake was adequate. But in 1887 another MS&L train was involved in a major accident at Hexthorpe, when the simple vacuum brake was ineffective. And in 1889 came the worst disaster ever (at that time), at Armagh, in which the simple vacuum brake was again implicated. Parliament at last made the automatic brake a legal requirement.

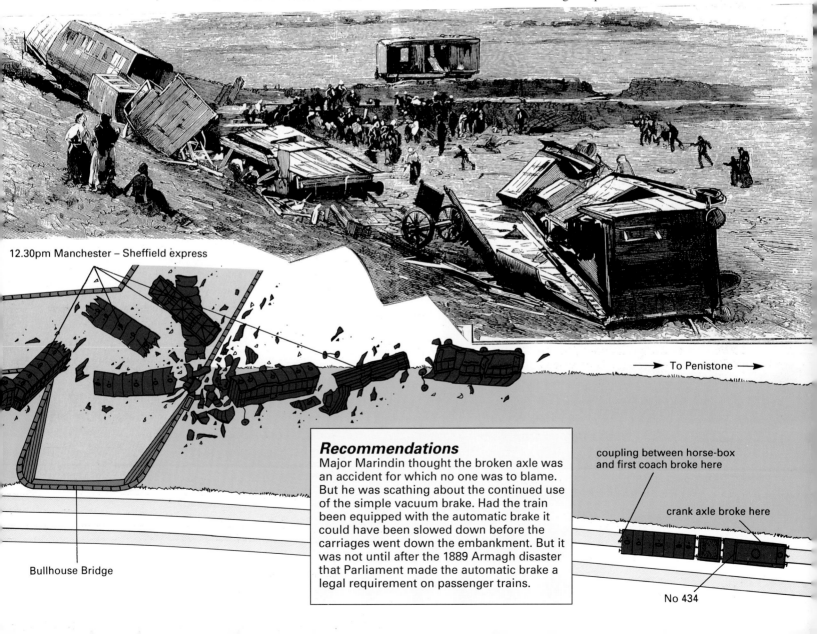

12.30pm Manchester – Sheffield express

To Penistone →

Bullhouse Bridge

Recommendations
Major Marindin thought the broken axle was an accident for which no one was to blame. But he was scathing about the continued use of the simple vacuum brake. Had the train been equipped with the automatic brake it could have been slowed down before the carriages went down the embankment. But it was not until after the 1889 Armagh disaster that Parliament made the automatic brake a legal requirement on passenger trains.

coupling between horse-box and first coach broke here

crank axle broke here

No 434

Manors Station 1926

**Three minutes from home, an electric passenger train
overran stop signals and crashed side-on with a goods train.
Rescuers found that the driver was missing and
the safety control had been put out of action.**

At 9.47pm on Saturday, 7 August 1926, a six-car electric multiple unit (EMU) left Newcastle Central station on a circular journey that would take it non-stop out to Monkseaton on the north-east coast. Thereafter it ran south, stopping at Whitley Bay, Cullercoats and Tynemouth, before turning west and calling at all stations back to Newcastle. It was a journey scheduled to take 63 minutes, but it ended abruptly, and in tragedy, just three minutes from home.

As the train approached Manors (East) station the guard, who had been writing up his notes, suddenly noticed that they were running too fast to stop, even though the signals were set against them. He applied his brake at once, but the train had overrun the signals and the speed was too great to be instantly overcome. Beyond the station lay a converging junction, and crossing this was a west-bound freight train, drawn by an 0-6-0 goods engine running from Heaton to Blaydon.

The EMU collided side-on with the goods train, striking it at the third wagon from the tender. The coaches withstood the impact well and there was no telescoping, but the motorman's end of the leading coach was very badly damaged. This coach not only bore the brunt of the impact with the goods train, but it also came into contact with the elevated overtrack signalbox before crashing against a parapet wall.

On board the EMU were 157 passengers. Fortunately, most of them were seated in the rear of the train. There were just three people in the leading coach: a young couple from Durham sitting towards the front, and a woman in another compartment. They all received injuries, although none serious, and the rest of the passengers experienced only minor cuts and bruising, or shock. But the driver was nowhere to be found.

▼The driver's cab and leading coach sustained most of the damage when the crash occurred. Consequently, the number of casualties was quite low – only three of the 157 passengers on board had injuries requiring treatment.

Driver missing

An extensive search of the wreckage convinced rescuers that the driver was not going to be found at the crash site and a police sergeant with a lantern was despatched to walk back along the track to search for him. Close to Heaton station the railway was crossed by a bridge carrying Heaton Park Road, and it was beneath this bridge that the body of the motorman was found.

The man's injuries, plus marks found on a bridge support pillar, indicated that he had been struck while leaning out of the door of his train, with his back to the bridge. Death would have been instantaneous and probably simultaneous with the body being dragged through the doorway.

With the discovery of the body it was clear that the train, travelling at approximately 35mph, had run the 1 mile 96 yards from Heaton to Manors without a driver.

What went wrong?

The technical operation of this train should have made the accident impossible. The 600V DC multiple unit was equipped with Westinghouse brakes on every axle – brakes which would automatically be applied if pressure was not exerted on a device known as the dead man's handle.

Two handkerchiefs, one red and one white, were to blame for the failure of the dead man's handle. The red handkerchief had been looped over the control handle and fastened in a triple knot, while the white one had been fastened

through the red in such a manner as to tighten it and further depress the device. This dangerous arrangement had not been present when the guard had entered the driving cab shortly before leaving Newcastle Central, so the motorman must have tied it into position just before leaving the station, or at some point on the journey.

It must have been in place when the train

▲Such was the extent of the damage to the driver's cab that on the night of the crash rescuers spent several hours scouring the debris before they decided that the driver's body was missing. It was found beneath a bridge just outside Heaton station.

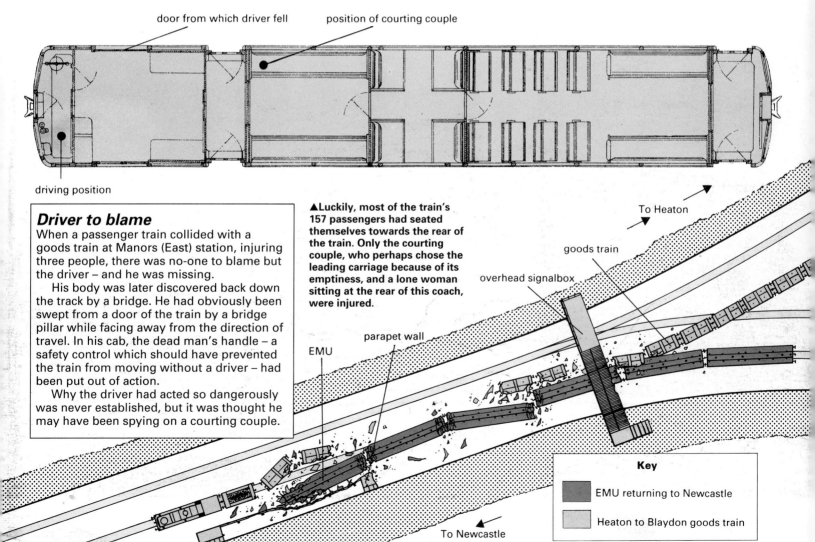

door from which driver fell

position of courting couple

driving position

Driver to blame

When a passenger train collided with a goods train at Manors (East) station, injuring three people, there was no-one to blame but the driver – and he was missing.

His body was later discovered back down the track by a bridge. He had obviously been swept from a door of the train by a bridge pillar while facing away from the direction of travel. In his cab, the dead man's handle – a safety control which should have prevented the train from moving without a driver – had been put out of action.

Why the driver had acted so dangerously was never established, but it was thought he may have been spying on a courting couple.

▲Luckily, most of the train's 157 passengers had seated themselves towards the rear of the train. Only the courting couple, who perhaps chose the leading carriage because of its emptiness, and a lone woman sitting at the rear of this coach, were injured.

To Heaton

goods train

overhead signalbox

parapet wall

EMU

To Newcastle

Key

EMU returning to Newcastle

Heaton to Blaydon goods train

was invariably carried out by railwaymen and was not only disreputable, but also highly dangerous and totally forbidden.

Of course there were many legitimate reasons why a driver might feel the need to look back down his train, but none of these would involve the dangerous practice of tying down the dead man's handle. If the suspicion of 'dogging' was at the back of everyone's mind, no one raised it at the inquiry, for the dead driver left behind a widow and five young sons.

However, it is significant to note that in early October 1926 the London & North Eastern Railway sent a circular to all of its staff asking them to 'respect the privacy of passengers'. Whether this was a gentle reminder to their employees of the possible dangerous consequences, or for some other reason altogether, also remains a mystery.

The Ministry of Transport investigation into the accident could do no other than lay the blame on the dead driver, stating: 'There is little object speculating upon his reasons for leaning out of the train as he did. They may have been legitimate or they may have been the reverse. In either case nothing can excuse his action in deliberately tying up a control upon which the security and even the lives of the passengers may at any moment depend.'

▲As police sifted through the wreckage for clues to what had caused the accident, they found that the dead man's handle, which should automatically have stopped the train if the driver was incapacitated, had been deliberately tied up with knotted handkerchiefs so that it was permanently in the running position.

arrived at Heaton station, for the driver had got out of his cab to talk to the station foreman while waiting for the guard to give the 'right away'. The handkerchief arrangement could not have been contrived in the time it took him to return to his seat and the train to travel 150 yards to the offending bridge pillar.

Quite why the motorman tied down the dead man's handle will always remain a mystery. Several theories were put forward at the time, although the official investigation refused to be drawn into speculation.

The layout of the driving cab is perhaps important to the issue, as is the position of the windows and doors. At the front of the train were three windows: a rectangular one in the centre, a larger rectangular one to the right and a porthole window to the left. Behind the porthole was the motorman's driving position. On the left or near side of the driving position was a sliding window, while on the right side of the train there was a fixed one. Immediately behind the driving compartment was a luggage van with fixed and barred windows, and behind that, a small vestibule with doors on either side of the train. The luggage van was provided with sliding doors on each side and it was from the right-hand side door in this van that the driver was swept by the bridge pillar.

Immediately behind the vestibule there was a first class compartment in which a courting couple were travelling. The presence of this couple may have led to the tragic consequences of 'dogging'. In railway terms the word 'dogging' was well known, for it referred to the practice of leaning out of carriage windows to watch courting couples in the compartments behind. This form of voyeurism

Dead man's handle
The initial pressure needed to bring down the spring-loaded dead man's handle was 25lb, while the running of the train required an additional pressure of between 3lb 12oz and 1lb 12oz. Any pressure less than this would cause the safety device to trip out immediately and make the brakes come on automatically.

The device was not infallible, but had the driver left the controls for any legitimate reason it should have prevented the accident which occurred on that fateful night.

Recommendations
There were few recommendations that the investigating officer could make, as everyone except the motorman had done their jobs diligently. He stressed the importance of not tampering with safety devices, yet he also noted that no similar case had been recorded in the 23 years of electric traction on Tyneside.

Had the guard noticed his train's position earlier, he might have stopped it by using the brake controls at his end. However, because the position of his windows was a mirror image of the driver's, he was not suitably placed to observe signals, his sliding window being on the wrong side. It was recommended that drop windows be provided on either side.

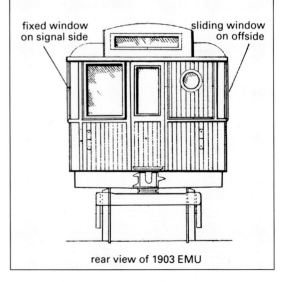

fixed window on signal side — sliding window on offside

rear view of 1903 EMU